Capitalist Property and Financial Power

A Comparative Study of Britain, the United States and Japan

John Scott

Lecturer in Sociology
University of Leicester

WHEATSHEAF BOOKS

First published in Great Britain in 1986 by
WHEATSHEAF BOOKS LTD
A MEMBER OF THE HARVESTER PRESS PUBLISHING GROUP
Publisher: John Spiers
Director of Publications: Edward Elgar
16 Ship Street, Brighton, Sussex

© John Scott, 1986

British Library Cataloguing in Publication Data

Scott, John, *1949–*
    Capitalist property and financial power:
    a comparative study of Britain, the
    United States and Japan
    1. Capitalism
    I. Title
    330.12′2   HB501

    ISBN 0-7450-0047-9
    ISBN 0-7450-0213-7 Pbk

Typeset in 11/12pt. Times British by Gilbert Composing Services
Printed and bound in Great Britain at
The Camelot Press Ltd, Southampton

THE HARVESTER PRESS GROUP
The Harvester Group comprises Harvester Press Ltd (chiefly
publishing literature, fiction, philosophy, psychology, and science
and trade books); Harvester Press Microform Publications Ltd
(publishing in microform previously unpublished archives, scarce
printed sources, and indexes to these collections); Wheatsheaf Books
Ltd (chiefly publishing in economics, international politics, sociology, women's studies and related social sciences); Certain Records
Ltd and John Spiers Music Ltd (music publishing).

Contents

Figures and Tables

Figures

Tables

Acknowledgements

The research reported in this book began a number of years ago with an investigation into the ownership of British companies. That research itself formed part of a collaborative international investigation of interlocking directorships. Contacts with colleagues during that research encouraged me to extend the analysis of share ownership into a comparison of Britain, the United States, and Japan. Through much of the period during which the British data were collected, Cathy Griff worked as Research Associate on the project and undertook the arduous tasks of liaison with part-time researchers and contact with companies, as well as engaging in data collection and analysis. Without Cathy this research could never have been completed. The part-time research assistants who burrowed away in the basement of Companies House were Stephen George, Tom Young, Brian Davies, Hanif Bhamjee, and Anoop Sethi, and further data processing was carried out at Leicester by Charlotte Kitson and Jill Scott. To all of them I am profoundly grateful.

The Registrar of Companies and his staff in Cardiff and London offered help above and beyond the call of duty, and fitted our many demands into their busy schedules at a difficult time for themselves. To all of them and to the Registrar I am grateful for the research facilities provided in one of Britain's greatest working archives. I must also thank the many companies which responded to inquiries about their shareholdings and ownership. I had originally hoped to name them all, but the number eventually proved too great—and some in any case requested that their help be unacknowledged. I remain in the debt of all the company secretaries and registrars who helped.

The American and Japanese data were obtained from published directories, but I am grateful to Jim Bearden and Beth Mintz for providing me with their list of top American companies and to Hiroshi Okumura and Yoshiaki Ueda for help with the Japanese data. Despite the help of my Japanese colleagues, my knowledge of written Japanese is very limited, and I have had to use the conventional anglicisations of Japanese names throughout. I apologise for any mistakes which may have been made.

The computer programs employed were written and made available to me by Peter Cowley, Martin Everett, and Clyde Mitchell. Clyde Mitchell, in particular, has helped with computing over the years. A number of the programs had to be modified at Leicester for use with large data sets. Much of this was carried out by Charlotte Kitson with the able support of the staff of the University of Leicester Computer Centre. A great deal of help was received from Sylvia West and John Beckett: the former wrote some programs for me, and the latter helped me to consume the University's budget on the Manchester super computer. Also at Leicester, I must acknowledge the help of the University library with its efficient interlibrary loans service and its important special collections on local and transport history.

The British part of the research was supported in its early stages by a grant from the Economic and Social Research Council, and continuing material support has been provided by the Department of Sociology at Leicester. Intellectual support has also been provided by my colleagues and by participants at various seminars and conferences; I apologise to all of them for stealing their ideas so unashamedly. Last but not least, Betty Jennings has again typed the bulk of the manuscript with speed and efficiency.

John Scott
Leicester, January 1986

1 Property Ownership and Corporate Control

The themes of this book are the changing and varying patterns of ownership and control to be found in the economies of the world today. These topics will be investigated through a detailed study of three economies: Britain, the United States, and Japan.

My argument is that the classic owner-controlled, generally family-controlled, enterprise has become a victim of the massive changes to which the capitalist economies of the world have been subjected.[1] But the form of business enterprise which is replacing the family firm is not the 'managerial' enterprise of liberal theory but a different form of owner-controlled enterprise. Modern businesses are just as much owner-controlled as their predecessors; but the identity of the owners has changed. The owners of the largest modern enterprises are other enterprises, which are, in turn, owned by yet other enterprises. The old system of personal possession, in which individuals owned and controlled 'their' companies, has been supplemented and replaced by a system of impersonal possession. In this system enterprises are linked to one another through chains of control which do not originate in the personal wealth and power of individuals and families. Rather, these chains are never-ending circles of connection—'vicious' or 'virtuous' circles according to taste. In a system of impersonal possession, enterprises are subject to the constraints inherent in the network of connections between enterprises, which are created by interweaving chains of intercorporate relations. Controllers and controlled alike are part of this same system of constraint. This is not to say that forms of personal possession have disappeared: far from it. But even the surviving individual–and family-controlled

1

enterprises have had increasingly to accommodate themselves to the system of impersonal possession.

Within particular economies, enterpreneurial capital remains a potent force alongside those enterprises in which impersonal possession prevails. Both state-and foreign-controlled enterprises are further units of capital in which impersonal possession is replaced by the control exercised by identifiable and powerful agencies. The extent and role of such forms of capital, however, varies from one economy to another, depending on the level of foreign penetration and the economic role pursued by the state. But impersonal possession itself is not a simple phenomenon. The concrete forms taken by depersonalised property vary from society to society according to the legal framework of business enterprise and the historical pattern of industrialisation.

Britain was the first nation to industrialise, and its industrialisation took place as a result of the myriad activities of small family-controlled enterprises which financed their operations from the wealth of their controlling families and with the support of local country banks. The big London banks which were active in the international money market and in government finance took no active part in funding the manufacturers, and those enterprises which sought to expand had to raise new capital through the sale of their shares in the stock exchange. Only in the inter-war years of the twentieth century did this situation begin to change as insurance companies and other financial intermediaries became active purchasers of company shares. The growth of 'institutional' share ownership—in which the big commercial banks eventually took a leading part—was responsible for the emergence of the system of impersonal possession in Britain. Families and individuals were increasingly supplemented by the financial intermediaries as the major owners and controllers of business enterprises.

Through a different route, the United States arrived at a similar destination. The later industrialisation of the United States allowed business interests to learn from the British experience and to experiment with alternative ways of mobilising capital. From the 1890s to the First World War a number of New York investment banks took the lead in the formation of big business through the amalgamation and reorganisation of existing family-controlled enterprises. The investment bankers were the dominant force on the New York stock exchange and ensured that the giant enterprises they created were floated onto a wide sea of ownership in which the original family holdings became weakened and considerably diluted. Thus, American enterprises emerged as larger than most of their British counterparts, but were dependent on the same system of capital mobilisation, and as in Britain, the financial intermediaries gradually became the dominant element in share ownership and corporate control.

In both Britain and the United States there has emerged a fusion between the capital involved in the production of goods and services and the capital which circulates through the credit system. The stock exchange and the financial intermediaries are the central mechanisms in the system of 'finance capital'. The funds required for investment in the various sectors of the economy do not come directly from the resources of families and individuals but are mobilised through the credit system—in the form of share capital, loan capital, and bank loans. The agents at the heart of this system—the financial intermediaries—are a diverse set of enterprises operating as insurance companies, pensions funds, investment trusts, financial advisers, savings institutions, and commercial banks. What unites them is their ability to mobilise the money made available to them by their many policy holders, contributors, clients, and depositors, and so to make it available for investment in other enterprises through the stock-exchange mechanism. Though not necessarily the most important of the intermediaries in terms of the amount of capital which they mobilise, the big commercial banks play an important role in coordinating capital mobilisation; and through the inter-locking directorships in which they are involved they are associated with loose and overlapping bank-centred spheres of influence. The bank at the centre of its sphere does, not by any means, control the operations of its associated enterprises. But it is extremely influential by virtue of the exchange of personnel that exists among their boards and by the bank's central location in the flow of information and capital through the business system. Banks are the central agents in a set of diverse financial intermediaries which dominate both the availability of capital and the information which is required to put that capital to use. This has been described as a situation of 'hegemony'[2], whereby the financial intermediaries are able to determine the conditions under which other enterprises must act. The power of these financial enterprises consists not in any ability to dictate to particular enterprises but in their power to set the limits and opportunities available to all major enterprises. Financial hegemony and bank-centred spheres of influence are the mechanisms through which the systems of finance capital and impersonal possession operate in the British and American economies.

But this is not the only form which a system of finance capital may take. In his classic statement of the concept, Hilferding[3] recognised the key role played by the banks in German development and laid the foundations for an interpretation of finance capital which claims a continuing and direct involvement of banks within the decision-making apparatuses of particular enterprises. While this thesis cannot be applied to the Anglo-American economies, there is rather more evidence in support of it as an interpretation of the Japanese economy. In Japan the stock exchange has always played a very limited role in industrial finance, being more important as a mechanism for buttressing the control of those who could determine the availability of capital. Japanese economic development occurred under the aegis of wealthy families which used the massive banks and trading companies which they owned to build up large manufacturing enterprises and to exercise control over their operations. This control, founded on the units of money capital and commercial capital, could be reinforced by the establishment of shareholding relations among the enterprises, but at no stage was the stock exchange *per se* an important element in the process.

Thus in Japan a fusion of capital in all spheres of the economy—the central element in the concept of finance capital—emerged earlier than in Britain and the United States and involved a radically different set of institutions. Despite the forcible removal of the wealthy families from positions of power after the Second World War, the institutional forms which they had created continued to be an important feature of capitalist development in Japan. Many of the largest business enterprises in Japan are members of combines which are centred around banks but which are organised on totally different lines from the bank-centred spheres of influence found in the British and American economies. The combines are tight interest groups in which the capital available to the constituent enterprises comes predominantly from the group bank, which plays a key role in the decision-making of the member enterprises. But even here the banks are not the ultimate loci of financial power. The power and influence of a bank derives from its position within a combine, and it is the combine which epitomises impersonal possession in Japan. As in Britain and the United States, there are no major centres of personal power and, within the combines, there is no single enterprise at which decisions originate. Nevertheless, the combine themselves each represent units of finance capital which are more or less distinct from one another and operate as separate loci of decision and coordination. The hegemonic institutions of the structure of impersonal possession in Japan, therefore, are not the separate financial enterprises but the combines; it is they which determine the conditions under which their member enterprises must operate.

The aim of this book is to explore the present structure of ownership and control in the three economies of Britain, the United States, and Japan in order to map in more detail their characteristic forms of organisation. Such a task has not been undertaken before and involves numerous problems of method and data. In each society there are sources of data with differing degrees of adequacy, requiring variations in method and technique. The United States and Japan have relatively permissive securities and companies legislation, with minimal requirements for public disclosure, and research on their economies must make recourse to unofficial sources of information. In the United States these are few and far between, and researchers have had to resort to estimation and guesswork based on the 'inside information' available—or not available—to them. Fortunately, a unique set of directories listing large shareholders for many major companies were commercially published at the time of the present research. Unlike earlier research on the United States, therefore, this study has had almost complete data available on most of the companies investigated. Japan has been well served by such commercial directories for many years, and Japanese researchers have made good use of them. Never before, however, have these sources been used for comparative network analyses.

In Britain there is a relatively tight framework of corporate legislation and, by international standards, a high level of public disclosure. Each company registered in Britain must normally make an annual return to a government department setting out the names and addresses of all its shareholders. This requirement has been in force for more than one hundred years, and all returns are available for public inspection. Paradoxically, the country with the greatest availability of data—Britain—has been the least researched. With few exceptions, British social scientists have ignored the mass of data available on company ownership and control. In the United States and Japan, where data is far less complete, there have been long traditions of such research.

The background and findings of previous research on ownership and control in the three economies will be briefly reviewed in later chapters of this book.[4] The bulk of the book, however, is concerned with the results of a systematic comparative study of corporate control, using conventional approaches to the definition and measurement of control as well as newer techniques of network analysis. Chapters 2 to 5 are mainly concerned with the British data, but introduce also the general concepts and procedures which are used in later chapters. The legal structure of ownership and corporate regulation in Britain is the topic of Chapter 2, which also contains a discussion of the various types of shareholder found in Britain. Because of the complexities of company law, the implications of such things as trusts and nominees are spelled out in some detail. Any researcher into the share registers must come to grips with these complexities, but rarely have they been made the subjects of sustained discussion. The second half of this chapter, therefore, will be of particular relevance to those who intend to carry out their own research; readers who are mainly interested in the results of the present research may prefer to skip read the final section of Chapter 2 and to use it as a reference source for topics raised in later chapters. Chapter 3 is concerned with the methodology followed in the research, and especially with a discussion of the ways in which the British data were collected and processed. Chapter 4 discusses the concept of control and presents the initial results of the British research. This chapter raises the question of the basis of the conventional measures and argues for the need to take more seriously models of voting behaviour. The formal dynamics of voting in coalitions and committees, it is argued, are relevant to understanding the balance among shareholders in corporate decision-making. These considerations are used to reconceptualise the results of the British research and to suggest further avenues of inquiry. Chapter 5 explores the voting dynamics of intercorporate networks and presents a description of the structure of the network of shareholdings in Britain. It is argued that techniques of network analysis are essential for mapping structures of hegemony.

The results of the research on American and Japanese companies are presented in Chapters 6 and 7, both of which draw upon the general arguments of the preceding chapters. In each case the dynamics of corporate voting are treated as the basis for the measurement of control, and the structures of hegemony are compared through network analysis. While each chapter can be read independently, in conjunction with the general arguments of earlier chapters, the full picture of any one economy emerges only from the comparison with the others. Some of the major lines of comparison are drawn out in Chapter 8, which returns to the general questions of capitalist property and financial power. Two appendices complete the book by setting out information which would interrupt the flow of the arguments in the main chapters. Appendix I gives a brief account of the selection of the companies studied and lists the British top 250, classified by mode of control. Appendix II discusses the methods of network analysis employed and should be of particular relevance to those intending to use these techniques. Technical issues have been kept to a minimum in the main chapters, but readers may wish to refer to Appendix II for clarification of particular points.

NOTES

1. This discussion draws on J. Scott, *Corporations, Classes, and Capitalism*, rev. edn., London, Hutchinson, 1985, and J. Scott and C. Griff, *Directors of Industry*, Cambridge, Polity Press, 1985. The reader is referred to these sources for more detail.
2. *See* B. Mintz and M. Schwartz, *The Power Structure of American Business*, University of Chicago Press, 1985.
3. R. Hilferding, *Finance Capital* London, Routledge & Kegan Paul, 1981 (1st edn, 1910).
4. A full discussion of previous research can be found in Scott *op. cit.*

2 The Legal Structure of Capitalist Property

In all of the advanced capitalist economies the prevailing legal form of business enterprise in the 'company' or 'corporation'. The large business typically comprises many such companies tied together through legal and economic relations and subject to the control of a 'parent' company. Yet the legal form of corporate business is extremely variable from one society to another. The aim of this chapter is to outline the nature of company law and administration that has developed in Britain, and an attempt will be made to highlight those features common to all systems of capitalist property. Only on the basis of a clear understanding of the legal structure of ownership is it possible to investigate the actually existing relations of control over property

THE DEVELOPMENT OF BRITISH COMPANY LAW

Industrial enterprises in earlier stages of capitalist development took the form of a family firm with little or no legal differentiation between the assets of the business and the assets of the household. The creation of the 'joint-stock company' allowed the firm and the household to be differentiated from one another, and so provided the basis for development towards large-scale enterprise. A joint-stock company has a permanent legal existence as a corporate body, an existence separate from that of the 'members' who jointly contribute to its stock of capital.[1] The first true joint-stock companies, as distinct from the 'regulated' companies of the medieval merchant adventurers, were the 'chartered' companies of the

9

seventeenth century; for example, the East India Company of 1600, the Hudson Bay Company of 1670, and the Bank of England of 1694. Operating in the commercial and financial sectors, these companies were formed by royal charters and experienced varying levels of parliamentary confirmation and approval of their activities. The charter for each company stipulated the appointment of a governor, a deputy governor, and a number of directors, all of whom were to be shareholding members of the company, and the directors were jointly responsible for running the affairs of the company. A number of unincorporated enterprises followed this model of business organisation, forming themselves through a trust deed rather than seeking a charter, but such 'companies' had no legal existence as corporate bodies. The failure of the chartered South Sea Company, and the speculative boom in company promotions which it had stimulated, led to the so-called Bubble Act of 1720, which restricted the right to act as a corporate body to those companies which were created through royal charter. This legal move, however, did little to affect the formation of unincorporated companies through trust deed and many businesses, in any case, were organised as partnerships, which had the legal right to own property in their own name. A business formed as a trust could not take legal action in its own name, but the trustees (the equivalents of company directors) could hold property on behalf of the subscribers, and it was possible for shareholdings to be transferred from one person to another. Despite the Bubble Act, the unincorporated enterprises had many of the advantages of the chartered companies and provided the basis for the business of many large undertakings.

The growth in the number of unincorporated businesses, and the associated difficulty in obtaining a royal charter from the government, led Parliament to create a new form of company in the eighteenth century. The 'statutory' company was a response to the canal boom and allowed for formation of an enterprise through a private Act of Parliament. When the canal boom was succeeded by a railway boom, the number of statutory companies grew enormously. The basis of such a company was not an individual charter but a particular Act introduced to Parliament by the promoters of the company and sponsored by their parliamentary associates. Railways, banks, and insurance companies were the main beneficiaries of this legal innovation, but it failed to adjust the law adequately to the changing character of business enterprise. Banking legislation of 1827 and subsequent legislation failed to resolve this problem and served only to complicate matters further, leading Parliament to set up a select committee in 1841 to investigate the situation and bring forth recommendations.

The committee recommended the introduction of a Companies Act to tidy up legislation in the area, and an Act was eventually introduced in 1844. The aim of this Act was not to alter the status of the chartered and statutory companies but to regularise the unincorporated companies by allowing them to become 'registered' companies. A business wishing to register under the 1844 Act was required to file a number of specified documents with the newly created Registrar of Companies, and in return was accorded full corporate status. This Act, therefore, permitted easy registration as a company and defined most of the now-familiar features of a joint-stock company: a board of directors, a general meeting, the appointment of auditors, and the requirement of public disclosure. A major feature missing from this list was limited liability, the principle under which the shareholders of a company were liable in law only for the amount of money represented by the value of their shares. A royal commission of 1853 reiterated the view that limited liability should not be permitted: honesty and good business practice could only be assured if shareholders were fully liable for all debts incurred by a company. A new Companies Act in 1856, however, allowed registered companies to limit the liabilities of their shareholders, and henceforth the designation 'Limited', or 'Ltd', became the normal suffix to a company name. The 1856 Act was, incidentally, the first to apply in Scotland as well as in England and Wales, as Scottish law had always been less restrictive towards company formation. Though Scotland retained, and still retains, its own system of company registration, the same legal requirements for company formation now operated throughout the British Isles.[2]

As the number of company formations continued to increase, in such areas as textiles, mining, and iron and steel as well as in the commercial and financial sectors, a new Act was passed in 1862 to consolidate and extend the earlier legislation.[3] Although minor changes to company law followed, it was not until 1907 that any major changes were introduced. The most important innovations made in the 1907 Act were the distinction between 'public' and 'private' companies, and the requirement for public disclosure of the balance sheet in all public companies.[4] A private company was defined as one with fewer than fifty members and which limited the rights of members to transfer their shareholdings. In a public company, which had to have more than seven members, there were no such restrictions on transfer and the company had to meet the full disclosure requirements of the Act. This system of company law provided the regulative framework for the expansion of business enterprises throughout the period up to the Second World War, though an Act of 1929 did introduce some limited changes.[5] In 1943 the Cohen Committee on company law was set up to consider amendments to the 1929 Act, the main stimulus to its appointment being the growing awareness that foreign share-ownership could be masked by the use of 'nominee' shareholdings. Some of the Committee's recommendations were embodied in an Act of 1947, which was then consolidated with previous legislation in a major Act of 1948. Further Companies Acts in 1967 and 1976 imposed new requirements to disclose large shareholdings and any interests of directors in the share capital or business of the company.[6] In retrospect it can be claimed that the basic framework of company law had been created by 1907, and that subsequent legislation has been concerned mainly to extend the range of matters which were to be publicly disclosed.

THE FRAMEWORK OF CORPORATE REGULATION

Under the system of company law which has been built in Britain, a distinct legal form of business enterprise has been created. A company is a continuing legal entity which is distinct in law from its members and comes into existence when its Memorandum and Articles of Association are deposited with the Registrar of Companies. The Articles specify how the company is to be administered and define the roles of the directors and members of the company. The company must have directors, who are nominally responsible to the members through an annual general meeting (AGM). The members, as shareholders in the company, do not own its assets, neither individually nor collectively. The company is legally the owner of its own assets, and the members have only the rights attached to their ownership of the share capital. The capital subscribed by the members is 'share capital': a share is a part of the capital of the company, and its face value—the price at which it was originally issued[7]—represents its proportionate contribution to the total share capital. The maximum share capital of a company, termed its 'authorised' or 'nominal' capital, is specified in the documents which create the company, and a company is empowered to issue shares with a total face value not exceeding that authorised.[8] Shareholders have a right to a dividend from the profits earned by their capital and a right to a voice in company decision-making, but the dividend and the voice will both vary with the type of share that is held; that is, company law permits the existence of distinct classes of shareholders, each with their own specific rights.

Ordinary shares, or 'equities', are those which carry a right to full participation in the profits of the company after allowing for any payments due to creditors. Because the dividend received is dependent upon the profitability of the company, ordinary shares are true 'risk-bearing' securities and so normally have a full voice in company affairs: rights to attend and vote at general meetings, to inspect various documents, and to take legal action against the directors and officers. Ordinary shares normally participate equally in voting, with one vote being given to each share,[9] and thus large blocks of votes can be accumulated by those with substantial shareholdings. A holder of 51 per cent of the shares, for example, would command 51 per cent of the votes. Though this principle of equal voting rights for each share is normally observed, company law permits a wide range of vote concentration to exist. Some companies have attempted to equalise voting rights among shareholders by creating a sliding scale of votes or by specifying the maximum number of votes which can be commanded by any shareholder. In yet other cases, however, a concentration of votes has been ensured by issuing two or more classes of ordinary shares, one of which (often termed 'A ordinary') has limited or no voting rights. *Deferred ordinary shares* are those which have a right to a dividend only after dividends have been paid to other ordinary shareholders, and such shares have generally been issued, credited as fully paid, to those who have sold their existing business to a newly formed company. Such shares are sometimes termed 'founders' shares' or 'management shares', and if they are given superior voting rights to the other ordinary shares a high degree of vote concentration is possible. Where deferred ordinary shares are issued, the remaining ordinary shares are often designated 'preferred ordinary' so as to indicate their priority as regards dividends.

Ordinary shares of all types, and however designated, are distinguished from *preference shares*, which take priority over all other shares in the receipt of a dividend and normally receive a fixed percentage payment.[10] Because of their preferential financial position, preference shares are not usually given a full voice in company affairs. Preference shareholders are members of the company who may vote only under certain specified conditions—normally if their dividend is in arrears. This rule is not, however, invariable, as some companies grant full or almost full voting rights to their preference shareholders. Where more than one class of preference shares has been issued by a company these are normally ranked as '1st' and '2nd' or as 'A' and 'B' preference shares.

A company may issue any mixture of the various types of ordinary and preference shares, and all those who subscribe to this share capital are legally regarded as members of the company. The situation is different for those who lend their money to the company. In law, money which is raised on loan is not part of the 'capital' but part of the 'debts' of the company, and thus lenders are creditors rather than members. For this reason, lenders have no voting rights in company affairs. Although companies may raise loans through normal bank borrowing, they may also do this by issuing certificates of indebtedness for sale to the public. Such a certificate is a debenture, which represents a loan for a specified period at a fixed rate of interest. Though they have no votes, debenture holders have priority in payment over the shareholders, and their loan is secured directly against the assets of the company. It is normal for a company issuing debentures to appoint trustees, whose responsibility is to ensure that the claims of the debenture holders are met. Where a company fails to meet these claims the trustees can act on behalf of the debenture holders by taking control of the mortgaged assets or appointing receivers. While directors were frequently appointed as trustees in the past, it is now more usual for corporate trustees to be appointed.

The task of balancing the claims of shareholders and creditors and of undertaking the management of the company is legally vested in the board of directors. In order for a company to be legally bound in contracts, it is necessary that all contracts be made by the directors or by those empowered to act on their behalf. Directors may delegate any or all of their powers, though there is no legal necessity to appoint a managing director or chief executive. In most large companies, however, such a role has been created and a *de facto* distinction between directors and executives has been established. While the executives manage the day-to-day operations of the company, the directors supervise the executives and are obliged to ensure that the company operates in the interests of its members. The directors are also required to make public disclosure of all those aspects of the companies' operations specified in company law. The Companies Act of 1844 established the principle that a company had to maintain an up-to-date register of its members, and since 1967 any holder of 10 per cent or more of any class of share capital was required to inform the company of the size of its holding and the directors were to record it in a separate register—in 1976 the notification level was reduced to 5 per cent. Further registers are to be maintained for the shareholdings of directors and their families and for debenture holders, unless the latter are simply issued 'to bearer'. Copies of all these registers are to be filed annually with the Registrar of Companies,[11] along with the audited financial statements. Companies seeking a stock exchange listing for their shares have had to meet an additional set of extra-legal requirements, often more stringent than the requirements of company law. Each listed company must publish an annual report, available free of charge to the general public, containing much of the statutory information. The report must list all holders of 5 per cent or more of any class of shares and must list the names and nationalities of all directors, together with details on their remuneration and shareholdings.[12]

The joint-stock company is not, of course, the only legal form of business enterprise, though it is by far the most widespread. The other major forms used to organise private undertakings are the mutual and cooperative societies and similar types of enterprise. These are not subject to the Companies Acts but variously to the Building Society, Friendly Society, and Industrial and Provident Societies Acts, and they are subject to the regulation of the Chief Registrar of Friendly Societies. The typical form for such societies corresponds closely to the joint-stock company, except that the members, though sometimes described as 'shareholders', are the depositors or customers of the society. In the case of mutual insurance companies, for example, the policy-holders, or a particular class of policy-holders, exercise all the voting rights in the company.[13] Enterprises in the public sector are typically organised as public corporations, though nationalisation sometimes results in a ministry becoming the sole shareholder in a joint-stock company.[14] Public corporations may be financed exclusively from government funds, raised through taxation and the issue of government stock, or partly by the issue of their own stock. The stockholders of the corporation, however, have no rights of participation in its decision-making and hold a position akin to that of the debenture holder in a company.[15] The legal differences between the public corporations of the post-war period and the earlier public 'boards' are of minor importance, relating mainly to the manner in which their board members (equivalent to directors) are appointed. In public enterprises organised by charter, as in the case of the British Broadcasting Corporation, the 'governors' are normally appointed by the Crown, while those corporations created by statute have their board members appointed by a minister. In practice these differences are irrelevant.

A large business enterprise, therefore, operates through the legals forms of the joint-stock 'company', the 'society', or the public 'corporation'. Individually owned businesses are limited in scale because they can draw only on the wealth of the individual owners, their families, and spheres of associates. The joint-stock company and the mutual society allow businesses to draw on a wider pool of capital, and the public corporation offers the same possibilities to public undertakings. The legal form regulates control over business assets, and the complex structure of a parent company and the subsidiary companies which it owns permits a diverse range of assets to be subjected to the control of whoever has the power to determine the composition of the parent board. Those who subscribe the capital may or not have this power, their opportunities of action being determined by the precise details of the legal form under which they operate and the actual pattern of distribution of the various classes of capital. The debate over the 'separation of ownership from control' has explored the possibility that directors or executives may be able to usurp some or all of the powers legally ascribed to shareholders. But while the shareholders are, indeed, legally separated from ownership of the business assets, they may not all be factually dissociated from participation in the effective control of those assets. The opportunities available to shareholding families, institutional investors, and banks, for example, are determined by the possibilities inherent in the legal structure of property, and it is necessary to investigate the interplay of legal forms and the social conditions in which they operate in order to understand the structure of strategic control in the business enterprise. The enterprise, as a social organisation, is dependent on the enabling properties of the joint-stock company, and the investigator of ownership and control must have a clear understanding of the legal rights of the various contenders for control.[16]

THE REQUIREMENT OF PUBLIC DISCLOSURE

Victorian individualism was a major force in establishing the principle of public disclosure, ensuring that those responsible for the ownership and management of an enterprise could not hide behind the anonymity of the corporate form. The current legal requirements of disclosure have been briefly reviewed above, chief amongst which is the maintenance of a full register of all shareholders and separate registers of substantial shareholders and of directors' interests, together with audited accounts. All except the full shareholders register form part of the published annual report required under stock exchange listing requirements,[17] and these reports comprise an important source of information for research purposes. The register of shareholders is maintained, up-to-date, at the company's registered office[18] and is to be available for public inspection at reasonable hours and at a nominal charge. All the documents held by the Registrar of Companies, including the register of shareholders, are similarly available for public inspection. This principle was established in 1856 and the Registrar's records, unlike those of most companies, are archival: all past records are retained and the investigator may examine records for each year of a company's history since its formation.

The Companies Registration Office, the headquarters of the Registrar of Companies, is the primary location for research into the ownership and control of companies registered in England and Wales.[19] The public inspection fee for documents held by the Registrar was one shilling (five pence) from 1856 to 1981, when it was increased to £1. This fee entitles the searcher to examine all the records for a particular company, including the register of shareholders. In the search rooms in Cardiff and London recent records may be examined in microfiche form, and the inspection fee includes the right to retain the microfiche copy. Share registers for large companies, however, are not available on microfiche. These long registers are stored at Cardiff and at various depositaries, though roll film copies for recent years are held in the London search room. Share registers have been maintained in a variety of forms, including trays of record cards, loose-leaf volumes, and computer printout. The most recent trend is for registers to be held on computer and provided to the Registrar as computer-readable microfiche, though this so far affects only a small proportion of the records held.

A typical share register now consists of one or more volumes of computer printout and must contain the name, address, and number of shares held by every ordinary or preference shareholder. Thus each share is registered in the name of an identifiable shareholder. By contrast with some other countries 'bearer shares', issued simply to the bearer rather than to a named holder, are not permitted under British law, though some companies issue 'share warrants' to bearer. These are warrants to claim a share and normally carry all the rights attached to the share itself, and where such warrants have been issued, the register will record only the total number in issue. It is normal, however, for debentures to be issued to bearer, but if 'nominative' debentures are issued (i.e. issued to named holders) the company must maintain a complete register. Share and debenture registers, however, are not required to note the ultimate beneficial owners of shares, but only the 'registered' holders. That is to say, if a person or company allows, say, a bank to administer their financial affairs, any shares held may be registered in the name of the bank. There is a widespread use of 'nominee' companies, run by banks and others, whose sole purpose is to act as the registered holders of shares beneficially owned by others. A major problem for the researcher—and also for public searchers—is to identify the interests which lie behind the nominees and bank accounts listed in company share registers. There has been no attempt to extend the principle of disclosure to counter this problem, though the 1976 Companies Act did allow a company itself to inquire into the beneficial ownership of any registered holdings in their register.[20]

One reason for the use of nominees is concealment. Nominees provide 'a convenient cloak for those who do not wish their ownership of the shares of a particular company to be known'.[21] Concealment may be thought necessary by an investor for tax purposes, to prevent the disclosure of insider dealings, or to enable strategic holdings to be built up prior to a takeover. Despite the legal powers recently given to companies to investigate the nominees on their own registers,[22] conceal-ment has always been difficult. The accumulation of shares prior to a takeover bid, for example, is always likely to involve large transfers of shares into particular nominees, and so it will always be clear that someone is building-up a stake. Since the number of likely candidates will tend to be small, the identity of the shareholder behind the nominee transactions will invariably be guessed. Nevertheless, nominees may indeed be widely used for the concealment of smaller holdings by those seeking to minimise their tax liability or to retain their anonymity. A second reason for the use of nominees is convenience. Personal shareholders, stockbrokers, and others may choose to leave their shares registered in the name of the bank which handles all the paperwork for them. Nominees run by lawyers and accountants frequently offer the same services. The use of such a nominee is sometimes a legal necessity, as section 117 of the 1948 Companies Act prevented the notification of any trust in the share register of a company registered in England.[23] Where family shareholdings are held in trust, therefore, they must be registered in the names of the individual trustees or through a nominee. The third reason for the use of nominees is in connection with normal banking activities. Banks which act as investment managers, trustees or executors, or which hold shares as collateral for loans will normally transfer the shares to one of their nominees, although the control they have over these shares will normally be far greater than in the case of those which they hold simply for the convenience of customers.

LEGAL FORMS OF SHARE OWNERSHIP

The most straightforward form of share ownership exists where a particular individual holds a block of shares in a company and is listed by name in the share register. But a number of personal shareholdings represent those held as trustees of family settlements or as executors appointed under a will. A trust is a legal device through which a number of people are able to hold property on behalf of others.[24] Trusts are typically used by families wishing to transfer a portion of their assets into the control of trustees who are given the power to decide the distribution of the income produced by the assets and who may have considerable power to influence any sale of the assets. The trustees have the legal title to the property under an agreement, called the trust deed, which specifies the persons who are to benefit under the trust. The use of a trust need not involve such a radical divorce of the family from its assets as at first seems the case, because the trustees may be drawn from among the beneficiaries, and the trust normally operates only for a specified period. Two types of trust are recognised in law, each of which comprises a major form of share ownership. A *private trust* is for the benefit of particular individuals, while a *charitable trust* is for the benefit of a general social group (such as the aged or the blind).[25] Both private and charitable trusts, therefore, may appear in share registers in the names of their individual trustees. But the share registers also include the names of nominees for special funds set up for charitable trusts which do not wish to be involved in the day-to-day matters of investment management. It is not legally possible for trustees to delegate their management responsibilities to those who are not trustees, but special arrangements have been made by the Charity Commissioners for charitable trusts to invest their assets in certain recognised investment funds which are run by professional managers. Two such funds have been recognised for general use by registered charities—the Equities Investment Fund for Charities ('Charifund') and the Charities Official Investment Fund[26]—and there are in addition specific funds recognised for use by particular charities: the 'common investment funds' for the colleges of Oxford and Cambridge universities, the Church Investment Fund for Church of England charities, and the Local Authorities Mutual Investment Trust.[27]

Each of these special funds appears in company share registers only through nominees, and an investigation of ownership and control must trace them back to those responsible for their management. Certain other nominees for charities, however, do not have this relationship to investment managers but relate to charities in a purely secretarial capacity. In law, trustees must act as both custodian and as manager, although in certain specified circumstances these two functions may be separated. The custodian trustee is legally regarded as the owner of the property and has the legal right to exercise the voting power of any shares held. Conversely, the managing trustee has all the powers of management, including directing how the voting power is to be exercised. This issue of voting power is crucial: the manager decides *how* the vote is to be exercised, while the custodian *enacts* that decision by actually voting. The custodian is bound to carry through any transactions of the managing trustees, unless this involves any breach of the trust deed.[28] Certain investments by smaller charitable trusts may be registered in the name of the Official Custodian for Charities, an officer of the Charity Commissioners, who acts purely in a custodian capacity. For this reason, shareholdings registered in the name of the Official Custodian must be disaggregated into numerous, small and independently managed trusts.[29] A slightly different role is played by the Public Trustee, an office set up under the Public Trustees Act of 1906, though not itself part of the Charity Commissioners. The Public Trustee acts as both manager and custodian for individuals, charities, and pension schemes, and most of the office's activities are operated through a number of special unit trusts.[30]

Corporate shareholders akin to charities include various Church of England bodies.[31] The Central Board of Finance was established in 1914 as the financial executive body of the Church and is responsible to the General Synod.[32] Dioceses provide funds to the Synod, which then votes funds to the Central Board. The main items of expenditure relate to the central services of the Church, and include financing convocation, synods, councils, the Church Information Office, Board of Education, and other departments. The Church Commissioners for England was established in 1948 on the basis of a much older organisation. Its income derives from its property and investments and is used to pay the clergy and to maintain church buildings and land. Although the Commissioners and the Central Board have been linked through a joint liaison committee since 1977 the investments of the two bodies have always been managed separately.

A further category of corporate shareholder to consider in this context includes various public bodies and overseas governments. British government departments appear in various registered names in lists of shareholders, their appearance invariably marking substantial stakes in the capital of the companies with which the government is widely known to be involved. By contrast, local authorities are frequent small

investors on behalf of their pension schemes, sometimes using
their own name and sometimes using nominees. An important
and active central government agency until the mid-1970s,
however, was the office of the Crown Agents, which set up a
massive banking and property operation between 1967 and
1974. The Crown Agents were hit by the financial collapse of
the mid-1970s and a Holding and Realisation Board was set up
to reconstruct their finances and investments.[33] Only one
overseas government appears at all regularly as an investor in
British companies, the Kuwait Investment Office. This office,
operating in great secrecy and exclusively through nominees,
determines and manages the British investments of the Kuwait
Ministry of Finance, which has similar offices in other
capitalist economies.

Personal shareholders and the various corporate bodies
discussed so far do not exhaust the whole range of
shareholders. There are, of course, shareholdings by companies themselves. While personal shareholdings have declined
considerably in significance in the post-war period, intercorporate shareholdings have greatly increased. These have
generally been discussed by lawyers and accountants within the
framework of parent–subsidiary relations.[34] Companies have
always been permitted to own shares in other companies,
though from 1887 to 1982 they were not permitted to purchase
their own shares.[35] A parent or holding company is one which
has a shareholding in excess of 50 per cent of either the capital
or the total vote in another, subsidiary company. Where the
holding exceeds 10 per cent, but is less than 50 per cent, the
target company is regarded as an 'associate'.[36] The terminology of 'parent', 'subsidiary' and 'associate' is, however,
insufficient to grasp the full variety of intercorporate
shareholdings. There are, in fact, four major categories of
intercorporate shareholdings: (1) those of financial and
holding companies, (2) those of portfolio and trade investors,
(3) those of insurance and provident investors, and (4) those of
fiduciary investors.[37]

Shareholdings by *financial and holding companies* are aimed
at securing the exclusive or shared control of other companies.
Parental holdings in subsidiaries and associates are, of course,
one form of this type of shareholding, a form in which the

parent aims at a high degree of control. Where two or more companies each have holdings in the same 'associate', such shareholdings can generate not only joint ventures but also more complex holding systems and combines.[38] A number of industrial enterprises involve such arrangements, but they are particularly common in the financial sector, where banks and insurance companies have formed numerous consortiums to provide the capital for special investment companies which may themselves take substantial stakes in other companies.[39]

Portfolio and trade investors aim at investment rather than exclusive control, but their portfolios of diverse small shareholdings often impel them to become involved in corporate control. Examples of such investors include stockbrokers and stockjobbers, investment trust companies,[40] and unit trusts. The legal form of the unit trust is derived from the private trust and involves a distinction between the trustees, who hold the investments, and the unit-holding beneficiaries. Department of Trade regulations require that the trust deed differentiate between custodian and managing trustees. All the shares purchased for the unit trust must be registered in the name of the custodian, generally a bank or insurance company, and the managing trustees are generally formed into a legally distinct management company. This form of organisation permits the management company to act as managing trustee for a large group of unit trusts, and since the trust deeds specify that voting power over the shares held is to be vested in the managing trustees, unit trust management companies become centres of voting power for the shares held by the trusts in their 'group'.[41]

Insurance and provident investors follow an investment strategy, but appraise the range and size of their investments on criteria different from those employed by other investment companies. Both insurance companies and pension funds invest in order to meet the long-term claims of their beneficiaries, and both the premium income and the rate of return on investments are calculated on the basis of actuarial estimates of the risks involved. Insurance companies are organised as joint-stock or mutual companies, but pension funds, like unit trusts, are mainly organised as trusts. Funded pension schemes[42] mobilise contributions from those in work in order to accumulate a fund which can be invested to earn sufficient income to pay pension commitments. Most pension funds are specific to the employees of particular enterprises, and the managing trustees are often employees of the enterprise. By contrast with such internally managed, 'self-administered', schemes, externally managed funds have banks, stockbrokers, or other financial companies as their day-to-day managers. Voting control over shares held by a pension scheme varies between these two cases. The custodian trustee of an internally managed scheme has sole responsibility for supervising the investment managers, and routine administration is delegated to a board appointed jointly by the custodian, the employer, and the employees. Managerial and secretarial work is the responsibility of the pension department of the enterprise, and voting control over shares is vested in the investment managers and the internal trustees, the custodian trustee being entitled to intervene only if it feels that the managers are acting contrary to the interests of the pensioners. In externally managed funds voting rights are rarely made explicit in the trust deed or management contract, but it is generally the case that voting is regarded as an indivisible aspect of investment management. In such circumstances the internal trustees will not seek to influence the ways in which these voting rights are exercised unless they feel that moral or political issues are involved (e.g. a concern over South African investments) or if the managers themselves have a financial interest in an investment. Even in these circumstances the managers will advise the internal trustees on how their voting powers should be exercised. Trustees normally act in a routine way and 'voting is in effect what the managing institutions choose to make it'.[43]

The final category of corporate shareholder, *fiduciary investors*, hold and manage shares on behalf of a diverse range of interests. While insurance and provident funds also involve a fiduciary responsibility, their investment management is ultimately constrained by actuarial considerations. The investors under consideration here have a more diffuse fiduciary relationship, often on behalf of personal clients, and are entrusted to meet executor and trustee obligations to the beneficiaries of family trusts as well as exercising investment authority delegated to them by their clients. Fiduciaries acting as executors and trustees have the legal right to the property and the right to exercise any voting power; but where they simply exercise delegated powers, these legal rights remain with the client. In the latter case the fiduciary is acting as 'agent' rather than 'trustee' and is bound by the specific agreement made between principal and agent. The agent, in law, is always acting under client's orders. It is normal, however, for the agency contract to specify the scope of the powers delegated to the fiduciary agent. These diffuse activities of fiduciary investment have increasingly formed an integral part of the operations of banking enterprises, and so are best considered in that context.

The largest banking enterprises in Britain, those which originated as 'clearing' or 'commercial' deposit banks, are involved in a range of activities within the financial sector, unlike more specialised lending enterprises such as building societies and consumer credit companies. The subsidiaries and associates of the big banks are involved in all four of the forms of shareholding discussed, making them key agents in the mobilisation of corporate capital. Bank shareholding has its origins in the trustee and executor business undertaken for clients. The core of this business has always been personal trust management, and as the banks came to take a more active role in managing trust holdings they have also taken on personal investment management.[44] Most of the big banks have organised their trust business into subsidiary trust companies which are regulated under the Public Trustees Act of 1906 and the various Insurance Companies Acts.[45] Discretionary investment management by trust departments has become mainly a service for the banks' largest personal customers, as the cost of managing small accounts has become prohibitive. Banks have, therefore, taken advantage of the growth of unit trust business and have sought to persuade smaller investors to put their money in a bank-managed unit trust. This has been part of a growing involvement of banks in the unit trust sector, with all four of the big banks operating their own unit trust management companies. They have also become involved with investment trusts, though only Midland Bank has a large group of managed companies,[46] and this has been a more important area for merchant bank involvement. During the 1970s and 1980s investment trusts have themselves tended to become specialised investment adjuncts of pension funds and insurance companies, and so have become less attractive to clearing bank trust companies. A further major area of investment management for bank trust departments has been their pension fund business, where the bank acts as manager and is given complete discretion within the guidelines set down by the funds trustees. Banks will additionally manage the pension fund for their own employees and also operate general pension funds for use by a number of smaller clients.[47]

In addition to personal and corporate fund management, clearing banks are heavily involved in custodian trusteeship and operate many nominee companies for this purpose. The use of nominees by clearing banks became important between the wars, when they began to accept shares as collateral for loans. Such shares had to be transferred to the bank, and instead of registering them in the names of bank officials—who were likely to retire, die, or move on to other jobs—nominees were used. Many of the large bank nominees, often described as 'branches' nominees, had their origins in this way and now act as custodians for a large number of individual clients. These nominees are often to be found among the largest shareholders in British companies and do not generally use separate account designations for specific clients, the allocation of shares to individual clients being made as a purely internal book-keeping arrangements by the bank.[48] Where nominees register shares in designated accounts (accounts with numeric or alphanumeric identifiers), this reflects the fact that the account is a custodian holding for a particular large client. An extension of this use of designated accounts in general nominees is the allocation of specific nominees to particular clients for their exclusive use. In all such cases of custodian trusteeship, the banks have no powers to determine the ways in which the shares will be voted.

The operations of bank trust departments, involving both custodian services and investment management, are just one branch of bank involvement in share capital. In addition to normal commercial deposit banking for industrial clients, the merchant banking or corporate finance department will be involved in loans, underwriting, share issuing, and take-overs, and may combine all of these with a share registration service. This clearly gives the banks immense potential for influence in corporate affairs. Where the trust and corporate finance departments have a customer in common, the trust department may take up a share issue which would not otherwise have been attractive, and this has led critics to suggest that managed funds are 'captive funds' which can be mobilised by the corporate finance department when necessary.[49] It is possible, however, that the potential conflict of interest which is involved in such situations—a conflict between the fiduciary responsibility to enhance the value of investments and the commercial interest of ensuring a successful share issue—will lead banks to ensure that trust and corporate finance business are kept distinct.[50] What is clear, however, is that all the activities described are integral parts of the coordinated corporate strategy pursued by banking enterprises and that it is important to investigate all aspects of their involvement in share ownership and control.

NOTES

1. Useful discussion on the development of British company law can be found in A.B. Levy, *Private Corporations and Their Control*, 2 vols., London, Routledge & Kegan Paul, 1950, and T. Hadden, *Company Law and Capitalism*, London, Weidenfeld & Nicolson, 1977.
2. Ireland, too, had its own system of registration, based in Dublin. On the formation of the Irish Free State, companies operating in Northern Ireland were permitted to register with the newly created Registrar of Companies in Belfast. Wales has never had a separate system of company law and was fully incorporated into the English system.
3. The 1862 Act introduced such new principles as the requirement to keep a register of mortgages and the power to issue share warrants to bearer.
4. A Limited Partnership Act was also passed in 1907, allowing partnerships to register with limited liability. This legal form was not especially popular because of the greater flexibility offered by formation as a private company.

5. The 1929 Act required disclosure of the nationality of non-British directors (an amendment first introduced during the First World War) and of directors' remunerations, strengthened the position of auditors, and, in the wake of the Hooley crash, attempted to limit the possibilities of fraudulent promotion.

6. Companies Acts of 1980 and 1981 have been concerned mainly with the harmonisation of company law throughout the European Community. The most important change was the creation of the new form of 'public limited company' (plc), under which all public companies had to reregister.

7. It is possible for the face value of shares to be altered after they have been issued, but this does not affect the argument here. The face value is simply to be distinguished from its market value on the stock exchange.

8. Alongside the authorised and issued capital must be mentioned the paid-up capital, which comprises the total amount of money contributed by those who have purchased the issued shares. Where shares are issued partly-paid, the shareholders being liable to pay the balance of the purchase price at a specified time, the paid-up capital will be less than the issued capital.

9. In some cases a share of, say, £1 will be accorded four votes (one vote for each 25p held), but the principle of equal voting rights still holds. In companies where the capital exists as 'stock' rather than 'shares', votes are allocated according to specified units of stock: for example, one vote for every 25p of stock held.

10. Participating preference shares are those in which the dividend may vary above the specified level when the company is particularly profitable. Cumulative preference shares have the right to accumulate unpaid dividends.

11. Since 1948 a company has been allowed to make a full return every three years, with updating returns in other years.

12. The annual report also contains the balance sheet, the profit and loss account and various financial statistics, all of which represent the 'consolidated' performance of the parent company and its subsidiaries. Non-financial information includes charitable and political donations, the location of the registered office, and the industrial activities of the company.

13. The legal forms employed by unit trusts and pension funds are parts of complex arrangements within and between enterprises organised as joint stock companies or public corporations. The specific features of these legal forms are discussed later in this chapter.

14. Ministerial shareholdings are generally held in the name of the secretary of state or the Treasury Solicitor.

15. In Britain, 'corporation' is used exclusively to refer to public bodies. In the USA the term is equivalent to 'company'.

16. The implications of this argument for patterns of ownership and control comprise the main topics of discussion in later chapters of this book. The general debate is reviewed in J.P. Scott, *Corporations, Classes, and Capitalism*, rev. edn, London, Hutchinson, 1985.

17. Unquoted private companies are, of course, exempt from this requirement, though a report must be lodged with the Registrar of Companies. Mutual and friendly societies are under no obligation to publish a register of their members.
18. Where a company employs a registrar, usually a bank or accountancy firm, to maintain its share register, the register may be retained at the registar's office.
19. The public inspection office was originally in London at Somerset House and then at Bush House. Companies House is now based in Cardiff, though search facilities are available at City Road in London. In Scotland, current records are held at Exchequer House and past records at the Scottish Record Office.
20. The results of any such inquiry must be maintained in a special register at the Company's Registered Office, but there is no requirement for it to form part of the annual return. This provision of the Companies Acts has not been widely used.
21. R. Stone *et al.*, *The Owners of Quoted Ordinary Shares*, London, Chapman & Hall, 1966, p.12.
22. Powers given under section 27 of the 1976 Companies Act. From the standpoint of the researcher the situation is little improved.
23. This provision does not apply in Scotland.
24. The trust, therefore, performs some of the same functions as a joint-stock company, and, before the passage of the Companies Acts, a number of businesses were organised as trusts. For a general discussion of the law of trusts, *see* G.W. Keeton and L.A. Sheridan, *The Law of Trusts*, London, Professional Books, 1974.
25. Each type of trust may be discretionary or non-discretionary. A discretionary trust is one in which the trustee has to exercise his or her own judgement as to the distribution of the income rather than being bound by rules laid down in the deed.
26. Charifund is a unit trust managed by the M & G Group; COIF is an investment trust managed from Winchester House by the investment office of the Church of England's Central Board of Finance.
27. LAMIT is subject to the same management as COIF. Its funds are mainly drawn from local authority superannuation schemes.
28. Keeton and Sheridan, *op. cit.*, p. 55.
29. If trustees of such charities wish to delegate their management, then the Official Custodian will, on their behalf, liquidate the assets and invest the proceeds in the Charities Official Investment Fund. On the law of charities, *see* D.G. Cracknell, *Law Relating to Charities*, London, Oyez Publishing, 1973, and C.P. Hill, *A Guide for Charity Trustees*, London, Faber & Faber, 1974.
30. These unit trusts appear in share registers as the FC1, FC2, and FC3 accounts of the Public Trustee. The Trustee also has a number of discretionary investment clients.
31. A number of shareholdings registered in the names of the fellows of Oxford and Cambridge colleges are in fact nominee holdings for the charitable trusts through which the colleges were founded.

32. *See Official Yearbook of the Church of England,* annually, London, The Church Assembly.
33. The investments of the royal family might be considered part of the public sector rather than as personal holdings. Such holdings never appear by name but in a special Bank of England nominee company.
34. Early contributions which set the terms of the discussion are A.J. Simons, *Holding Companies,* London, Pitman, 1927, and G. Garnsey, *Holdings Companies and Their Published Accounts,* London, Gee, 1923.
35. Exceptions to this prohibition were allowed for employee benefit trusts, such as pension schemes.
36. In the absence of any attempt to influence the strategy of the target company the holding may be regarded simply as a trade investment.
37. This typology draws on that presented in J. Revell, *The British Financial System,* London, Macmillan, 1973.
38. *See* J. Scott and C. Griff, *Directors of Industry,* Cambridge, Polity Press, 1984, Figure 1.1.
39. Examples of such special investment companies include Finance For Industry and the Agricultural Mortgage Corporation, both of which are owned by consortiums of large clearing banks.
40. A distinction can be made between investment companies and investment trust companies. The latter are not 'trusts', in the legal sense, but they do have certain fiscal privileges. This is discussed further in Chapter 5.
41. M.J. Day and P.I. Harris, *Unit Trusts,* London, Oyez Publishing, 1974. Unit trusts are exempt from the provision requiring disclosure of interests in holdings of 5 per cent or more of the capital in joint stock companies.
42. Some public sector pension payments are met from current taxation rather than from invested funds.
43. R. Minns, *Pension Funds and British Capitalism,* London, Heinemann, 1980, p.104. Under the Trustee Investment Act all trustees, except those for family trusts, national savings, the Post Office, and the Trustee Savings Bank, must have advisers qualified to provide written advice on proposed investments. This strengthens the power of external managers.
44. Though acting as agent the bank normally requires complete discretion as to the management of investments.
45. National Westminster is the only one of the 'big four' not to have a separate trust company.
46. The Scottish clearing banks have always had closer relations with investment trusts than have the English banks.
47. The operation of bank trust departments is described in: The London Clearing Banks, *Evidence . . . to Committee to Reorganise the Functioning of Financial Institutions,* London, Committee of London Clearing Banks, 1977; and Wilson Committee, *Evidence on the Financing of Industry and Trade,* vol. 3, London, HMSO, 1978.
48. Some general nominees are operated as custodians for specific types of client. Manually operated nominees in branches near the stock exchange, for example, are often reserved for use by stockbrokers.

49. Minns, *op. cit.*
50. This has been argued for the American case in E.O. Herman, 'Commercial Bank Trust Departments', in M.J. Rossant (ed.), *Abuse on Wall Street*, Westport, Conn. Quorum Books, 1980.

3 Method and Measurement in the Study of Property

It has been shown in the previous chapter that the legal structure of property ownership and the requirements for public disclosure have created great opportunities for researchers interested in questions of ownership and control. Yet the mass of material stored at Companies House and in company records has been remarkably underutilised. Few studies have used these resources to the full, and there has been little attempt to use company records to push forward our knowledge of the structure of property ownership.

Two series of studies, however, stand out from all others in this area, and an understanding of their methods remains an essential starting point for other investigators. A group of researchers based at the Cambridge University Department of Applied Economics[1] were involved in a larger attempt to construct a national balance sheet of income and wealth, and initially collected aggregate shareholding data to remedy inadequacies in published statistics. Beginning with the year 1957, the Cambridge researchers subsequently investigated 1963 and 1970, and their time series has been continued into 1975 by the Department of Industry and 1981 by the Stock Exchange.[2] Despite differences in methods from year to year, the Cambridge researchers established a core of procedures that are of continuing relevance to other researchers.

The second series of studies to be considered was directed by Sargant Florence and was concerned not with aggregate national data but with the details of ownership in particular companies, the aim being to discern trends in corporate development. A pilot study for 1936 was followed by systematic investigations of large companies in both 1936 and 1951.[3] Despite the originality and sophistication of Florence's

33

methods and theorisation, no researchers attempted to follow his lead until the early 1970s, when the research which is reported in the bulk of this book was begun.[4]

AGGREGATE TRENDS IN SHARE OWNERSHIP: THE CAMBRIDGE STUDIES

The Cambridge researchers investigated samples of quoted companies stratified by the market value of their capital. All quoted companies with a capital above a cut-off point (£100m in 1962 and £145m in 1970) were selected, and progressively smaller sampling fractions were used in lower size bands. In the 1957 survey they had used the share registers at Companies House in London but discovered that this led to considerable problems of timing. A register relates to the situation fourteen days after the date of the AGM, and so the register date varied considerably from company to company. It was impossible, therefore, to study the ownership of all the selected companies for exactly the same date. To overcome this problem, the later studies investigated the registers held at the transfer offices of the company registrars.[5] As these registers were continually updated, it was possible to collect data relating to the same date for each company. This alternative was not without problems of its own, as it was necessary to obtain the cooperation of a large number of registrars, to train sufficient staff to visit all the transfer offices, and to coordinate activities for the particular target day. Having selected a list of companies to investigate, and after having deleted all those with complex changes in share capital during the year and all those whose registrars would not cooperate, the Cambridge researchers draw a stratified sample of holdings from the registrars of all companies remaining in the sample. For the majority of the registrars a sample of 1 in 100 holdings was drawn, this fraction being modified for the smaller registrars, and the intention was to produce a list of between 500 and 1,000 shareholders for each company. This sample provided the backdrop to a separate investigation of large shareholders. In the 1957 study the researchers drew up a list of the major insurance companies and other 'institutional' shareholders in order to investigate the size of their holdings in the registers, but this involves the obvious difficulty that the researchers can obtain no information about large shareholders which do not appear in their original list. Furthermore, holdings by companies on the list cannot be identified when they are registered in the names of nominees. In the later studies, therefore, the researchers adopted a more systematic approach of selecting all registered holdings above a certain cut-off level, the level chosen for each company being an attempt to ensure that the selected holders would account for 15 per cent to 20 per cent of the total capital.

The end result of this complex process of data collection was, for each company, a list of registered shareholders, and the researchers used these lists as the basis for constructing lists of beneficial shareholders. This involved an attempt to identify the beneficiaries of nominee holdings so that aggregate figures for types of beneficial holder could be compiled. Table 3.1 presents a summary of the results of the 1969 study. Almost one-fifth of all shares were registered in nominee accounts, resulting in a serious underestimation of certain categories of beneficial shareholding. Unit trusts, as trusts, are not permitted to register shares in their own names, and all their shares were, therefore, registered through nominees. Holdings by pension funds and unit trusts were also considerably underrepresented in the lists of registered holdings, as were overseas shareholders. In order to compile the data summarised in Table 3.1, therefore, the Cambridge researchers had to devise ways of reallocating nominee holdings to their beneficiaries. As they were interested only in aggregate figures, and not with the identity of particular nominees, they were able to write to the banks which operated the nominees to request a breakdown of the categories of beneficiary for a sample of the nominee holdings. These figures were then taken as multipliers for all such nominee accounts and enabled the reallocation of nominee holdings to be carried out.[6] In this way the Cambridge researchers believed that they had obtained an accurate quantitative picture of shareholding without breaching normal banking confidentiality.[7]

Table 3.1: *Share ownership: the Cambridge results (1969)*

Category of owner	% Shareholders	
	Registered	Beneficial
Persons	44.7	47.4
Nominees	19.8	–
Insurance	10.6	12.2
Pension funds	4.9	9.0
Investment trusts	4.2	7.6
Unit trusts	–	2.9
Banks	1.4	1.7
Other finance	1.2	2.5
Charities, etc.	1.8	2.1
Non-financial companies	3.9	5.4
Public sector	3.8	2.6
Overseas	3.7	6.6
Totals	100.0	100.0

Source: J. Moyle, *The Pattern of Ordinary Share Ownership 1957–70*, (Cambridge University Press, 1971), Tables 1 and 2.1

TRENDS IN CORPORATE DEVELOPMENT: THE WORK OF FLORENCE

The Cambridge researchers concentrated their attention on the relative importance of personal and corporate shareholdings, and carried-out no separate analysis of large shareholders and their participation in control. The latter issues were, however, central to the research of Florence. The main concern of his studies was to formulate a 'realistic' approach to business administration, an approach to business leadership which recognised the constraints within which managers must act. Florence addressed his own research to American writing on the relationship between ownership and control,[8] and so was interested in distinguishing companies with dominant shareholders from those with dispersed share ownership. Florence's research began in the same way as the 1957 Cambridge study, using the records at the Companies Registration Office in London as his source.[9] He decided, however to concentrate, on registered shareholdings and make no attempt to identify the beneficiaries of nominee accounts. His assumption was that nominees tended to hold for large numbers of individuals and, therefore, did not constitute cohesive voting blocks. For this reason, he argued, they could be ignored in a 'realistic' study of business leadership.[10] This assumption may well have been correct for 1936—though it was by no means true of all nominee holdings—but the Cambridge researchers have shown that many nominees in the post-war period have been custodians for substantial shareholders, and it must be recognised that Florence's analysis of the 1951 data may be considerably flawed by his focus on registered holdings. Nevertheless, the methods of analysis which Florence applied to his data remain of paramount importance for other researchers.

The 'realistic' approach led Florence to concentrate on voting in corporate decision-making. Shares were seen not simply as sources of material benefit but also as political resources, and so the central problem was to determine, for any particular enterprise, the locus of key voting blocks of shares. Florence defined the total vote in a company as the sum of votes, measured over all classes of capital with full voting rights, which could be exercised at a shareholders' meeting.[11] Any group seeking to determine corporate policy must hold sufficient shares to give it a good chance of winning any contests which might arise at a shareholders' meeting. Recognising the importance of the claim by Berle and Means that this was possible with less than a majority of the shares, Florence aimed to reconstruct the notion of 'minority control'. This form of control exists where a single shareholder or a cohesive group of shareholders possess the largest block of shares and the remaining shares are widely dispersed. Clearly, the critical mass required will vary with the overall distribution of the company's voting capital, but Berle and Means argued that minority control was normally possible with a voting block of 20 per cent and Florence attempted to justify this particular cut-off level for minority control on the basis of a model of decision-making. Florence advocated what he called the 'twenty-twenty rule', whereby a resolute group of twenty or fewer shareholders can exercise minority control in the face of a mass of indifferent shareholders so long as the group held at least 20 per cent of the shares.

Florence's argument is that a group of twenty or less is able to cooperate for purposes of control, while a group with more than twenty members is unlikely to be able to cooperate in this way. While some kind of direct contact is possible among a group of twenty, this becomes more difficult to sustain in larger groups. He adds to this point the empirical claim that the size distribution of shareholdings in the large companies of 1936 and 1951 is such that the percentage holding of each shareholder declines sharply after the twentieth holder. Additional shareholders could add only a very small percentage to the concentration of votes. Thus the existence of twenty large holders with 20 per cent of more of the shares is *prima facie* evidence for the existence of a controlling group.[12] The researcher must then go on to demonstrate that the twenty holders do actually constitute or contain a coherent and resolute group; for example, a group of holders with the same family name or with kinship or business links. The case for the existence of minority control is strengthened, he argues, if it can be demonstrated that some members of this group do actually participate as directors or officers in the administration of the enterprise.[13] The choice of 20 per cent as the cut-off for a critical block is justified by Florence on the basis of two arguments. He firstly argues that it is unlikely that small and medium-sized shareholders will unite to form a potent opposition group. Most shareholders are unable or unwilling to spend time and money attending brief shareholders' meetings held at some considerable distance from where they live. Many such shareholders will not bother to make a postal vote or to appoint someone as their proxy. Those who do vote, argues Florence, will vote in such a way that their total vote is distributed at random, ensuring that their votes for and against a proposal will cancel one another out. If the assumption of random voting does not hold in any particular case, argues Florence, the bias in the vote is most likely to be in favour of the established controlling group because of their control over the voting proxy forms which are sent to those shareholders unable to attend the AGM.

The second argument that Florence proposes is based on theories of rational choice. A resolute group, especially if represented on the board, could be reasonably certain of voting success with a holding lower than 20 per cent. Following Penrose,[14] he shows that in a company with a total vote of 1,000 and a mass of indifferent shareholders, a block of sixty votes held by a resolute group can enable the group to pursue their policies with a 96 per cent probability of success. Florence hesitates to conclude that a 6 per cent block is sufficient for minority control, because he recognises that the indifference of the smaller holders cannot be taken for granted, and he therefore makes the pragmatic decision to regard 20 per cent as a secure basis for minority control. Holdings of between 10 and 20 per cent he sees as representing rather more marginal cases.

Thus the Cambridge researchers have proposed ways of handling nominees and converting from registered to beneficial holdings, while Florence has provided a set of methods and measures for handling the mobilisation of voting capital. The research on British companies which is reported in the following chapters was explicitly designed to learn from the contributions made by these earlier studies, and it is now possible to review the methods followed in that research.

DISCOVERING CORPORATE VOTE-HOLDERS: AN ALTERNATIVE

The research on British companies reported in this book was carried out at Leicester University and was part of a larger investigation of corporate structure. Lists of the 250 largest enterprises of 1904, 1938, and 1976 were compiled for use in a study of interlocking directorships,[15] and ownership data were collected for all the enterprises on the 1976 list. In addition, less systematic ownership information was collected for some of these enterprises in earlier years and for those on the 1904 and 1938 lists. Initial ownership information was collected from Annual Reports and other published sources, and this made it possible to identify most cases of majority and minority control. A large residue of enterprises with no obviously dominant shareholding interest remained, and it was decided to examine the share registers at Companies House in order to compile lists of the largest shareholders in each of these enterprises. The same information was collected on some of the enterprises believed to be majority or minority controlled as a check on the results available from public sources. In all, the registers of approximately 140 companies were investigated.[16]

The Cambridge researchers recognised the central difficulty in using Companies House as a resource base: the fact that registers for a particular year in fact cover a very wide range of dates. However, it was felt that the present research would lose little of value by employing these registers, and the resources necessary to train and pay a large team of researchers to visit transfer offices were not available. Companies House is a unique repository of research information, and the help of the staff was of inestimable value in allowing a large number of companies to be investigated in the time available. Actual data collection took place at the Cardiff office, where the original hard-copy share registers for 1976 were stored. The aim was to compile lists of the largest shareholders in each of the selected companies, and the part-time research workers who collected the data were sent an information card for each of the companies giving the cut-off level of shareholding to be used for that company and specifying any further data (such as family holdings) which were to be collected.

The cut-off was chosen on the basis of 'guesstimates' of the distribution of capital and with the intention of identifying the sixty to one hundred largest registered holders in each company. In many, perhaps most, cases these estimates proved wide of the mark and the written instructions issued to the research assistants told them to alter the cut-off level if they had selected many more or many fewer than twenty to thirty holders by the time one-third of the register had been covered; that is, when the letter H was reached in the alphabetical list. Where the cut-off level had to be raised, because too many holders were being selected, the researcher was simply to continue using a revised cut-off. When the cut-off level had to be reduced, because too few holders had been identified, it was necessary for the researcher to return to the start of the register and begin collecting again with the lower cut-off. It was found that in practice researchers were soon able to make such decisions at an early stage in the analysis of a register. The routine collection task for the researchers was merely to examine each page in the register to identify any shareholder above the cut-off and make a note of the name, address, and number of shares held. In the case of enterprises which were known or suspected to have been family controlled in the recent past, the information card instructed the researcher to make an additional search for specified family names in order that an estimate could be made of any surviving elements of family participation. In addition, family holdings which were split into a large number of separate trusts and holdings may have been missed by the simple cut-off level selection procedure, and a separate search for family holdings enabled this problem to be overcome. This procedure could only be used, however, where a family name could be specified and where the name was not so common that numerous unrelated individuals would be identified; this meant searching for names such as Tate and Barclay in the relevant registers, but making no search for names such as Smith and Jones. In practice it was discovered that the amount of shares registered in such common names was surprisingly low and that large aggregate holdings in *any* name were likely to reflect substantial holdings by one or two related individuals.

The raw data collected by the researchers were recorded, normally, as alphabetical listings[17] and were returned to the project office at Leicester for further processing. The aim was to compile lists of the twenty largest *vote-holders* in each company, and so the immediate task was to reduce the long lists of registered holders to the shorter lists of vote-holders. This involved both deletion and aggregation of registered holders. Nominee holdings which were mere custodians for a large number of individuals and did not represent a cohesive voting block, had to be identified and deleted, while family holdings and commonly managed investment and unit trust holdings had to be identified and combined to form distinct vote-holding groups. The first step was to ensure that the parent company of each registered corporate shareholder was known, as many corporate holdings were registered in the names of subsidiaries. Use of *Who Owns Whom* and similar sources[18] allowed all holdings by a particular parent to be identified and aggregated into a single holding. A similar procedure was followed for family holdings, combining together all holdings in the same family name and by individuals known to be related but having a different surname. *Who's Who, Kelly's Handbook, Burke's Landed Gentry* and similar biographical sources were essential to this task.[19] Where an individual had an address in what was suspected to be a commercial district, this was investigated through telephone and street directories and in membership directories of the professional bodies representing lawyers and accountants. Most such cases were, indeed, offices of lawyers and accountants acting as nominees for the family trusts of their clients.[20] Personal shareholders were also checked in such sources as *Directory of Directors, City of London Directory*, and *Leviathan* to obtain further information on their business connections. This often provided the basis for connecting family groups and locating their primary business interests. These could often be cross-checked through the *Stock Exchange Official Yearbook* and the *Register of Defunct and Other Companies*.

Nominee holdings had to be treated somewhat differently from other corporate shareholders, as not all of them indicated the name of the parent bank, and few nominee companies are listed in *Who Owns Whom*.[21] To trace the parent banks of nominee companies, street directories were used to check on the addresses given. If it was known, for example, that 'Kingsman Nominees' had its offices at 55 King Street, Manchester, a search in *Kelly's Directory of Manchester*, which gives a street-by-street listing of commercial addresses, would show this to be one of the Manchester offices of the National Westminster Bank. In all but a few cases the street directories for the major cities enabled the parents of nominees to be identified, and the residual cases were resolved by visits to the address to inspect brass name plates.[22] Before the final aggregations and deletions of nominee and other holdings could be made, it was necessary to approach the banks themselves so as to discover the nature of the nominees as a prelude to discovering the identities of the beneficiaries and vote-holders. The procedure used by the Cambridge researchers could not be followed, as the interest of the project was in the identity of vote-holders rather than simply aggregate levels of shareholding. Previous research had suggested that most nominees were single purpose—either custodian or manager but not both—and banks were asked if they would allocate each of their nominees appearing in the lists of registered shareholders to one of the following categories:

Type 1. Where the bank acts as investment manager for the shares held by the nominee; for example nominees holding for the bank's own pension fund or for its investment clients.
Type 2. Where the nominee acts as custodian for one particular beneficiary, but the bank does not itself have any management or voting responsibility for the shares.
Type 3. Where the nominee acts as custodian for a large number of individuals and companies, and the bank has no management or voting responsibility for the shares.

In most cases it was found that banks were willing to provide thi: information, though they did not always wish this help to be acknowledged in public. While disclosing no information about particular clients and their affairs, the classification of nominees in this way enabled the processing of the data to be pushed one stage further. All nominees of type three were deleted, as none of the individual beneficiaries was likely to be large enough to qualify as one of the top twenty vote-holders. Exceptions were made to this rule when type-3 nominees listed separate alphanumeric accounts in a register. In such cases each separate account was regarded as the equivalent of a type-2 nominee. In the majority of cases, however, type-3 nominees held shares in a single 'plain', undesignated account and could reasonably be deleted.[23] Type-1 nominees were aggregated under the name of the parent bank and combined with any holdings which the bank held in its own name.

The remaining problem, therefore, was to identify the vote-holders for the many type-2 nominees which appeared in the share registers. This problem was resolved through a two-step procedure. First, a list was drawn up of all corporate shareholders which were likely to be large shareholders in the companies studied but which did not appear in the share registers. This was done by scouring business directories to compile lists of large institutional investors. The major examples of such 'absent' investors were the various unit-trust groups and pension funds which, as trusts, had to be registered in the name of a custodian. Other examples were charities, some insurance companies, investment trust companies, and some family holdings. The second step was to try to match each member of this list with a corresponding name in the list of type-2 nominees. In some cases an intelligent guess could be made if the name of the nominee or the account designation contained some clue to the identity of the beneficiary; for example, through the use of the initial letters of the company name as an acronym. In all such cases, however, the guess was checked by writing to the suspected beneficiaries and asking for confirmation. In the remaining cases beneficiaries were approached and asked if they would disclose the name of their nominee(s). In very few cases was there a flat refusal to cooperate, and it eventually proved possible to identify the vote-holders for almost all of the type-2 nominee holdings.[24]

Having completed the task of identifying nominees, a directory and code-book were compiled for use in the project,[25] and this was used to complete the aggregation of connected holdings. Groups of commonly managed investment trusts and unit trusts, for example, were identified from the published yearbooks.[26] The most difficult task was to process information on pension fund holdings, as the available data were limited in both quantity and quality. Fund holdings which appeared to be managed 'in-house' by the pension department of the enterprise concerned were allocated to that enterprise, while those which were externally managed were allocated to the managers. Having carried out this final grouping it was possible to construct, for each company, a list of the twenty largest vote-holders, and these lists became the basic source data for all further analyses. These lists were the basis for the final allocation of enterprises to the categories of majority and minority control, and they made it possible to identify a group of one hundred enterprises in which there was no dominant shareholding interest.

By drawing on the methods and procedures pioneered by

Florence and the Cambridge researchers, it was possible to arrive at a systematic and comprehensive analysis of the structure of share ownership in large British companies. For the first time it was possible to view the distribution of votes among the dominant shareholdings in these enterprises and to map the contours of capitalist property. The chapters which follow will present the results of that investigation.

NOTES

1. Though based at the DAE for some time, the research continued after the original group dispersed. *See*: R. Stone, J. Revell and J. Moyle, *The Owners of Quoted Ordinary Shares*, London, Chapman and Hall, 1966, and J. Moyle, *The Pattern of Ordinary Share Ownership, 1957–70*, Cambridge University Press, 1971.
2. M.J. Erritt, et al., *The Ownership of Company Shares: A Survey for 1975*, London, HMSO, 1979; The Stock Exchange Fact Service, *The Stock Exchange Survey of Share Ownership*, London, The Stock Exchange, 1983.
3. P.S. Florence, 'The Statistical Analysis of Joint Stock Company Control', *Journal of the Royal Statistical Society*, 110, Part I, 1947; *idem.*, *Ownership, Control and Success of Large Companies*, London, Sweet & Maxwell, 1961.
4. This began with an investigation of Scottish companies, and the emergence of the methods and ideas developed in this book can be glimpsed in: J. Scott and M. Hughes, 'Ownership and Control in a Satellite Economy: A Discussion from Scottish Data', *Sociology*, 10, 1976; *idem.*, 'Capital and Communication in Scottish Business', *Sociology*, 13, 1979; *idem.*, *The Anatomy of Scottish Capital*, London, Croom Helm, 1980.
5. Maintenance of the share register and administration of share transfers has increasingly been devolved from the company itself to bankers and accountants who act as registrars for large numbers of companies.
6. This procedure was carried out in 1961 and the same multipliers were used in 1970. This involves a possible underestimation of beneficial shareholdings (such as those of pension funds) which were growing in significance over the period.
7. Vernon carried out a similar investigation of one particular 'blue chip' company and followed up with a postal questionnaire sent to a random sample of the personal shareholders. *See* R.A. Vernon, *Who Owns the*

Blue Chips?, Epping, Gower Press, 1973. Earlier work in the same tradition as the Cambridge research is reported in H. Parkinson, *Scientific Investment*, London, Pitman, 1932 and *idem.*, *Ownership of Industry*, London, Eyre & Spottiswoode, 1951.

8. A.A. Berle and G.C. Means, *The Modern Corporation and Private Property*, New York, Macmillan, 1932.
9. Florence investigated only English companies, as Scottish records are stored in Edinburgh.
10. Florence, *Ownership, Control and Success*, p.118.
11. *Ibid.*, p.45.
12. As Florence remarks, an American official enquiry had come to similar conclusions. *See* R.W. Goldsmith and R.C. Parmelee, *The Distribution of Ownership in the 200 Largest Nonfinancial Corporations*, Monograph no. 29, Temporary National Economic Committee, US Senate, 76th Congress, 3rd Session, Washington, Government Printing Office, 1940.
13. Florence, *Ownership, Control and Success*, pp. 45ff; *idem.*, 'The Statistical Analysis', pp.4–5.
14. L.S. Penrose, 'Elementary Statistics of Majority Voting', *Journal of the Royal Statistical Society*, 109, Part I, 1946.
15. This research is reported in J. Scott and C. Griff, *Directors of Industry*, Cambridge, Polity Press, 1984, and F.N. Stokman, R. Ziegler, and J. Scott (eds.), *Networks of Corporate Power*, Cambridge, Polity Press, 1985. Further details on the selection of companies can be found in Appendix I, p. 205, below.
16. The information was collected for English-registered companies only. Shareholding information on Scottish companies was taken from the earlier research reported in note 4, though this related to 1973/4 rather than to 1976. It was, unfortunately, not possible to collect new information for the Scottish enterprises.
17. Some companies, for example Unilever, did not have alphabetical registers, and many kept a separate listing of bank holdings.
18. Other sources used at this stage included *Banker's Almanac, Issuing Houses Yearbook, Jane's Major Companies of Europe, Key British Enterprises*, and *Kompass*.
19. Use of the voluminous Burke publications was much eased by the publication of *Burke's Family Index*, an alphabetical index to all families listed in the Burke publications since their inception.
20. This was confirmed wherever possible by writing to the lawyers or accountants or, in some cases, to the families themselves.
21. Some time after the completion of data processing it was discovered that a *Directory of Nominees* is published, which does give this information for most nominees.
22. A useful adjunct to street directories is *Oliver's Guide to the City of London*, which prints large-scale maps of the City showing streeet numbers and the ground plans of buildings.
23. A problem arises when one beneficiary holds shares in two or more such nominees. It is impossible to know to what extent this occurred.
24. A number of residual cases could be resolved by the use of data supplied

by Richard Minns, who had investigated the 'Section 27 Registers' of nominees maintained by some companies. Unfortunately, the existence of his data was not known until most nominees had already been identified. As the section 27 provisions were something of a novelty at the time of Minns' research, it is likely that the registers consulted by Minns were the result of short-term curiosity on the part of particular company secretaries. It is unlikely that much of this curiosity has been sustained, and many companies have made no enquiries about nominee holdings in their registers. It is likely, therefore, that the methods pursued in the present project are likely to be the most useful for future researchers.

25. J. Scott and C. Griff, *A Directory and Codebook of Nominee Companies*, Leicester, Company Analysis Project, 1983. This booklet is available from the British Lending Library and certain other libraries, and copies are stored in the national copyright reference libraries.

26. *Investment Trust Yearbook*, London, Fundex, annually; *Unit Trust Yearbook*, London, Fundex, annually. These yearbooks also give some information on the major holdings of particular trusts, which helped in identifying particular nominees.

4 Corporate Control in Britain

The conventional approach to studying corporate control has been to use sources which are easy and quick to consult and to use a fixed cut-off level of shareholding to identify cases of minority control. Typically these sources have been Annual Reports and directories, perhaps backed-up by short visits to Companies House to resolve awkward cases. The paucity of detail which is available from such sources has meant that the assignment of enterprises to particular categories of control has been undertaken by reference simply to the size of the largest known shareholding. This approach should not, however, be underestimated. It is an efficient and powerful means of drawing the broad outlines of corporate structure in a particular economy, and it provides a solid basis for broad international comparisons.[1] If the intention is to use a classification of control for further research, however, a more adequate—but more time-consuming—procedure must be followed. Both the sources of data and the categories of control must be refined. The use of a simple size criterion for identifying minority control—for example, all situations where the largest shareholder controls between 10 per cent and 50 per cent of the shares—necessarily generates marginal cases where control appears to be exercised with less than the requisite proportion of shares or a minority controller is subsequently ousted from control. Zeitlin has correctly emphasised that, for this reason, research must dispense with fixed cut-off points and determine the mode of control in an enterprise with reference to 'the corporate situation within the corporation and the constellation of intercorporate relations in which it is involved'.[2] The control status of an enterprise can be known only through a detailed investigation of the capital, commer-

cial, and personal relations in which it is enmeshed. To this end, Zeitlin and his co-workers proposed a paradigm for handling such data in their study of Chilean business.[3]
The data collected from the British share registers in the present research allows that research to proceed in the direction suggested by Zeitlin, and enables a more satisfactory categorisation of corporate control to be made. In earlier research and in earlier reports on the present data an attempt was made to approximate this procedure by introducing categories of 'shared' and 'limited' minority control,[4] but such a solution still depended upon coarse shareholding data and required the making of *ad hoc* decisions. This same procedure will be followed in the first section of this chapter so as to outline the broad features of corporate control in Britain and to present the data in a form comparable with other studies. The theoretical basis of this classification will then be considered, and it will be suggested that the forms of minority control must be thoroughly reconceptualised. Information from share registers will be used to present a reanalysis of the same enterprises in terms of this revised categorisation of control.

A PROVISIONAL VIEW OF CORPORATE CONTROL

Analyses of corporate control invariably find their starting point in the categories bequeathed by Berle and Means.[5] Recognising that the institution of the joint-stock company creates a novel legal and economic framework for business, they were concerned to show the conditions under which owner control could still be exercised. To this end they introduced the concept of majority control to describe the situation where a person who no longer owns the business assets *per se* may nevertheless be able to exercise similar powers of control by virtue of holding a majority of the issued shares of the company. A person—and by extension any corporate body—which holds a majority of the shares in a company may be able to act in much the same way as the traditional capitalist entrepreneur. Berle and Means recognised, however, that it

may also be possible to exercise these powers of control with
less than a majority of the shares. As has been shown in the
previous chapter, the category of 'minority control' which they
introduced to handle this situation has been a powerful, but
not unproblematic, stimulus to research. Most researchers
have accepted the validity of adopting a specified threshold
level of shareholding, below which the exercise of minority
control is unviable. Berle and Means adopted a cut-off point of
20 per cent in their own research, and later researchers have
suggested 10 per cent, 5 per cent, or even less.[6] In the
provisional analysis which follows, a threshold of 10 per cent
will be adopted.[7]

The major concern behind Berle and Means' discussion of
minority control was to delineate the conditions under which
'management' control becomes possible. Where no single
interest or group of associates was in a position to exercise
minority control, argued Berle and Means, the top executives
and directors of an enterprise can become a self-perpetuating
oligarchy largely independent of any control by shareholders,
and so are able to pursue alternative goals to those of the
profit-maximising capitalist entrepreneur. Critics of the
behavioural implications which some have sought to draw
from the concept of management control have attempted to
counter the Berle and Means thesis by asserting the renewed
importance of minority control. The growth of shareholding
by financial intermediaries, and especially by bank trust
departments, has been seen by writers such as Zeitlin and Kotz
to be the basis of 'bank minority control'.[8] The big banks,
owning substantial blocks of 5 per cent to 10 per cent of the
shares in large enterprises, are seen as exercising, perhaps
jointly, control over the affairs of these enterprises. In a recent
review of the American debate on this issue, Herman[9] has
argued that such critics put the case against managerialism too
strongly. Financial intermediaries, argues Herman, are not
typically minority controllers; there is, rather, a situation of
'constrained management control' in which they are able to
exercise a significant constraint over managerial decision-
making because of the high proportion of shares which they
collectively hold. Herman presents a sophisticated defence of
some of the key elements in the managerialist position, but his

rejection of the ideas of Zeitlin and Kotz is perhaps overplayed. It is argued here that neither 'bank minority control' nor 'constrained management control' are adequate descriptions of the complexities of corporate control in large enterprises. In enterprises where financial intermediaries are the dominant shareholders but none is able, individually, to exercise minority control, the category of control through a constellation of interests is a more adequate description to employ.[10] Where the twenty largest voting shareholders, who, as Florence argued,[11] comprise the key members of any voting block, collectively hold sufficient shares for minority control, the mode of control differs from both the minority and the management forms. The twenty largest shareholders comprise a diverse constellation of capitalist interests and no stable coalition can exercise the full powers of minority control. The fact that the members of the constellation have divergent and conflicting interests, however, means that the board of directors can indeed achieve some degree of autonomy from any particular interest. The top shareholders may be able to cooperate to determine the composition of the board, the outcome of this cooperation depending on the balance of power among them, but they are unable to act in concert over a sustained period. The concept of control through a constellation of interests aims to grasp the dynamics of this situation.

'Majority control', 'minority control', and 'control through a constellation of interests', therefore, are the major concepts required to understand contemporary corporate structure. A full analysis of control, however, must recognise certain other important modes of control which cannot be fully assimilated to these. The most straightforward of these other modes is that where majority control involves ownership of *all* the outstanding shares. Such 'wholly owned' companies may be either personally owned or subsidiaries of other enterprises.[12] Also of importance are the 'public corporations', corporate bodies formed by a department of state, having no share capital, and being directly responsible to a 'sponsoring' ministry or department. In some respects the public corporation is analogous to the wholly owned subsidiary, though its specific legal form and its direct links to the state apparatus rather than to a parent company make it advisable to distinguish it from all other modes of control. Mutual and friendly companies, too, must be distinguished from other corporate forms. The powers of control in these companies are legally vested in individual depositors and policy-holders, and it is rarely possible for votes to be accumulated by particular interests. The resulting rule of 'one person, one vote' means that, paradoxically, such enterprises may come closest to the situation of the 'managerial' enterprises conceptualised by Berle and Means. Finally, some intermediate forms of control must be recognised. The powers of majority and minority control may not be exclusively exercised by one particular interest but may require the sustained cooperation of a small group of associates. Such cases—which would include any true cases of joint 'bank minority control' as suggested by Zeitlin and Kotz—should be distinguished both from the exclusive forms of control and from control through a constellation of interests. In other cases the dominant shareholders may be represented on the board but have rather less than the percentage shareholding required for full minority control. Such cases have been described as 'limited minority control'.

Table 4.1 uses the various concepts which have been defined to present a provisional overview of corporate control in Britain. It can be seen that the largest single category is that of control through a constellation of interests, defined residually as those enterprises in which there was no dominant shareholding interest.[13] Forty per cent of the top 250 British enterprises of 1976—eighty-four non-financial and sixteen financial—were controlled in this way, and a further eight enterprises (building societies and life insurance companies) were subject to mutual ownership. The next largest category, encompassing almost one-third of the enterprises, was that for majority control, including the wholly owned, exclusive, and shared variants. The thirteen public corporations may legitimately be included in this total, as they were controlled by a single interest with no 'minority' challengers, and the enlarged category accounts for 36 per cent of the top enterprises. Finally, one-fifth of the enterprises were subject to various forms of minority control. Taking all 250 enterprises together, 112 (45 per cent) seemed to have had a *single* controlling interest.[14] Among these enterprises, the state had a

Table 4.1: *Corporate control in Britain: provisional classification (1976)*

Mode of control	Corporate				State	Mixed	Other	Totals
	Personal	British	Foreign	Mixed				
Public corps.	–	–	–	–	13	–	–	13
Wholly owned	7	1	28	0	2	0	0	38
Exclusive majority	14	1	9	0	1	2	0	25
Shared majority	0	7	1	4	1	2	0	15
Exclusive minority	19	12	5	0	0	0	0	36
Shared minority	0	2	0	0	1	8	0	11
Limited minority	3	1	0	0	0	0	0	4
Mutual	–	–	–	–	–	–	8	8
Constellation of interests	–	–	–	–	–	100	–	100
TOTALS	43	24	43	4	18	110	8	250

Note: The 100 enterprises controlled through a constellation of interests have all been allocated to the 'mixed' category, though it would, of course, be possible to subdivide them under various headings. This possibility is pursued in Chapter 5.

controlling interest in sixteen, personal shareholders controlled forty, and the remaining fifty-six were controlled by
corporate interests. Those controlled by corporate interests
were predominantly foreign owned, the largest single group
being the twenty-eight foreign wholly owned subsidiaries.
British and foreign corporate interests were also important
among the controllers of the enterprises subject to shared
control, though a number of the 'shared minority' cases
involved joint control by corporate and personal interests.
Overall it can be concluded that 71 enterprises were controlled
by corporate interests, 43 by personal interests, 18 by the state,
and 118 by rather more diverse groupings.[15]

CAPITAL AND CONTROL: RECONCEPTUALISING THE LINKS

The classification of modes of control which has been used in
the preceding section provides an overview of corporate
control in Britain, but it cannot be assumed to give an
unproblematic view. All scientific classifications are theoreti-
cally-grounded; they are not mere neutral, technical instruments of description. What, then, is the theoretical basis of the
typology which has been used here and which is common to the
majority of the studies in this area? The underlying theoretical
framework of this typology concerns the mechanisms of
majority voting. This involves an understanding of the
conditions under which particular shareholding interests can
achieve victory in a contested poll. These mechanisms and the
conditions under which they operate, however, have been left
largely untheorised by previous researchers—they have been
assumed to be unproblematic except in marginal cases of
minority control, where residual problems could be resolved
by arbitrary and *ad hoc* criteria. Such procedures can only be
avoided if the theoretical basis of the classification is made
clear and an attempt is made to resolve as many of its
theoretical problems as possible. Only then would it be
possible to return to the empirical classification given in Table
4.1 and to appraise its adequacy as a representation of
corporate control in Britain.

It was shown in Chapter 3 that Florence initially defined his concept of minority control by reference to a model of voting behaviour. His argument was that the holders of a small proportion of the shares could, in certain circumstances, depend upon a 96 per cent probability of success in corporate voting. In order to follow Florence's lead it is necessary to turn to political sociology, where an influential strand of thought has investigated rational choice in majority voting systems. Buchanan and Tullock[16] have proposed a particularly relevant analysis of the use of 'logrolling' in votes on a series of issues. Logrolling, or vote trading, may be explicit or tacit and allows a minority interest to gain sufficient support to form a majority coalition by attracting the votes of other interests who feel that they may, in return, be able to gain the support of the minority interest in the future.[17] This argument depends upon the existence of varying levels of involvement in particular issues on the part of the various voters. The majority coalition must be built by those with a strong interest in the outcome of the vote being able to persuade a sufficient number of those who are indifferent to support them on this particular issue.[18] In a future vote, when the strength of the involvements are reversed, the reciprocal exchange of support can be effected.

The relevance of this argument to corporate decision-making can be illustrated by the situation where A has 26 per cent of the shares in a company and B has 25 per cent, the remaining shares being widely dispersed. If A feels strongly on an issue but B is indifferent, then a successful strategy of coalition-building by A will result in a vote of 51 per cent in favour of A's views: the coalition led by A can win even if all the small shareholders vote against A. From this illustration it can be seen that the size of holding necessary for minority control depends not only on the distribution of the remaining shares but also on the distribution of opinion and indifference among the other shareholders and on their propensity to vote. That is to say, A's chances of success in the illustrative case are far greater if it can be assumed that the small shareholders are likely themselves to be indifferent to the outcome of the vote, or that they will split equally 'for' and 'against', or that many of them are unlikely to vote. If any of these conditions hold—or any combination of them—then A may be victorious with the support of a holder with far less than 25 per cent. Indeed, A may be successful without needing deliberately to try to build a coalition. For example, if it is assumed that shareholders representing 20 per cent of the total vote will not vote and that the remainder will divide equally on the issue, then A can be sure of getting 50.6 per cent of the poll without the support of B.[19] If A can assume that the small voters are indifferent and that it is possible to persuade the majority of the voters to support A's view, then A will be able to gain an overall majority in the poll with a personal holding of far less than 26 per cent.

This fictional illustration may usefully be compared with voting behaviour at an AGM of one of the enterprises studied in the present project.[20] National and Commercial Banking Group has been classified in Table 4.1 as subject to exclusive minority control because of a holding of 16 per cent by Lloyds Bank. In 1982 the enterprise, which had by then changed its name to the Royal Bank of Scotland Group, was involved in an unusually contentious AGM in which some of the smaller shareholders sought to block the reappointment of the vice-chairman as a director. In the poll 59,142,399 votes were cast in favour of the director, who had the support of Lloyds Bank, and just 398,295 votes were cast against. Thus the motion to reappoint the director was passed with a majority of more than 99 per cent. As measured by the issued voting capital, however, the total possible vote in Royal Bank of Scotland Group was 225.6m, meaning that the number of votes cast was only 26 per cent of the total possible vote. Thus, to obtain a 99 per cent majority in a 26 per cent poll, the Lloyds Bank holding needed only to attract the support of the holders of a further 10 per cent of the voting shares. To outvote Lloyds Bank on any issue at the Royal Bank of Scotland AGM, a dissident group would have to mobilise sufficient votes to increase the level of the poll to just over 32 per cent (twice the Lloyds Bank holding)[21] and ensure that all the voters except Lloyds were 'against'. If Lloyds were able to gain the support of any of the voters, then they would have a majority on the poll. Thus, to the extent that Lloyds is able to attract voters to its side, the dissidents will have to increase the size of the poll even further.[22]

A model of majority voting, therefore, shows the possibility of minority control with small shareholdings, but it does not generate a fixed threshold level for the exercise of this control. The conditions under which minority control is possible are so variable that no such level will hold in all cases. Florence's[23] analysis of the dynamics of corporate voting showed that minority control could be exercised with as little as 6 per cent of the shares, but Florence recognised that the conditions for the realisation of this success were not always to be met and that, for this reason, any fixed threshold would have to be set at a higher level so as to minimise the number of dubious cases. Florence's choice of a 20 per cent cut-off, therefore, reflected his attempt to combine two incompatible procedures. On the one hand, he wanted to construct what he termed a 'realistic' model of the dynamics of voting in corporate decision-making; and on the other hand, he sought clear-cut boundaries between minority and other forms of control. It should be apparent by now that an attempt to utilise a voting model can only be successful if the search for an absolute percentage cut-off is abandoned.

A solution to Florence's dilemma comes, paradoxically, from his own argument that attention should be directed to the twenty largest shareholders in any company. Following the logic of Florence's argument, reviewed in the preceding chapter, it should be clear that any contender for minority control will be found among an enterprise's twenty largest shareholders[24] and that the remaining nineteen will have to provide the basis for any rivalry to this control. Thus, true cases of minority control can be identified by examining the distribution of votes among the twenty largest vote-holders. In cases where there is no dominant controller, the top twenty shareholders remain an important group to study. If the mass of small shareholders can be virtually disregarded, as they will not vote or their vote will be divided equally, then the twenty largest shareholders will be more-or-less equal participants in a twenty-person 'game'. In such conditions it is necessary for a coalition only to receive a majority of the votes held by the top twenty, though any such coalition will be nebulous and transitory. This is precisely the situation described earlier as ·'control through a constellation of interests'.

These considerations may now be used to reassess the data in

Table 4.1. The use of a shareholding cut-off level of 10 per cent to identify exclusive minority control necessarily generates a number of marginal cases where the ostensible minority controller can, in fact, be outvoted by the remaining nineteen large shareholders. The rationale for reducing the cut-off from Berle and Means' 20 per cent to 10 per cent, a procedure followed by numerous other researchers, was the great dispersal of shareholdings which had taken place since the 1930s. It has to be recognised, however, that the last two decades have seen a remarkable reconcentration of share-holdings as a result of the growth of 'institutional' shareowner-ship, which has put considerable pressure on the surviving personal shareholders. It is likely, therefore, that a number of the enterprises classified as subject to exclusive minority control in Table 4.1 may actually be subject to more limited forms of minority control.

There were thirty-six enterprises classified as subject to exclusive minority control with the original 10 per cent cut-off, and in seventeen of these the presumed controlling interest was below 20 per cent.[25] Wherever information on the twenty largest voteholders in these enterprises was available, the distribution of votes between the largest holder and the remaining nineteen was investigated. It was found that in all cases where the largest holder controlled less than 14 per cent of the votes, the remaining nineteen holders could jointly outvote this interest. This was not possible in any case where the largest holding was in excess of 18 per cent. There were three cases where the size of the largest block lay between 14 and 18 per cent, all involving holdings of about 16 per cent, and these showed some variation in voting dynamics, suggesting that the boundary between 'secure' and 'limited' minority control was to be found somewhere around 16 per cent. This imprecision is deliberate, as the notion of a fixed threshold has already been discarded. If secure minority control is defined as the situation where the largest single shareholder cannot be outvoted by any coalition drawn from the remaining nineteen holders, an examination of the three marginal cases may cast some light on the conditions for its establishment. The three enterprises were National and Commercial Banking, Standard Chartered Bank, and Unilever. The situation of National and

Commercial has already been referred to, and an examination of its twenty largest vote-holders in 1976 showed that the Lloyds Bank holding could not be outvoted by the unified opposition of the other large shareholders. The Midland Bank held 16.94 per cent of Standard Chartered's voting capital, and while this holding could just be outvoted by the remaining nineteen holders, Midland could normally rely upon the support of one of these holders. This was MAIBL, in which Midland was a 45 per cent shareholder, and the two holdings together constituted an unassailable 18.63 per cent.[26] In Unilever the Leverhulme Trust held 16.55 per cent and could be outvoted, though one of the other large shareholders was the Unilever pension fund with a holding of 0.67 per cent. If the Leverhulme trustees—the Lever family and a mixture of past and present chairmen—could rely upon the support of this 'in-house' holding, they would have an unassailable voting block of 17.22 per cent. Thus it would appear that dominant interests with insecure 16 per cent holdings could secure their position if they had support from associated and other in-house holdings. Minority controllers without this possibility were likely to remain in an insecure position of control. Those with 14 per cent or less are not so likely to co-exist with in-house holdings of a sufficient size to guarantee them success, and so are more likely to be dependent on the support of other shareholders and/or on divisions among the other large shareholders.[27]

It is possible, however, that some of the cases where family minority control seems to have been based on holdings of less than 14 per cent may have involved an underestimation of the family holding. The Stein family, for example, were found to have held 12.68 per cent of the shares of Ladbroke Group and could have been outvoted by the next nineteen holders. The latter included some unidentified 'tax haven' holdings which may have been owned by the Stein family and would have brought its total of votes to 17.01 per cent.[28] Such a holding would have been a secure basis for control because a number of the other large shareholders were, unusually for the enterprises studied, individuals and families who may well have been associates of Cyril Stein and his fellow directors. Those exercising limited minority control have to form unstable and impermanent coalitions.[29] On this basis ten enterprises were

reclassified to this category,[30] and the original cases had to be
re-examined. In Table 4.1 this involved the following four
enterprises: Marley, Pilkington, and Mercury Securities
all showed large family holdings, by the Aisher, Pilkington,
and Warburg families, respectively; Wheatsheaf Distribution
and Trading had Ranks Hovis McDougall as its largest
shareholder, the residue of an earlier 100 per cent holding,
and had a number of directors recruited from the RHM
executive. Despite the fact that each of the families could
rely on in-house or associated holdings, this was in no case
sufficient to give them secure minority control.[31] Similarly,
RHM could be outvoted by the next three shareholders in
Wheatsheaf and had no associated holdings. Each of the four
enterprises, therefore, can be allocated to the newly defined
category of limited minority control.

It is important to distinguish cases of limited minority
control from cases of control through a constellation of
interests, and some pointers in this direction come from a study
by Cubbin and Leach.[32] Using data on the twenty largest
registered shareholders in eighty-five large British companies
between 1970 and 1971[33] they discovered that the twenty
holders collectively had a large enough block for voting control
in all eight-five enterprises, but this was not generally true of
the largest holder alone. Of particular interest was their
discovery that a 'controlling' holder could be identified in a
significant number of those enterprises where the largest
shareholder held less than 10 per cent. The latter enterprises
were those in which the largest shareholder typically held
between 5 per cent and 10 per cent, but Cubbin and Leach
make the important point that such a holding was a far less
secure base for control when the largest holder was a financial
intermediary rather than a person or a non-financial
enterprise.[34] What seems to be suggested by Cubbin and Leach,
though it is largely implicit in their paper, is that it is necessary
to distinguish relatively stable minority control from more
limited forms, and to distinguish both of these from enterprises
where shareholdings are concentrated in the hands of a diverse
group of financials.

Cubbin and Leach, then, provide an argument for re-
examining those enterprises subject to control through a

constellation of interests but which had a large holder with 5 per cent or more of the votes. There were five enterprises where a personal or non-financial shareholder had such a holding: C.T. Bowring and Cadbury Schweppes had dominant family shareholders, while Guinness Peat, BICC, and Tootal had dominant corporate shareholders. In each case, however, there are good reasons for retaining them in their original classification rather than reclassifying them as subject to limited minority control. In both Bowring and Cadbury the dominant holding was in the hands of a large group of allied families—'kinecon groups' in the terminology of Zeitlin *et al.*[35]—and in neither case was the kinecon group supported by in-house or associated holdings.[36] The largest shareholder in Guinness Peat was an in-house holding by the enterprise's own merchant banking subsidiary, Guinness Mahon,[37] and this was faced with two strong and potentially rival holdings: Aer Lingus in second place and the Kissin family third. Guinness Peat represents, in many respects, the clearest example of a balance of power among competing members of the controlling constellation. Tootal had ICI as its largest holder—partly as a direct holding and partly through its pension fund—but ICI had no supporting shareholder in the top twenty and was, in any case, pursuing a policy of non-intervention and no board representation in Tootal's affairs. Finally, BICC was a participant in a liaison scheme with General Cable of the USA, its largest shareholder, but this liaison was in process of dissolution. At the time of the study General Cable had no board representation and no associated holdings in the top twenty. All five enterprises, therefore, differ substantially from the cases of minority control.

The classification used in Table 4.1 employed two categories of shared control, and it is necessary to see whether any of the enterprises allocated to these categories should better be regarded as subject to control through a constellation of interests or, perhaps, to other forms of majority or minority control. 'Shared minority' should strictly be used not simply for enterprises in which two or more substantial shareholders can be identified. Rather, it should be restricted to those cases where two or more associated but independent shareholders cooperate to determine the corporate strategy of their 'joint associate'.[38] This implies that their joint holding cannot be outvoted by the remaining large holders. Four of the eleven enterprises fell unambiguously into this category—ICL, UDT, Bunzl Pulp & Paper, and Gill & Duffus—but the remaining enterprises were less certain candidates for true shared minority control. In those enterprises where a corporate shareholder acts essentially as a support for a personal holder, the normal categories of minority control are more appropriate. This applied to four enterprises: in Trafalgar House the Commercial Union acted as a support to Nigel Broackes's limited minority control; in Wood Hall Trust the Midland Bank supported Michael Richards; in Land Securities the Legal & General and the Prudential Assurance buttressed Lord Samuel's exercise of minority control; and in Hill Samuel the Samuel family had the support of Philip Hill Investment Trust and its associates.[39] In each of these cases the degree of cooperation between the dominant shareholders was such that they could not be regarded as separate interests coming together to form a joint associate; they formed unified controlling blocks. In the case of Lonrho, 'Tiny' Rowland's minority holding of 12.76 per cent was supported by another personal holding—a stake of 21.37 per cent held by Sheikh Nasser of Kuwait. The strongest case of this form of minority control occurred in Whitbread, where the Whitbread family holding was supported by an enterprise which was itself controlled by the family. The last of the enterprises originally classified as subject to shared minority control, British Sugar, can be reclassified unambiguously as a case of secure minority control, as the two largest shareholders were government agencies and the share registrations were purely nominal arrangements masking the position of the Ministry of Agriculture as the sponsoring department.

Those enterprises classified under 'shared majority' control were less in need of reclassification, as most were examples of joint ventures between British and foreign corporate interests. Closer examination showed that just three required reallocation, in each case from shared majority to secure minority. British Petroleum, like British Sugar, had the controlling state shareholding split between two government bodies—the Bank of England and the Treasury—and was a clear case of majority control. Lazard had 78.8 per cent of its shares held by S. Pearson and the bulk of the remainder held by Lazard of Paris, of which the British Lazard company held 33.33 per cent. This was effectively a case in which the Pearson majority holding was reinforced by an associated holding. Similarly in British and Commonwealth Shipping the Cayzer family had the support of Caledonia Investments, a company which was itself controlled by the family.

The results of the reclassification which has been discussed are shown in Table 4.2.[40] The broad features of majority and minority control are unchanged from those apparent in Table 4.1, though the two central categories of minority control—secure and limited—have a firmer theoretical basis than the earlier categories. The most obvious changes in the distribution are the transfer of three cases of shared majority to majority control and seven cases from shared minority to other forms of minority control; but the most important changes are in the distribution of enterprises between the two categories of minority control. Instead of limited minority control being treated as a residual category, it is now a more adequately theorised mode of control derived from an understanding of the dynamics of corporate voting. It may be concluded that the provisional classification and the methods on which it is based do indeed give a broad-stroke picture of the features of corporate control, and so can be regarded as a legitimate approach to use for many purposes. Research which tries to relate the control of particular enterprises to other aspects of corporate behaviour, however, would be seriously misleading if it employed the same methods. While incorrect classifications of majority-controlled, state-controlled, and constellation-of-interests-controlled enterprises would be relatively few, serious misrepresentation of the variants of minority control would take place. The discussion in the rest of this book is based upon the classification given in Table 4.2.

As a final note, it should be made perfectly clear that the emphasis on corporate voting in the construction of the typology should not be taken as indicating that corporate decision-making is dependen⁺ on continuous formal voting. Overt battles of the kind depicted in the discussion of National and Commercial Banking are rather rare. The normal,

Table 4.2: *Corporate control in Britain: final classification (1976)*

Mode of control	Corporate				State	Mixed	Other	Totals
	Personal	British	Foreign	Mixed				
Public corps.	–	–	–	–	13	–	–	13
Wholly owned	7	1	28	0	2	0	0	38
Majority	15	2	9	0	2	0	0	28
Shared majority	0	7	1	3	0	1	0	12
Secure minority	13	9	3	0	1	3	0	29
Limited minority	11	4	2	0	0	1	0	18
Shared minority	0	2	0	0	0	2	0	4
Mutual	–	–	–	–	–	–	8	8
Constellation of interests	–	–	–	–	–	100	–	100
Totals	46	25	43	3	18	107	8	250

Type of controller

routinised processes of corporate decision-making do, however, rest upon a power potential: formal majority voting can generally be avoided when the outcome of any such vote is predictable. The power potential inherent in the voting blocks is expressed in the pattern of constraints which structures recruitment to the board and the decision-making routines. These constraints determine the composition of the dominant coalition which has the power to determine the strategy of the enterprise. But there is the ever-present possibility that the normal processes will breakdown and the underlying conflict of interests among the large shareholders will be actualised in a struggle for control in which the ability to achieve a majority in a poll may be crucial.[41]

CORPORATE CAPITAL, STATE CAPITAL, AND ENTREPRENEURIAL CAPITAL

The dominant controlling interests in the 142 enterprises which were neither mutual companies nor controlled through constellations of interests (see Table 4.2) comprised state capital, corporate capital, and entrepreneurial capital, the three entering into various shared and supportive arrangements to produce the enterprises with 'mixed' controllers. The largest group of companies was that controlled by entrepreneurial capitalists: forty-six such enterprises were subject to the personal control of individuals and families, and a further seven had personal controllers allied with corporate interests. Foreign corporate capital accounted for 43 of the top 250, was allied with entrepreneurial capitalists in 2, and formed 3 joint ventures with British enterprises. British corporate capital, in addition to the three joint ventures with foreign capital, controlled twenty-five enterprises and was allied with entrepreneurial capital in the control of five other enterprises. Smallest in terms of number of enterprises was the group of enterprises controlled by the state—18 out of the top 250, with an indirect share in the control of a further 2.

The public sector in Britain was built mainly in the period since the Second World War, though enterprises such as the British Broadcasting Corporation and London Transport had a longer history. It was the nationalisation of many vast undertakings in the transport, energy, and heavy industrial sectors which set the outlines of the public sector that persisted until the end of the 1970s. Public enterprise remained concentrated in these areas[42] with only a weak presence in the banking sector through the nationalised Bank of England and the latter's participations in Finance for Industry (FFI) and the Agricultural Mortgage Corporation (AMC). Perhaps the major, but short-lived, innovation was the National Enterprise Board (NEB), and its predecessor the Industrial Reorganisation Corporation (IRC).[43] The NEB was formed as a state holding company and investment bank, but by the mid-1970s its role as a life-support system for ailing businesses had been firmly established: in 1976 the two main subsidiaries were Rolls-Royce and British Leyland.[44] The public enterprises studied in the present research comprised thirteen public corporations and seven joint-stock companies which the state controlled, directly or indirectly, or shared in control. An important feature of contemporary public enterprise is its highly centralised character by comparison with the early public undertakings, which were frequently organised on a local or municipal basis. Just one of the twenty enterprises subject to state control was responsible to a municipal body—London Transport was controlled by the Greater London Council—all the others were directly supervised by 'sponsoring' ministries in the central government. Nine government departments participated in state control, with the Department of Industry alone controlling six enterprises. Not only was the Department of Industry the sponsoring ministry for British Steel and the Post Office, its responsibility for the NEB gave it substantial leverage over Rolls-Royce and British Leyland.[45] The Department of Energy sponsored British Gas, the National Coal Board, and the Electricity Council, and the Department of the Environment supervised British Rail, National Bus, and National Freight. The Treasury sponsored no corporations, but held all the shares of the Bank of England, managed the government stake in BP, and had an indirect influence over FFI and AMC. Three Departments were each responsible for one enterprise—the Department of Trade for British Airways, the Scottish Office for the South of Scotland Electricity Board, and the Home Office for the BBC—and the

Ministry of Agriculture acted jointly with other departments in supervising two enterprises: with the Scottish Office it appointed the chairman and two directors of British Sugar, and with the Welsh Office and the Treasury it appointed three directors of AMC.

The public enterprises were important not only in the industrial sectors in which they operated but also in the whole structure of property ownership through their massive pension funds, which participated in the controlling constellations of many of Britain's largest enterprises.[46] Minns has correctly argued that this gives the state a great potential for intervention in business decision-making throughout the economy,[47] yet this potential has never been used. Although the power of government to determine the policies of enterprises is as great, if not greater, than that of a family or a multinational in a wholly owned enterprise, governments have typically not exercised this power and have resorted to *ad hoc* interventions in such matters as prices and wages. The prevailing principle is that operational matters should be decided by commercial, market criteria, and this implies that pension investments should be judged in actuarial terms rather than used as instruments of industrial policy. No British government has yet been willing to depart from this practice.

Foreign enterprises controlled 43 of the top 250 companies, and shared control in 3 joint ventures. As shown in Table 4.3, the largest single contingent came from the United States: one-third of all foreign-controlled enterprises were wholly owned subsidiaries of American multinationals, and one-fifth had weaker levels of American control. Next in importance were the five French-controlled enterprises, the four Canadian, and the two South African.[48] Though France was the single most important source for European parents, enterprises from five other European countries had subsidiaries operating in Britain.[49] Most of the European subsidiaries were wholly owned and the only case of shared control was Danish Bacon, where two Danish food producers held the bulk of the shares and many more were held by an extensive consortium of small Danish farmers and slaughterhouses. Though not included in Table 4.3, both Shell and Unilever formed the British constituents of large Anglo-Dutch enterprises which retained

Table 4.3: *Foreign control in Britain (1976)*

	Domicile of parent enterprise				
	USA	Canada	Europe	Other	Total
Wholly owned	17	3	7	1	28
Majority	4	1	1	3	9
Shared majority	3	0	1	0	4
Secure minority	2	0	0	1	3
Limited minority	1	0	1	0	2
Totals	27	4	10	5	46

Note: Two enterprises with 'mixed' controllers—Bunzl and Gill & Duffus—are not included

separate parent companies in both countries.[50] Other countries with enterprises with large British operations were the USSR (Nafta), Bolivia (Amalgamated Metal, controlled by the Patino group), and Argentina (Bunge).[51]

The discussion of foreign ownership has, so far, been concerned with the 'immediate control' of the subsidiary or associate.[52] While this is, for many purposes, the appropriate level of analysis, it is also important to examine the ultimate control of the parent enterprises. Unfortunately, such information is not available for all the enterprises studied. In the case of American subsidiaries, however, it is possible to use the sources employed in Chapter 6 to discover parental control. A majority of the British companies controlled by American enterprises were subject, ultimately, to control through a constellation of interests, though more than one-third of the parents had dominant corporate or personal controllers. Six of the ten parents which were majority or minority controlled had family controllers.[53] Table 4.4 shows that American enterprises which were themselves majority controlled tended to retain majority stakes in the British operating companies, while those which were controlled through constellations of interests were sometimes willing to

Table 4.4: *Ultimate control of US subsidiaries in Britain (1976)*

Immediate Control of subsidiary	Control of parent enterprise				Totals
	Majority	Minority	Constellation	Not known	
Wholly owned	3	3[a]	10	1[b]	17
Majority	0	2	2	0	4
Shared majority	0	1	2	0	3
Secure minority	0	0	2	0	2
Limited minority	0	0	1	0	1
Totals	3	6	17	1	27

Notes:
a. Anglo-Chemicals & Ore was a subsidiary of Engelhard Minerals, which was minority-controlled by the Oppenheimer group of South Africa. The latter also had a direct stake in the British top 250 through its control of Johnson Matthey.
b. No information was available on Primary Industries, the parent of Lonconex.

share control or to take minority holdings in British enterprises.[54]

Twenty-five enterprises were controlled by British corporate interests, and a further five were joint ventures. A large number of the controllers of these enterprises were banks or other financials: clearing banks controlled ten, other financials controlled six, non-financials controlled eleven, and three enterprises had other corporate shareholders. Eight of the ten enterprises controlled by clearing banks were themselves banks: Midland, Barclays, and Lloyds all had Scottish clearing bank subsidiaries or associates, Midland and Lloyds held minority stakes in overseas banks, and all four banks were members, together with the Bank of England, in three consortiums which controlled specialist banks.[55] The only non-financial enterprises controlled by banks were two minority-controlled trading companies.[56] In addition to shipping and commodity trading, these enterprises carried out such activities as insurance broking, leasing, and agriculture, and thus reinforce the conclusion that clearing-bank control was limited to the financial and commercial sectors. This was true also of the other financial controllers, as the enterprises which they controlled were involved in investment, credit, property, and commodity trading. One of these was a straightforward case of exclusive control,[57] one was a joint venture in hire purchase credit,[58] but the others involved more complex shared forms of control. Unit trust group M & G was jointly controlled by merchant bankers Kleinwort Benson and the Fairbairn family, and M & G itself shared control of commodity trader Gill & Duffus with Dutch investment interests. The Save & Prosper unit trust group was jointly controlled by two merchant banks and an investment partnership, though the leading role was taken by the Robert Fleming merchant bank.[59] Perhaps the most complex case was that of the investment trust management company Touche Remnant, which was formed by accountants Touche Ross and then sold to the various investment trusts managed by the company. Thus, Touche Remnant's shares were held equally by twelve trusts, and the company was the focus for the common management and administration of these same trusts. The trusts were, in turn, linked to one another through cross-shareholdings.[60] This mechanism of aligned participations— common in investment trusts but unusual in other sectors— ensured that ultimate control rested with the key directors and investment managers of the constituent trusts.

Six of the enterprises controlled by non-financials were joint ventures, three with American enterprises and three all-British. Among these, ICL was notable for the fact that the state, via the Department of Industry, had a small participation. This resulted from an earlier and larger minority holding but was not necessary as a support for the minority controllers. Neither Plessey nor GEC could exercise minority control alone, and the presence of the state holding served merely to reinforce this fact.[61] Three of the enterprises controlled by a non-financial operated in the food and tobacco sector, and each was minority controlled by parents which had family shareholders in their controlling constellations.[62] The only financial to be controlled by a non-financial was Lazard, minority-controlled by S.

Pearson which was itself family controlled. Finally, among the enterprises controlled by non-financials, Carrington Viyella was majority-controlled by ICI, though there was an agreement that ICI would not exercise these powers to the full. Shortly after the period of this research, ICI reduced its stake to a minority holding.

The three remaining cases of control by corporate interests were rather different from those already discussed. Perhaps the most straightforward was the meat distributor FMC, which was controlled by the NFU Development Trust. This trust was run by the National Farmers' Union, and FMC was operated as a commercial meat-marketing board. In this case, therefore, the ultimate controller lay outside the corporate system. Globe Investment Trust had Cable Trust as its minority controller, but both trusts were part of a trust management group, and Globe was, in turn, the minority controller of Cable. As in the case of Touche Remnant, the trusts in the group were allied through aligned participations—but in this case there was no separate management company.[63] The liaison arrangement between Globe and Cable, therefore, ensured that each was effectively controlled by its own board of directors, their boards being almost identical. In Lucas Industries a different legal device ensured that control was vested in the directorate, as the minority controller was the enterprise's own, internally managed pension fund. The Lucas directorate could successfully face a challenge from any large shareholder as the directors had the secure voting power of the pension fund behind them. Although this is a widespread practice in the United States, Lucas was the only case discovered among the top 250 British enterprises.

The corporate interests controlling major British enterprises through majority and minority holdings, whether foreign or British, were predominantly controlled through constellations of interests—a fact which strengthens the conclusions drawn earlier about the importance of this mode of control in the modern capitalist economy. Nevertheless, a number of cases of ultimate control by personal and family interests were discovered, and it is important to assess the extent of the control which such entrepreneurial capitalists exercised over enterprises in Britain's top 250. Entrepreneurial capitalists comprise all personal capitalist interests involved in the ownership and control of large enterprises and may variously be individual 'tycoons', founders, or inheritors of businesses, nuclear families or extended family groups, or groups of associates linked through bonds of friendship or common business activities.[64]

Strategic control by entrepreneurial capitalists was found in thirty-nine enterprises, with a further six having enterpreneurial interests sharing control with companies. A further seven enterprises were controlled by private trusts and foundations which generally had a continuing connection with a founding family or other personal interest. These enterprises were overwhelmingly drawn from a narrow range of economic sectors, predominantly those concerned with financial and commercial activities. Seventeen enterprises were involved in merchant banking, investment, insurance broking, commercial property, and leisure services; nine were involved in the related areas of construction and construction goods; and thirteen operated in various areas of wholesale and retail distribution. The only area of manufacturing industry to show a significant representation of personally controlled enterprises was food and drink, where seven such enterprises were found. The size of the dominant shareholding in the thirty-nine enterprises where personal interests had exclusive control varied from just below 10 per cent in Pilkington, Marley, and Mercury Securities, to 100 per cent in Baring, Rothschild, Heron, Littlewood, and Union International, but the bulk of the enterprises showed personal holdings in the range 30 to 70 per cent. In the majority of these enterprises a single family, sometimes an extended family, held the controlling stake, but in enterprises such as Robert Fleming, J. Lyons, W.H. Smith, and Tesco the family group was extended to include collateral kin with differing family names. Just one family, the McAlpines, held a controlling block in more than one of the enterprises— two branches of the family, each controlling a separate construction business.[65] All except one of the controlling families was British, though a number of their members may have been partially resident abroad for tax reasons; certainly a number of their holdings were registered in the names of Channel Island and Bermuda nominees.[66]

Many of the family holdings were registered on behalf of family trusts and private foundations, but seven enterprises were controlled by trusts which had a more tenuous relationship with groups of enterpreneurial capitalists. These fell into three broad categories: those controlled by charitable trusts, those controlled through voting trusts, and one controlled through a 'partnership' scheme. Rank Organisation, Rowntree Mackintosh, Unilever, and Wellcome Foundation were all controlled by trustees of charitable trusts, and all except Wellcome had representatives of their founding families among the trustees. The Rank Foundation held a majority of the shares in the Rank Organisation,[67] and its trustees included various directors of the enterprise and of Ranks Hovis McDougall.[68] Similarly, two Rowntree trusts formed a controlling minority block in Rowntree Mackintosh, holding their shares through the Official Custodian for Charities, and the trustees included a former chairman of the company and members of the intermarried Rowntree, Seebohm, and Barclay families. In the case of Unilever the Lever family link with the controlling Leverhulme Trust was rather more tenuous: though the family received three-quarters of the income from the trust, a majority of the trustees were past and present chairmen of the company and the only family trustee was Lord Leverhulme. Wellcome Foundation shows a complete dissociation of the founding interest from the charitable trust, though the enterprise may reasonably be characterised as controlled by the persons who had the power to vote the controlling holding. Sir Henry Wellcome, the founder, had no family to inherit his business and had established the Wellcome Trust to fund medical research from its earnings from the ownership of the Foundation. Wellcome's will stipulated merely that the trustees were to include representatives of both business and science. In this case, therefore, the trust holding was the basis for the trustees to constitute themselves as a self-perpetuating group of controllers.[67]

Where Wellcome Foundation shows a testamentary transfer of control from an individual to a group of trustees without family succession, John Lewis Partnership shows how such arrangements can coexist with family control. The 'partnership' scheme created by John Spedan Lewis has generally been seen as an example of the most extreme form of democratic employee control,[70] though a closer investigation showed that control was in fact highly concentrated. A partnership trust was created by Lewis through a settlement of his shares in trust for the employees and, in 1950, a transfer of their voting power to trustees. The trustees, a majority of whom are elected by the employees' 'central council', appoint the chairman and deputy chairman of the company, while the chairman appoints a half of the directors and the central council appoints the other half. The chairman of the trustees is automatically the chairman of the company and has the power to nominate a successor. Considerable power, therefore, was vested in the chairman, who could be removed from office only if a two-thirds majority of the central council passed a motion of no confidence: under such circumstances the elected trustees could exercise their only legal power, to dismiss the chairman. These legal mechanisms which strengthened the position of the chairman resulted in the recruitment of John Lewis's nephew to the chair in 1972. Control over Trust Houses Forte and Leslie & Godwin also was dependent on the existence of trustee shareholdings, but both cases involved special voting rights for shares held by trustees. The complex voting arrangements in THF derived from the merger in 1970 of the Forte family business with the old Trust Houses group. Special 'trust shares' accounted for 0.13 per cent of the capital, but their trustees had a legal right to 50 per cent of the votes. The Forte family held a substantial minority stake to buttress the trustee holdings. The Leslie & Godwin capital included a 0.5 per cent block of 'management shares' which had extra voting rights so long as they were held by duly appointed trustees. In these circumstances, which held at the time of the research, the trustees were entitled to cast votes equivalent to one-third of the votes represented by the remaining shares. Through this complex arrangement the trustees were able to vote a 25 per cent block in any poll, and this holding was reinforced by Rothschild Investment Trust's holding of 7.11 per cent as Jacob Rothschild was one of the trustees. In Both THF and Leslie & Godwin the consequences of share dispersal in large enterprises were at least partially offset by the maintenance of the legal device of a voting trust.

In addition to the enterprises in which family and personal

shareholders were the dominant interests, a large number of the enterprises with no dominant interest had family participants in their controlling constellations. The latter enterprises showed less of a concentration in the financial and commercial sectors than was the case in those with dominant family controllers, though two-thirds were to be found in finance, distribution, property, construction, and food and drink.[71] Table 4.5 shows that fifty-five families were found among the top twenty shareholders in thirty-six of the enterprises classified as controlled through a constellation of interests.[72] One enterprise, S. & W. Berisford, had four separate family groups among its twenty largest shareholders, but a majority of the enterprises had just one large family shareholder. Two-thirds of the enterprises with family participants had these family interests represented on their boards of directors, with the likelihood of board representation increasing with the number of families included in a controlling constellation. The mean size of a family holding in these thirty-six enterprises was 1.64 per cent, and it was discovered that the size of a family's holding was associated with the probability of it having at least one board seat. Table 4.6 shows that there was a three-to-one probability that a family with 1 per cent or more would be represented on the board. By contrast, there was a three-to-one probability that families with a holding below this level would not have board representation. An interesting discrepancy in the detailed figures shown in Table 4.6, however, is the fact that families holding less than 0.5 per cent had the highest probability of board representation, perhaps indicating that they comprised mainly current directors who had rapidly and actively acquired their holdings.[73]

Disregarding those personally controlled enterprises which were controlled by non-family trustees,[74] about one-third of the top 250 enterprises had a significant level of family control or influence: 49 with family control and 36 with family participation in their controlling constellations. Managerialist writers have suggested the existence of a long-term decline in family capitalism, and this figure of eighty-five enterprises with family control or influence is surely remarkable; but it is, nevertheless, important to try to assess the level of family

Table 4.5: *Family participations in controlling constellations: Britain (1976)*

No. of families participating	No. of enterprises	Total no. of families
4	1	4
3	3	9
2	10	20
1	22	22
Totals	36	55

Table 4.6: *Size of family participations: Britain (1976)*

| | Size of family shareholding block (%) | | | | | |
	<0.5	0.5–0.9	1.0–1.9	2.0–2.9	>3.0	Total
With board membership	4	6	13	4	6	33
Without board membership	1	13	4	3	1	22
Totals	5	19	17	7	7	55

control and influence which existed in the heyday of family capitalism. Unfortunately, comparable information on shareholdings in earlier years is not available, and so it is necessary to use estimated figures.[75] To obtain an estimate of the extent of enterpreneurial capital prior to the First World War the top 250 enterprises of 1904 were investigated, using board membership as an indicator of family control and active influence.[76] All those enterprises which met any one of three criteria were selected as showing family influence or control, the three criteria being (1) one or more directors having the same name as the company (2) one or more of the directors was known to have been, or to be descended from, a dominant shareholder in the enterprise's history and (3) two or more directors had the same surname.[77] A total of ninety-one non-financials and nineteen financial family enterprises were selected in this way. These 110 enterprises included many clear-cut cases of family control: the Charrington, Guinness, and Courage breweries, Reckitt, Vickers, S. Pearson, and Shell were all on the list. Also included were enterprises where control was shared by associated families (Furness Withy, Linen Thread, North British Locomotive) and by large coalitions of families in such massive amalgamations as Bleachers Association, Fine Cotton Spinners, Associated Portland Cement, and Imperial Tobacco. A number of the selected enterprises, such as the large railways and the clearing banks, were likely to have involved families participating alongside corporate interests in enterprises with no dominant shareholder—the precursors of the modern constellations of interests.[78] The selection procedure is likely to have resulted in an unmeasurable underestimation of family control and influence, owing to the existence of cases where a controlling or influential family had a name different to that of the enterprise and had only one board representative, but the most important underestimation concerns influential families without board representation. If these 'passive' family shareholders are deleted from the 1976 list, however, a fair comparison of the extent of family control and active influence in the two periods can be made. On this basis, the 110 enterprises of 1904 should be compared with a total of 73 in 1976. 'Active' family control in the top 250, therefore, would seem to have declined from over 44 per cent to 29 per cent between 1904 and 1976.

The growth of corporate shareholdings—especially those by financial intermediaries—has been a major factor in bringing about this decline in family shareholding, and the implications of this will be reviewed in the following chapter. Another important factor, however, was the sheer growth in size of enterprises, which made it progressively more difficult for families to retain sizeable stakes. Yet other family enterprises were taken over by larger enterprises, giving the families a diluted holding in the new parent. Five enterprises appeared to have withstood these forces and showed family control in both

1904 and 1976; they remained large enough to appear in the top 250 in both years and they remained under family control. These enterprises were Baring Brothers, N.M. Rothschild, Arthur Guinness, S. Pearson, and Whitbread.[79] One further enterprise, Imperial Tobacco, experienced massive growth over the period and moved from family control to active family influence.[80]

CORPORATE CONTROL AND CORPORATE INTERLOCKING

Where one enterprise holds shares in another, an intercorporate capital relation is established; but this is not the only form of intercorporate relation. An interlocking directorship exists wherever one person is a director of two enterprises: the presence of the person on both boards creates a link between the two enterprises which may be used for the communication of information between them or to aid the coordination of their actions. These uses of interlocks will be explored in the following chapter, but it is necessary here to examine the tendency to interlock shown by the various types of enterprise. For this purpose an interlock will be recognised only if it exists between two members of the top 250; board connections with smaller enterprises are not of immediate concern.

Table 4.7 shows that 189, just over three-quarters, of the top 250 enterprises were interlocked, but there was considerable variation from one category to another. Mutuals, majority-controlled, and wholly owned enterprises showed a below-average propensity to interlock, with fewer than a half of the wholly owned enterprises being interlocked. The highest rates of interlocking were found in the enterprises subject to the forms of shared control, while significantly above-average interlocking was also found among the public corporations and those controlled through constellations of interests. Virtually all of the enterprises exclusively controlled by British corporate interests were interlocked, often with the controlling interest but also with other enterprises.[81] About one-third of the foreign subsidiaries, wholly owned and majority controlled, were interlocked, and this proportion rose to two-

Table 4.7: *Mode of control and interlocks: Britain (1976)*

Mode of control	Number of enterprises		
	Interlocked	Uninterlocked	Total
Public corps.	11	2	13
Wholly owned	16	22	38
Majority	15	13	28
Shared majority	11	1	12
Secure minority	24	5	29
Limited minority	14	4	18
Shared minority	4	0	8
Mutual	6	2	8
Constellation of interest	88	12	100
Totals	189	61	250

thirds amongst the securely controlled foreign associates. The weaker the foreign control in an enterprise, the more likely was it to interlock.[82] This finding is confirmed by the fact that only one of the four enterprises with shared majority control (Danish Bacon) was uninterlocked. While Danish Bacon was controlled by a coalition of Danish producers with minimal British participation, the remaining three (Rank Xerox, British Aluminium, Morgan Grenfell) were joint ventures between American and British enterprises. Only a quarter of the wholly owned American subsidiaries were interlocked, those with parents controlled through constellations of interests being more likely to interlock than those whose parent had a dominant controller.

Just under two-thirds of the enterprises controlled by enterpreneurial capitalists were interlocked, the propensity to interlock varying with the strength of family control. While almost three-quarters of those enterprises subject to personal limited minority control were interlocked, this was the case for less than a half of those wholly-owned by personal interests. All categories of enterprises subject to enterpreneurial capital control showed a below-average tendency to interlock. The relationship between the strength of family control and the propensity to interlock was confirmed by the pattern of interlocks found among the enterprises controlled through constellations of interests. Just twelve of these enterprises had no interlocks, and eight of these had family participants. Put another way, twenty-eight of the thirty-six enterprises with family participants were interlocked—a rate higher than that found in any of the categories of family control.[83]

In this chapter it has been argued that the composition of the board of directors of an enterprise is constrained by the nexus of capital relations which forms its control situation. An examination of the twenty largest shareholders in an enterprise will disclose the dominant shareholding interest, if such an interest exists, or will show the composition of the controlling constellation. The distribution of control over the voting shares among those large holders determines the potential which any interest or coalition of interests may have to attain and retain a share in deciding the corporate strategy pursued by the enterprise. State capital, corporate capital, and enterpreneurial capital have been shown to make up the controlling groups in those enterprises having a dominant interest, and they also comprise the main participants in the controlling constellation of the remaining enterprises. In the following chapter the composition of these constellations will be examined further, and it will be argued that an understanding of the dynamics of corporate control rests upon an analysis of the network of intercorporate relations which these capitalist interests create. This network is built from the commercial relations in which enterprises engage, the capital relations which determine their mode of control, and the personal relations—predominantly interlocking directorships —which structure the ability of the corporate boards to transform the environment in which the enterprise operates.

NOTES

1. This approach was the basis of the comparisons presented in J. Scott, *Corporations, Classes, and Capitalism*, rev. edn, London, Hutchinson, 1985.
2. M. Zeitlin, 'Corporate Ownership and Control: The Large Corporation and the Capitalist Class', *American Journal of Sociology*, 79 (1974), 5: 1107–8.
3. M. Zeitlin, L. Ewen, and R.E. Ratcliff, ' "New Princes" for Old: The Large Corporation and the Capitalist Class in Chile'. *American Journal of Sociology*, 80 (1975) 1.
4. *See* particularly J. Scott and M. Hughes, *The Anatomy of Scottish Capital*, London, Croom Helm, 1980, Appendix.
5. A. Berle and G.C. Means, *The Modern Corporation and Private Property*, New York, Macmillan, 1932.
6. R. Larner, *Management Control and the Large Corporation*, New York, Dunellen Press, 1970; P.H. Burch, *The Managerial Revolution Reassessed*, Lexington, Mass., Lexington Books, 1972.
7. This criterion was used for the comparisons presented in Scott.
8. Zeitlin *op. cit.*; D. Kotz, *Bank Control and the Large Corporation*, Berkeley, University of California Press, 1978.
9. E.S. Herman, *Corporate Control, Corporate Power*, Cambridge University Press, 1981.
10. This concept was first proposed in the first edition (1979) of Scott.
11. P.S. Florence, *Ownership, Control, and Success of Large Companies*, London, Sweet & Maxwell, 1961.
12. Berle and Means *op. cit.*, introduced the category of 'private ownership' to refer to majority control with 80 per cent or more of the shares. It is preferable to avoid this arbitrary threshold and to distinguish simply wholly owned enterprises from other cases of majority control.
13. It will be shown in Chapter 5 that these enterprises can, in fact, be identified positively as controlled through constellations of interest.
14. The categories are public corporation, wholly owned, exclusive majority, and exclusive minority.
15. A full listing of the 250 enterprises together with their controlling interests can be found in J. Scott, *Corporate Control in Britain*, Working Paper for Company Analysis Project, University of Leicester, 1985. This is available from the British Lending Library, the national copyright libraries, and various other libraries. Tables 4.2 and 4.3 in an earlier report (*Directors of Industry*) contained an error, as Whitbread was originally believed to be subject to shared majority control. Further evidence suggests that shared minority control is the appropriate category, with the two interests holding 40.38 per cent. Whitbread appeared in the 'uninterlocked' columns of those Tables. *See* J. Scott and C. Griff, *Directors of Industry*, Cambridge, Polity Press, 1985.

16. J.M. Buchanan and G. Tullock, *The Calculus of Consent*, Ann Arbor, University of Michigan Press, 1962.
17. *Ibid.*, pp.134 ff.
18. On the analysis of indifference through the use of preference curves, *see* D. Black, *The Theory of Committees and Elections*, Cambridge University Press, 1958.
19. The shares of the small shareholders who vote account for 29 per cent of the shares, and 14.5 per cent will be voted in support of A's 26 per cent. Thus A's proposal will receive 40.5 (26 plus 14.5) of the eighty votes cast, even if B's 25 per cent and the remaining 14.5 per cent are voted against. A block of 40.5 per cent of the shares in an 80 per cent poll is equal to a 50.63 per cent majority vote.
20. The information in the following paragraph is drawn from *The Financial Times* for the relevant period during January 1982.
21. The actual size of the holding at this time was 16.4 per cent.
22. The core of any rival coalition to Lloyds Bank would have to be the second-largest holder in Royal Bank, the Kuwait Investment Office, with 8 per cent. The KIO, however, has a firm policy of not voting any of the shares which it holds—a strategy which, in this case, would enhance the control exercised by Lloyds.
23. Florence *op. cit.*
24. In Florence's work he investigated the twenty largest registered shareholders. For reasons given in Chapter 3, the present research examines the twenty largest vote-holders.
25. *See* Scott, *Corporate Control in Britain.*
26. This was further reinforced by the fact that 19 per cent of the shares in MAIBL (Midland and International Banks) were owned by Standard Chartered itself.
27. It must be emphasised that the specific percentage figures relate to large British companies in the mid-1970s and cannot be transplanted to any other context. The underlying principles, of courses, are of general application.
28. In any cases where the annual report disclosed a director's holding in excess of those discovered in the register, the higher figure was that used in the research.
29. *See* Buchanan and Tullock, pp.151–2.
30. The total of twenty-six includes the two marginal cases of Standard Chartered and Unilever. This category also includes BAT Industries, where Imperial Group held 15.77 per cent, though the 1976 share registers for this company could not be analysed as it was in the process of reconstruction during the year.
31. Marley was difficult to analyse as the Annual report seemed deliberately ambiguous and the register included a large number of nominees which may, in fact, have been family holdings. It is estimated, however, that the Aisher family had 8.75 per cent and could perhaps rely on a block of shares held by the Hill Samuel merchant bank. The Pilkington block of 6.51 per cent was backed-up by a company pension-fund holding, and the Warburg holding was fortified by in-house-managed funds of the

Mercury group itself.

32. J. Cubbin and D. Leach, 'The Effect of Shareholder Dispersal on the Degree of Control in British Companies: Theory and Measurement', *Economic Journal*, 93 (1983).
33. The source of their data is D. Collett and G. Yarrow, 'The Size Distribution of Large Shareholdings in Some Leading British Companies', *Oxford Bulletin of Economics and Statistics*, 1976.
34. Cubbin and Leach, p.366.
35. Zeitlin *et al., op. cit.*
36. In the case of Cadbury Schweppes the enterprise's own pension fund and its merchant bankers, Kleinwort Benson Lonsdale, were important holders outside the top twenty. A full list of the twenty largest shareholders in each of the enterprises controlled through a constellation of interests can be found in J. Scott, *The Controlling Constellations*, Working Paper for Company Analysis Project, University of Leicester, 1984. This is available in various libraries as mentioned in note 15.
37. This block represented bank-managed funds and may have included some Guinness family holdings.
38. J. Scott and C. Griff, *Directors of Industry*, p.22.
39. Trafalgar House: Broackes 2.65 per cent and Commercial Union 7.57 per cent. Wood Hall: Richards 1.69 per cent and Midland 18.41 per cent. LSIT: Samuel 6.73 per cent, Legal & General 9.76 per cent, and Prudential 6.41 per cent; both insurance companies held as trade investments rather than as 'institutional' holdings. Hill Samuel: Samuel family 12.8 per cent and PHIT 17.9 per cent. The two Samuel families were not related.
40. A full listing of the final classification can be found in Appendix II. Table 4.2 includings a new heading for 'mixed' corporate controllers to bring out the number of Anglo-foreign joint ventures.
41. *See* Scott and Griff, pp.4–5.
42. The denationalisation of iron and steel from 1951 reduced public involvement in heavy industry for a time; the large steel enterprises were renationalised, to form British Steel, in 1967.
43. *See* S. Young and A.V. Lowe, *Intervention in the Mixed Economy*, London, Croom Helm, 1974. D.C. Hague and G. Wilkinson, *The IRC: An Experiment in Industrial Intervention*, London, George Allen & Unwin, 1983.
44. The NEB was a public corporation, not a joint-stock company, and so its subsidiaries appear under the state-controlled heading in Tables 4.1, 4.2, and in Appendix II. Since 1976 the NEB has been dissolved and a number of other state enterprises have been privatised.
45. At the time of the research British Telecommunications remained a part of the Post Office. The DOI also administered a small shareholding in ICL.
46. The large electricity and coal industry pension funds were managed in-house by the corporations themselves, while the funds for the Post Office and British Rail were substantially managed externally by merchant banks.

47. R. Minns, *Pension Funds and British Capitalism*, London, Heinemann, 1980; *idem*, *Take Over the City*, London, Pluto, 1982.
48. The latter includes the Belgian–South-African Rupert group, controllers of Rothmans.
49. Germany, Switzerland, Belgium, the Netherlands, and Denmark.
50. 'Shell' Transport and Trading held 40 per cent of the Royal Dutch-Shell group, the remainder being held by its Dutch partner, and operated purely as a holding company for the British operations of the group. A similar, but equal, relation existed in Unilever, and in both enterprises management of group operations was internationalised.
51. The controlling families of Bunge were resident in a number of South American countries.
52. *See* Scott and Griff, p.105, for a discussion of immediate and ultimate control.
53. The Ford, Reynolds, Cargill/Macmillan, Mars, Heinz, and Hoover families. The South African Oppenheimer group, controller of US parent Engelhard Minerals, was also family controlled.
54. Twenty of the US parents were among the top 252 US enterprises studied in Chapter 6. The exceptions were Carter Hawley Hale, Chrysler, Engelhard Minerals, Hoover, Ingram, Mars, and Primary Industries.
55. These were AMC, FFI, and Yorkshire Bank. Midland Bank and the Bank of England did not participate in Yorkshire Bank.
56. Barclays controlled Tozer, Kemsley, and Millbourn; Midland controlled Mitchell Cotts.
57. Eagle Star Insurance controlled English Property.
58. United Dominions Trust was controlled by Eagle Star and Prudential Assurance.
59. Fleming's associates were Barings Brothers and Ivory & Sime, the latter being a Scottish-based investment trust group. Further details on Ivory & Sime can be found in J.P. Scott and M.D. Hughes, *The Anatomy of Scottish Capital*, London, Croom Helm, 1980. After the completion of this project Robert Fleming partly bought-out its associates and acquired majority control of Save & Prosper.
60. The largest were Industrial & General Trust and Atlas Electric & General Trust. *See* annual reports and the booklet *An Introduction to Touche Remnant International Investment Management*, London, Touche Remnant, n.d.
61. For this reason, ICL was not included under the 'mixed' heading in Table 4.1 or 4.2.
62. BAT Industries was controlled by Imperial Group, Linfood by Guinness Peat, and Wheatsheaf by Ranks Hovis McDougall.
63. Electra Group Services provided common administration, but was a wholly owned subsidiary of Globe. Cable was acquired by Globe during 1977.
64. The term 'family holdings' will often be used to refer to shareholdings by entrepreneurial capitalists, whether individuals or families.
65. Marchwiel and Newarthill were the two McAlpine parent compaies. Two unrelated Laing families were discovered, one controlling John

Laing and the other United Biscuits. Similarly, the Samuels controlling Hill Samuel and LSIT were unrelated.

66. The exception was the Al Fayed family, controlling Costain.The Bunzl, Beaumont, and Schoenberg families, variously resident in Germany, Australia, and the United States, shared control of Bunzl with Imperial Group and their own American Filtrona company.

67. This was held through a private holding company.

68. Other Rank family charitable trusts participated in the controlling constellation of RHM, and there were a number of common trustees.

69. Wellcome might be considered as showing a pattern of 'internal' control similar to that found in Lucas. The main difference is that the recruitment of the Wellcome trustees, who appoint the directors, was restricted by the conditions of Sir Henry Wellcome's will, whereas the recruitment of directors to Lucas involved no such restrictions.

70. *See* A. Flanders, *Experiment in Industrial Democracy*, London, Faber & Faber, 1968.

71. Five in finance, commercial property, and leisure; one in construction; nine in retail and wholesale distribution; and nine in food and drink.

72. Provisional results in an earlier report showed a lower figure because the Clark interests in EMI had not been included and because of the omission of the Berisford family. *See* J. Scott, 'The British Upper Class', in D. Coates, R. Bush, and G. Johnston (eds.), *A Socialist Anatomy of Britain*, Cambridge, Polity Press, 1985. Other discrepancies in figures reported arise from the differential treatment of trustee holdings in that report.

73. The five blocks involved were Pybus in AAH, Percival and Aston in Berisford, and Peake and Harper in Harrisons & Crosfield. The Aston holding, held by a woman, was the only one not to be associated with board representation.

74. Those enterprises disregarded here are Leslie & Godwin, Wellcome Foundation, and Trust Houses Forte, though the trustees in the latter were associated with the Forte family.

75. The study of Florence relates to too recent a date. Resources were not available in the present research to collect the appropriate data from share registers.

76. These enterprises were those studied in Scott and Griff.

77. One enterprise where there was known to be a family controller without board representation, Meux Brewery, was added to the resulting list. Similarly, British Westinghouse, where a family director represented the holding of the American parent, was deleted. Some cases where the family representation reflected a holding by a family bank or holding company were included in the list as these could not easily be identified and the banks and holding companies were generally closely controlled by families.

78. Families appearing among the controllers of two or more enterprises were Rothschild and Hoare (two branches of the Hoare family) and members of the Barclay and Lloyd clans. All except Rothschild were part of the great Quaker cousinhood. *See* Scott and Griff, Ch.4.

79. Pearson declined in size during the inter-war period as the family wound down the original contracting business and expanded their other corporate involvements. Pearson's position in 1976 reflects the company's resurrection as the parent for the family's myriad business activities.
80. Two other enterprises with family participants in 1976 (Coats Patons and Reckitt & Colman) had predecessor enterprises in the 1904 list which were family controlled.
81. The only exception was Wheatsheaf Distribution.
82. Note that this did not hold between wholly owned and majority-controlled subsidiaries.
83. The rate of interlocking was found to be lower among those enterprises where family participants were represented on the board than among enterprises where family participants had no board representation.

5 The Controlling Constellations

Perhaps the most important feature of share ownership in the period since the 1930s has been the growth in shareholdings by financial intermediaries, which has reduced the overall level of personal shareholding and put considerable pressure on the family controllers of large enterprises. Control through a constellation of interests, it has been argued, is now characteristic of the majority of the large British enterprises: 100 of the top 250 enterprises in 1976 have been claimed to fall into this category. In such enterprises no single shareholder is dominant, but the twenty largest participants jointly hold a substantial proportion of the shares. The largest shareholders, however, are typically unable to act in concert in order to vote their holding as a single minority block, and so the composition of the board of directors comes to depend on the balance of voting power among the leading participants.

So far the evidence presented in support of this view has been circumstantial, and it is necessary to demonstrate the existence of controlling constellations in the largest British enterprises. The growth of the various types of financial intermediary will first be investigated, and the consequences of this growth for corporate control will then be shown. It will be argued that the evidence supports the claim that large enterprises with no dominant shareholding interest are subject to control through a constellation of interests and that their corporate strategies are constrained by the distribution of votes among the participating interests. It must be recognised, however, that the practice of nominee shareholding means that the participants and directors themselves will rarely have full knowledge of this distribution and that this uncertainty can enable a board of directors to achieve a relative autonomy from the particular interests of the leading shareholders, or may allow a coalition of associated shareholders to wield greater influence than their voting strength would indicate. Both of these possibilities, however, depend on the maintenance of uncertainty and the continued lack of involvement of many of the largest shareholders. The key to understanding control through a constellation of interests is that these conditions are liable to constant alteration, making the temporary dominance of any specific interests precarious in the extreme. Boards which recruit their directors from a wide range of corporate interests can be seen, in effect, to be minimising the risk that the interests of their own controlling constellation will be ignored—the financial interests shared by their own participants are also shared by the participants in other enterprises, and so the strategy formulated by the board is likely to accord with the common concerns of their own large shareholders. This raises two important questions: in what ways are the controlling constellations of the various enterprises interlinked, and what is the connection between this 'interlocking' and board interlocking? Answers to these questions depend on an analysis of the networks of intercorporate relations which are established between large enterprises, and a major concern of this chapter is to show how such networks can be investigated. On this basis it is possible to examine the main constraints on corporate decision-making that exist in Britain.

THE GROWTH OF INTERCORPORATE HOLDINGS

Throughout the post-war period there has been a massive increase in the proportion of shares held by financial 'institutions', and a corresponding decline in the holdings of individuals and families. As a result, there has grown a network of intercorporate shareholdings—a web of connections which ties many of the largest enterprises into an extensive system of capital linkages. This process has been the force behind the rise of control through a constellation of interests. In the vanguard of 'institutional' ownership were the insurance companies, which began to invest in British industry on a large scale during the 1930s.

Fire and marine insurance companies date from the seventeenth and eighteenth centuries, both being concerned with commercial premises and property, and life insurance became of importance from the late eighteenth century.[1] As insurers expanded into other areas, the division between 'life' and 'general' insurance became an important feature of the sector. From the middle of the nineteenth century, 'industrial' insurance—based on small, weekly, door-to-door collections from the working class rather than annual premiums from the middle and upper classes—came to be more important, with Prudential Assurance rapidly dominating this market. During the twentieth century, however, the boundaries between the various branches of insurance became rather more blurred, though companies generally retained separate departments and investment funds for life and non-life business. Insurance company funds were typically invested in government and foreign stocks, but growth in their assets in the inter-war years made them significant investors in corporate securities, and they began to shift the balance of their investments towards commerce and industry. Much of the impetus to industrial investment came from the mutual insurers rather than the joint-stock companies, largely because the former's concentration on endowment policies enabled them to act like investment companies: the writing of endowment policies as a form of investment likened their operations to the issuing of shares by a joint-stock investment company. While the mutual Scottish Widows had 30 per cent of its assets in ordinary shares by 1951, for a half of the joint-stock insurers, the level was below 10 per cent.[2] By 1956 insurance companies collectively held around 6 per cent of ICI and Dunlop, 15 per cent of General Electric, and 34 per cent of the Steel Company of Wales. Among non-life companies the biggest were Royal Insurance, Commerical Union, and General Accident; and the largest life companies were the Prudential, Legal & General, and Norwich Union. The Prudential dominated insurance company investment: in 1956 it held 6 per cent of the shares in Marks & Spencer, British Oxygen, Tube Investments, and AEI, and held 8 per cent of the Steel Company of Wales.[3] This leading role of the Prudential survived into the period of this research. In 1976 its life funds stood just ahead of Legal & General, Commerical Union, and Standard Life; Commerical Union was also important in non-life business, just ahead of Royal Insurance, General Accident, and Guardian Royal Exchange.

Alongside the growth of insurance investment has been a growth in investment and unit trust business, though their involvement in industrial shares originated in the nineteenth century. The first securities investment companies were formed in the 1860s, at the same time as the many specialised mortgage, land, and overseas investment companies.[4] The Foreign and Colonial Government Trust, formed in 1868, was the first to adopt the name and practices of the 'trust' company, and this example was followed by John Pender's Submarine Cables Trust in 1871 and, in Dundee, Robert Fleming's Scottish American Trust in 1873. These enterprises operated in much the same way as a modern unit trust and generally made periodic 'first', 'second', and 'third' issues of their trust certificates, using the proceeds to purchase further stocks and shares. Enterprises such as the Government Stock Investment Company and Pender's Globe Telegraph and Trust, while adopting similar practices, were in fact organised as joint-stock companies and issued shares instead of 'certificates'.[5] A court case which raised doubts about the legality of public shareholding trusts encouraged promoters to reorganise the early trusts as joint-stock companies, and, by the time that an appeal court decision had clarified the legal position, most of the investment vehicles had adopted the corporate form—and this legal form dominated the development of the sector until a rash of 'unit trust' promotions in the 1930s.[6] The main arenas of investment for the early companies were the railways and ranches of the American West, Australasia, and Argentina, and the proportion of their investments which went abroad stood at about four-fifths until the First World War. The First and Second World Wars proved catalytic in reorientating the trusts towards British industry as the government took control of their foreign holdings to improve its foreign-exchange position, and by the 1970s overseas investment accounted for only one-third of their investments.

The number of investment trust companies had risen to twenty-eight in 1886, but the Baring crisis and the ensuing prolonged depression in share prices sharply reduced the number of new promotions. By 1900, however, there were eighty-two companies, and the total had risen to 209 by 1935 and 347 by 1964.[7] These totals, however, mask the presence of a rather smaller number of decision-making centres. The practices of the founders, who promoted 'second' and 'third' versions of the original companies and organised overlapping syndicates to finance associated trusts, led, early on, to the adoption of group organisation by many investment companies. The promoters, often merchant banks or firms of lawyers or accountants, would generally continue to provide administrative services to all the trusts which they had promoted, and would frequently manage their investments as well. In such cases, the legally independent trust companies became a legal fiction obscuring the presence of a large and coordinated investment combine centred on the founding enterprise. Even when centralised management did not occur, many trusts were members of looser communities of interest or holding systems which were tied together through interlocking directorships and aligned shareholdings.[8]

In 1936 four groups each contained ten or more trusts—the Touche, St Davids, Crichton & Govett, and Brown Fleming & Murray groups[9]—and six more groups comprised between seven and nine trusts.[10] Some groups which contained smaller numbers of trusts, however, more than matched these four in terms of assets and influence. The Robert Fleming group, for example, was based around just two trusts, but it ran three trusts jointly with the Robert Benson group[11] and was closely affiliated with Brown, Fleming & Murray[12] and the Scottish American group of Dundee.[13] The tightest of the investment trust groups to exist in the 1930s were the St Davids, Benson, Touche, and Fleming groups, and these were allied with one another and with the slightly smaller Crichton & Govett group in an extensive City of London community of interest. Through Fleming the City was linked to the investment trusts of Glasgow and Dundee, but the Edinburgh trusts had most of their affiliations with the Scottish banking and insurance enterprises.[14]

During the post-war period, and especially in the 1950s and 1960s, a number of trust amalgamations and mergers took place. At the same time, numerous electric, telegraph, plantation, and mining companies whose original assets, in Britain and overseas, had been nationalised converted themselves into investment trusts; perhaps the most important was Cable & Wireless, the telegraph and radio combine originally financed by the Pender investment trusts, which was converted into an investment trust after the Labour government of 1945 had nationalised the operating units.[15] In this period, the larger groups adopted increasingly tighter forms of organisation, new management groups were created, and a number of unaffiliated trusts joined management groups. By 1964 the four largest groups in terms of the number of trusts managed were Robert Fleming, Drayton (formerly St Davids), Hill Samuel, and Baillie Gifford, though the largest groups by assets were Robert Fleming, Touche Ross (formerly Touche), and Electra House (the Cable & Wireless group).[16] This continuity in the identity of the leading groups was also apparent in 1976, with the largest groups, measured by number of trusts, being Robert Fleming, Drayton Montagu (part of the Midland Bank), Gartmore, and Touche Remnant. The largest groups by assets were Robert Fleming, Touche Remnant, Electra House, Drayton Montagu, and Baillie Gifford, though merchant banks such as Hambros, Kleinwort Benson Lonsdale, Barings, and Schroders managed important investment trust groups, and the Philip Hill trusts were associated with Hill Samuel.[17]

During the 1930s a number of new investment groups, following American practice, reintroduced the original legal form of the trust to purchase shares with proceeds from the sale of trust certificates. The first of these 'unit trusts' was formed by Municipal & General Securities, the British financial subsidiary of the American electrical contractors J.G. White. George Booth acquired a holding in the company and it soon came under the joint control of Booth and Ian Fairbairn.[18] The so-called M & G Group soon managed a number of unit trusts, though these involved a fixed set of investments and required little in the way of active management. Other groups were set up to form trusts, and gradually the rigid 'fixed' trusts gave way to the actively managed 'flexible' trusts, the unit trust groups coming to resemble investment trust groups in their centralised investment management. By 1939 there were fifteen groups operating a total of eighty-nine unit trusts, the largest groups being the National, Fifteen Moorgate, M & G, British General, and British Industrial Corporation groups.[19] The unit trust sector experienced much reorganisation and expansion after the Second World War, with many of the old groups disappearing. The five largest groups of 1976 were Save & Prosper, M & G, Barclays Unicorn, Britannia Arrow, and Allied Hambro, but all except Barclays had pre-war origins.[20]

The growth of insurance and investment funds represents a growth in the voting power of the enterprises which formed the funds. By contrast, the expansion of pension fund assets has only partly enhanced the voting power of the enterprises whose employees are their beneficiaries. The enterprises which have acquired the bulk of the massive voting power represented by the pension funds have, in fact, been the very fund managers who dominate the investment sector. Pension funds grew rapidly during the 1960s and 1970s, and at the end of this period about one-third of all pension fund assets were under external management. The external managers included stock-brokers and insurance companies, but the most important fund managers were merchant banks.[21] The largest pension funds by 1981 were those of the Post Office, National Coal Board, British Rail, Electricity Council[22] and British Steel—all public sector funds—and two of these were substantially managed by merchant banks.[23] The more active investors among the large, internally managed private sector funds in 1976 were the funds of ICI, Imperial Group, Shell, Unilever, and the big four clearing banks, with the management of many other large funds being delegated to external managers.[24] Delegation of pension fund management to external groups has enhanced the voting power of those already involved in investment and unit trust management, and while figures on pension fund investment are difficult to obtain, the largest managers in 1976 included Hill Samuel, Mercury Securities, Morgan Grenfell, Robert Fleming, and Schroders.[25]

THE RISE OF THE CONTROLLING CONSTELLATIONS

It has been shown that the growth of 'institutional share-holding has resulted in the rise to dominance in the capital market of a relatively small group of enterprises involved in fund management. Clearing banks, merchant banks, insurers, and investment groups, together with a handful of large industrial pension schemes, have achieved a virtual monopoly over the mobilisation of capital. Based principally, but not exclusively, in the City of London, these enterprises were the major participants in the constellations of interests which controlled many of Britain's largest enterprises. This can be illustrated by Table 5.1, which shows the members of a

Table 5.1: *The controlling constellation of Imperial Group (1976)*

Shareholder	Holding (%)
Prudential Assurance	2.4
Legal & General Assurance	1.8
Hill Samuel	1.4
National Westminster Bank	1.4
National Coal Board	1.4
M & G Group	1.0
Barclays Bank	0.9
Britannic Assurance	0.9
Royal Insurance	0.8
Kuwait Investment Office	0.7
Save & Prosper Group	0.7
Cooperative group	0.6
Commercial Union	0.6
Norwich Union	0.5
Wills family	0.5
Mercury Securities	0.5
Pearl Assurance	0.4
Midland Bank	0.4
General Electric	0.4
Sun Life Assurance Society	0.4

Table 5.2: *Share concentration in controlling constellations: Britain (1976)*

% of shares held by top 20	Number of enterprises		
	With family participation	Without family participation	Total
More than 50	0	0	0
40–9	1	3	4
30–9	3	10	13
20–9	26	35	61
10–19	6	16	22
Less than 10	0	0	0
Totals	36	64	100

particular constellation.[26] Imperial Group, one of the biggest manufacturers in food, drink, and tobacco, had 17.4 per cent of its voting shares held by its twenty largest shareholders, just about the level at which a dominant shareholder could have exercised secure minority control. Yet the constellation of interests comprises a diverse set of competing capitalist interests. With the exception of the Wills family and the Kuwait Investment Office, the participants were drawn from the fund managers discussed in the previous section: nine insurance companies held 8.3 per cent,[27] five banks held 4.6 per cent, two unit-trust groups held 1.6 per cent, and two internally managed pension funds held 1.7 per cent. This constellation of interests could not act as a cohesive group, and the largest single shareholder, the Prudential, had insufficient votes to make it a dominant force in the enterprise. The Imperial board could, therefore, detach itself from the interests of any particular member of its controlling constellation—though it was, in fact, interlocked with the Midland Bank—but it could not operate independently of the constellation as a whole. The success of any attempt to raise new capital through a rights issue would depend on the ability of the enterprise and its advisers to persuade these shareholders to take up their rights;[28] and if the enterprise were to run into serious difficulties, any reconstruction would have to meet with their approval. Such passive constraints on the strategy pursued by the board can easily shade over into active intervention when one or more members of the constellation seeks to achieve board representation or to mobilise support for a challenge to the board. In such circumstances the distribution of votes within the constellation and between it and the remaining shareholders becomes crucial.[29]

How typical is Imperial of the enterprises without dominant interests? Table 5.2 shows that the twenty largest shareholders held more than 10 per cent in all 100 enterprises and that in no case did they hold more than 50 per cent. The controlling constellations held collective minority control on the basis of the conventional measures, though it has been argued that to talk of financial minority control would be misleading in view of the diversity of the interests making up the controlling constellations. In most cases the constellation held between 20 and 29 per cent, and they were slightly more likely to hold below this level than above it. The enterprise with the most dispersed capital was British Home Stores, where the controlling constellation held 10.27 per cent. At the other extreme the controlling constellation in Steetley held 41.57 per cent, seven of its participants holding in excess of 2 per cent each. In neither of these cases was there a family participant, and Table 5.2 shows that the distribution of enterprises with family participants was little different from that for those without. The important factor in explaining the size of the block held by the controlling constellation was not the presence or absence of one or two extremely large holdings but the overall level of holdings among the constellation as a whole. Clearly, size was an important factor: the larger the enterprise, other things being equal, the more difficult was it for even the largest of institutions to tie up sufficient funds to give them a large percentage holding; conversely, a large institution could acquire a significant holding in a smaller enterprise with a relatively modest outlay.

Some insight into the emergence and growth of the controlling constellations can be gained from a comparison of the results of the present research with those of Florence's studies. Unfortunately, his unpublished listing of the twenty largest registered holders in enterprises with no dominant interest have not survived,[30] and so the comparison must, for the most part, rely on the aggregate figures for 1936 and 1951 given in his published report.[31] Florence gives such information for twenty-five of the enterprises which were controlled through constellations of interests in 1976, and nineteen of these showed a U-curve trend of shareholdings: a dispersal of shareholdings between 1936 and 1951, as family majority and minority holdings were diluted, and a subsequent reconcentration of holdings as the financial intermediaries increased the size of their investments. In the case of Courtaulds, for example, the twenty largest holders in 1936 held 21.0 per cent; by 1951 this had fallen to 7.1 per cent, but by 1976 it had risen again to 18.5 per cent. In two enterprises the trend followed an inverted U-curve, with the figure for 1951 being substantially higher than that for 1936, and each involved the presence in 1951 of a dominant corporate shareholder.[32] Three enterprises showed a continuous decline in the percentage held by the top twenty, two of these involving the survival of extremely large family majority holdings in 1936 and, in consequence, a belated dilution of the controlling block.[33] Finally, one enterprise, Dunlop, showed a continuous increase in the percentage held by the top twenty, reflecting the existence of an abnormally low holding by the top twenty of 1936. This extreme early dispersal was due to a major reconstruction of the enterprise during the 1920s, when the former controlling group had been ousted and a substantial amount of capital had been taken up by financial intermediaries. The reconcentration of shareholdings in Dunlop was moderate between 1936 and 1951, but by 1976 the level was comparable with the majority of the enterprises controlled through constellations of interests.[34]

In most of those enterprises controlled through constellations of interests for which there is longitudinal data, therefore, the key transition took place between 1936 and 1951. This was the period in which family control was lost or diluted and in which occurred the share dispersal which made possible the growth of 'institutional' holdings. Florence's data relate only to manufacturers and distributors, and many of the large enterprises in transport, banking, and insurance experienced a

much earlier dispersal of shareholdings. This can be illustrated
by one of the few such enterprises for which adequate
information is available. The twenty largest shareholders in P
& O held 12.92 per cent in 1938, 14.39 per cent in 1957, and
20.23 per cent in 1976.[35] Personal holders, generally represented on the board, accounted for 4.95 per cent in 1938, but
their holdings had declined to 2.71 per cent in 1957 and had
disappeared completely by 1976. Between 1938 and 1957 there
had been a substantial increase in the percentage held by
insurance companies and, to a lesser extent, by investment
trusts, which replaced a number of the holdings previously
taken by other shipping lines. By 1976 the increase in pension
fund holdings had squeezed out the final vestiges of personal
shareholding from the controlling constellation. This example
suggests that, for certain purposes, it might be useful to
subdivide the category of control through a constellation of
interests in order to distinguish constellations in which a
mixture of personal, corporate, and financial interests prevail
from those in which financial interests are dominant. The
former subtype, epitomised by P & O in 1938, corresponds to a
period in which financial intermediaries have not yet become
the key agents in capital mobilisation; yet it cannot be
assimilated to the conventional category of mangement
control, as a subset of the personal shareholding interests will
generally be found to comprise a significant element in the
board of directors.[36] During the 1930s the manufacturing and
distribution sectors began to show the same weakening of
family and personal control which had occurred much earlier
in transport and finance; and in many of the largest enterprises
family control gradually gave way to amorphous constellations of personal and financial interests. Through the 1950s
and 1960s the financial intermediaries enhanced their position
at the expense of many of the family participants, resulting in
the observed pattern of control through a constellation of
interests discovered for 1976. By that time the bulk of the
controlling constellations—about two-thirds (see Table 5.2)—
had no personal participants at all; and many of those family
participants which did survive were inactive and passive
'rentier' shareholders.

The growth of institutional shareholdings, and the consequent increase in the proportion of votes held by the financial enterprises which make up the controlling constellations, has been offset in some enterprises by the adoption of legal forms which minimise the voting power of the financials. In one of the enterprises studied in 1976, Lloyds Bank, this involved the adoption of limitations on the voting rights of large shareholders. The Articles of Association specified that no shareholder could exercise more than 500 votes, no matter how many shares were held. Thus the twenty largest shareholders, with 16.26 per cent of the capital, could exercise only 0.01 per cent of the votes.[37] It was not possible for any group to constitute the twenty largest vote-holders, as *all* holders with 500 or more shares had equal voting rights. In legal terms, therefore, Lloyds Bank seems a clear case of management control.

The importance of shareholding, however, lies not only in the voting power it accords but also in its role in the provision of new capital: an enterprise seeking to raise new capital through a rights issue will have to attract the support of its leading shareholders. The Lloyds Bank board could choose to ignore the interests of its leading shareholders, as their votes count for no more than those of any other shareholders, but the need to ensure the success of capital issues creates a pressure on the board to treat the largest institutional shareholders *as if* they were the largest vote-holders.[38] Indeed, institutional pressure caused Lloyds to alter its voting regulations in 1978, bringing the distribution of votes into line with the distribution of capital. This reinforces the argument that the emergence of control through a constellation of interests is tied closely to the expansion of institutional holdings, which has cast large and assertive financial shareholders into the leading positions in many of Britain's largest enterprises,[39] and for this reason Lloyd's Bank has been regarded as controlled through a constellation of interests. The mutual enterprises, however, have avoided the implications of institutional shared owner-ship through the adoption of a different legal form.[40] In the mutual company the policy-holders or depositors are the voting members, and voting rights do not vary with the size of the policy or deposit. No matter how many separate policies or accounts may be held by a member, only one vote may be exercised.[41] Building societies and mutual insurance companies acquire their capital for investment through the commercial practices of attracting 'customers' (as depositors and policy-holders) and not through the issue of shares, and for this reason they are relatively isolated from the constraints imposed on joint-stock companies by the rise of institutional share ownership. The mutual enterprises, therefore, were the closest approximations to management-controlled enterprises,

Table 5.3: *The largest participants: Britain (1976)*

Investor	No. of participations in controlling constellations
Prudential Assurance	88
National Coal Board	75
Cooperative group*	64
Legal & General Assurance	64
Norwich Union Insurance*	64
Pearl Assurance	64
Barclays Bank	60
Hill Samuel	55
Robert Fleming	52
Electricity Council	48
Mercury Securities	48
Royal Insurance	46
'Shell' Transport & Trading	45
National Westminster Bank	44
Commercial Union Assurance	42
Britannic Assurance*	39
Midland Bank	39
Church Commissioners*	38
General Accident	38
Save & Prosper Group	37

Note: The shareholders marked with an asterisk were not members of the top 250. In the terminology of graph theory, discussed later in this chapter, the shareholders are ranked by their 'out-degree'.

though their board composition hardly accorded with the
expectations of some of the stronger statements of the
managerialist thesis. Though far less likely to interlock than
were any of the other enterprises, the building society boards
had a regional character and were dominated by local gentry
and those active in the construction and housing sectors.[42]

Who, then, were the major participants in the controlling
constellations, and what was the pattern of their investments?
Excluding those few nominees which could not be identified,
192 shareholding groups participated in the constellations
which controlled 100 of Britain's top 250 enterprises. Sixty of
these shareholders were themselves members of the top 250, 55
were the family groups discussed in Chapter 4, and 87 were
other British or foreign interests. The 60 corporate participants
from the top 250 held just over two-thirds of all the
participations in the 100 enterprises,[43] demonstrating clearly
their dominant position in the structure of capital and control.
This relatively small group of enterprises could accumulate
such a high proportion of the total participations because so
many of them took shareholdings in a vast number of large
enterprises. While fifteen of them had only one participation,[44]
thirty-five participated in ten or more enterprises. Very few of
the participants from outside the top 250 matched this scale of
investment: just 11 of the 87 participated in 10 or more
enterprises.[45]

Table 5.3 shows the participants with the largest number of
participations in the 100 constellations. These 20 shareholders,
only 4 of whom were not members of the top 250, held over a
half of all participations. Nine of the 20 derived most of their
investment funds from insurance, with the Prudential alone
investing in 88 of the 100 enterprises, and 6 of the top
participants were banks.[46] A number of the banks and insurers
acted as managers for pension funds, but the top twenty
participants included three large self-administered schemes:
those of the NCB, the Electricity Council, and Shell. The two
nationalised schemes headed a group of eight public
corporation pension funds holding 13 per cent of all
participations; and while Shell headed a much larger group of
private sector funds, only five of these were substantial
participants.[47] These holdings by 'non-financial' enterprises

should not be sharply distinguished from the holdings of 'financials'. The growth of internally managed pension funds has reinforced the trend for all large enterprises to become units of 'finance capital', to engage in a spread of activities which cannot easily be divided into industrial, commercial, and banking categories. A large 'non-financial' may be involved in the production and distribution of commodities, in currency trading to finance its overseas operations, and, through its pension fund, in the provision of loan capital on a massive scale. The conventional categories of 'financial' and 'non-financial', therefore, should not obscure the fact that most large enterprises may be regarded as units of finance capital. The bulk of the money committed to pension funds, however, was managed by banks, and so inflates their influence in the economy. Table 5.4 lists the ten largest fund-managing participants, including those involved in all branches of investment management. Investment and unit trust business was especially important for all these enterprises—the three clearing banks appearing in the list mainly because of their involvement in this sector—but the merchant banks were massively involved in pension fund and general discretionary investment management.[48]

Table 5.4: *The largest fund managers: Britain (1976)*

Enterprise	No. of participations in controlling constellations
Barclays Bank	60
Hill Samuel	55
Robert Fleming	52
Mercury Securities	48
National Westminster Bank	44
Midland Bank	39
Save & Prosper Group	37
M & G Group	33
Schroders	32
Touche Remnant	26

Twenty foreign enterprises participated in the controlling constellations, but they were not generally to be found among the largest participants. The prime exception to this was the Kuwait Investment Office, which participated in thirty-eight constellations—no other foreign enterprise was involved in more than five constellations. The most important source of foreign participants, after Kuwait, was the United States, a number of American banks holding shares on behalf of owners of American Depositary Receipts: Morgan Guaranty participated in five enterprises, Bankers Trust in two, Citicorp in two, and the Bank of New York and Irving Trust each participated in one. SICOVAM participated in a similar capacity on behalf of French investors in five enterprises, but the remaining foreign participations were predominantly insurance company investments from Australia, Canada, and West Germany.[49]

Perhaps the most obvious conclusion to be drawn from Tables 5.3 and 5.4 should be underlined: a relatively small

Table 5.5: *Leading influences in controlling constellations: Britain (1976)*

Enterprise	No. of times appearing as largest shareholder
Prudential Assurance	43
Kuwait Investment Office*	7
Hill Samuel	6
M & G Group	5
National Coal Board	3
Britannic Assurance*	3
Norwich Union Insurance*	3
Barclays Bank	2
Morgan Guaranty Trust*	2
Pearl Assurance	2
Save & Prosper Group	2
SICOVAM*	2

Note: The enterprises marked with an asterisk were not members of the top 250. The table shows the number of the times each enterprise is ranked first among the twenty largest shareholders.

number of major investors participated on a massive scale in the one hundred controlling constellations. Nine enterprises each participated in the control of fifty or more other enterprises. One particular enterprise, Prudential Assurance, participated in eighty-eight constellations and, as shown in Table 5.5, was the largest shareholder in forty-three of these. The dominance of the Prudential in the British capital market is clear from the fact that it was one of the three largest participants in sixty-nine constellations:[50] in only twelve enterprises did the Prudential not appear as a member of the controlling constellation. No other shareholder appeared as a leading influence on such a scale, though there was a close correlation between those which were the largest participants and those which were the leading influences. Two exceptions to this were foreign intermediaries holding large blocks of shares on behalf of overseas investors, their holdings being concentrated in those enterprises which were especially popular with foreign investors: Morgan Guaranty Trust was the largest shareholder in Burmah Oil and EMI, and SICOVAM was the largest shareholder in Consolidated Gold Fields and Rio Tinto Zinc.[51]

Table 5.6: *Non-corporate participants in controlling constellations: Britain (1976)*

Shareholder	No. of participations in controlling constellations
Church Commissioners	38
Greater London Council	6
West Yorkshire County Council	4
Crown Agents	3
West Midlands County Council	3
Derbyshire County Council	1
Essex County Council	1
Hampshire County Council	1
University of Hull	1
University of Manchester	1

Note: Personal participants are not included above.

The bulk of the participations in the controlling constellations were British and foreign enterprises which generally
invested in numerous other enterprises. Most non-corporate
participants were families which confined their participations
to single enterprises. There was a group of participants,
however, which were neither personal interests nor corporate
business enterprises. These were the ten local authorities,
agencies, and semi-public bodies[52] shown in Table 5.6, the
most important of which were the Church Commissioners,
who participated in thirty-eight constellations. County Councils, through their internally managed pension funds, were not
major participants, though there was some concentration in
their investments. Both the Greater London Council and
Derbyshire County Council participated in Thos. W. Ward,
while the West Midlands, West Yorkshire, and Essex County
Councils participated in Dalgety. There was little sign that
local authority pension funds made any attempt to invest in
and influence the policies of enterprises which had substantial
operations in their areas.[53] The two university shareholders,
however, did have their participations in local enterprises, and
both holdings seem to have been the result of a benefaction of
the founding families: the University of Hull participated in
Reckitt and Colman, and Manchester University participated
in Simon Engineering.

Scottish investors showed some sign of regional preferences
in their patterns of investment. Fifteen Scottish corporate
interests accounted for 6 per cent of all participations, the
largest Scottish participants being the General Accident and
Standard Life insurance groups.[54] All five of the Scottish
enterprises which were controlled through constellations of
interests had at least one Scottish participant—Scottish &
Newcastle Breweries had five—and General Accident participated in all five constellations. The Murray Johnstone
investment group and Standard Life each participated in two
Scottish enterprises, and Coats Patons, Scottish Widows, and
Ivory & Sime each participated in one. The bulk of the large
investments made by Scottish enterprises were, of course, in
the much larger number of non-Scottish enterprises, but there
does seem to have been a willingness on their part to
participate in the capital of Scottish companies.[55]

Table 5.7: *The blue-chip investments: Britain (1976)*

Enterprise	Top 250 members in Constellation
Boots	18
Commercial Union Assurance	17
Glaxo Holdings	17
Guest Keen & Nettlefolds	17
Marks & Spencer	17
Prudential Assurance	17
Taylor Woodrow	17
Beecham Group	16
Consolidated Gold Fields	16
Courtaulds	16
Delta Metal	16
Distillers	16
Eagle Star Insurance	16
Grand Metropolitan	16
Hawker Siddeley	16
Pearl Assurance	16
Peninsular & Oriental	16
Redland	16
Reed International	16

Note: In the terminology of graph theory, discussed later in this chapter, the enterprises are ranked by their 'in-degree'.

While the major investors show a wide spread in their participations, certain enterprises were extremely popular targets for investment. As a constellation has, by definition, 20 members it was possible, in principle, for an enterprise to have 20 members of the top 250 participating in its controlling constellation. In fact the highest level of participation by top 250 members was found in Boots, only 2 of whose participants came from outside the top 250.[56] Table 5.7 lists the 'blue chip' investments, each of which had 16 or more top-250 participants. Ten of these nineteen blue-chips were, in fact, included in *The Financial Times* industrial Ordinary Share Index (the so-called '30-Share Index'). It is noticeable how few of the blue chips were to be found among the largest participants themselves (see Table 5.3). This was due in part to the fact that many of the largest participants were public corporations, mutuals, or were family controlled, and so had no controlling constellations themselves; but it also reflects the fact that major private sector industrials were insignificant investors in other large enterprises. The largest participants were overwhelmingly involved in banking, insurance, and investment management, while the blue-chip investments were mainly involved outside these sectors. The three enterprises appearing in both Table 5.3 and Table 5.7—the Prudential, Pearl Assurance, and Commerical Union—were all insurance companies. Enterprises with family participants in their controlling constellations were less likely to be popular targets for investment by top-250 enterprises: 8 of the 13 enterprises with fewer than 12 top-250 participants had substantial family shareholders, and none of them appeared in the 30-Share Index.

It can be concluded that a relatively small number of large investors dominated the controlling constellations and so held a hegemonic position in the mobilisation of capital. Whether classified as 'financial' or 'non-financial', these enterprises are units of finance capital which stand at the heart of the corporate system and determine the conditions under which other enterprises must act.[57] By virtue of their intersecting participations, however, a definite pattern of connections is created between enterprises. There is a structure to financial hegemony, and the power and influence available to an enterprise depends upon its position within this structure. An attempt to understand the power relations between enterprises, therefore, requires a mapping of this structure.

THE STRUCTURE OF FINANCIAL HEGEMONY

In order to map the structure of financial hegemony, the appropriate techniques of analysis are required. These techniques, commonly described as 'social network analysis', reflect a growing awareness that existing approaches to the study of social structure are inadequate. Social agents—for example, persons and enterprises—enter into relations with one another, and these relations exhibit a definite structure. Social structures are generally produced as the unintended consequences of actions and have properties which are irreducible to the actions of the agents which produced them, though these actions are, of course, a necessary condition for the existence of the structures. The various approaches to 'social network analysis' provide the tools necessary for studying the properties of social structures. A central feature of recent advances in social network analysis has been the use of rigorous mathematical models of the formal properties of social structures, and a number of these models will be used to map the structure of financial hegemony.[58]

The starting point for such a mapping is the matrix of connections between the agents being studied, and the various mathematical approaches differ in terms of the operations they apply to this matrix. 'Graph theory', perhaps the most widely used approach, is an implementation of matrix algebra, which draws on the conventional image of a 'network' to depict all structures as sets of 'points' connected by 'lines'.[59] From this point of view, agents are embedded in webs of connections, and it is, in principle, possible to draw a diagram of the structure in which each agent is represented as a point and the social relations of this agent are represented as lines connecting points. For all but the simplest structures, of course, such diagrams become too complex to draw and to read, and their properties must be studied more abstractly. But the metaphor of a web of connections is a powerful image in understanding and applying the more abstract tools of graph theory. Two of the most important concepts developed in graph theory are 'adjacency' and 'centrality'. Two points are said to be adjacent if there is a line connecting them, and the adjacency, or 'degree', of a point is simply the total number of other points to which it is connected in this way. The adjacency of a point is one of the most important indicators of its centrality within the network, as a comparison of the adjacencies of various points shows the extent to which each is well connected into the rest of the network. The point with the highest adjacency may be regarded as the most central point in the network. Some, but not all, social relations can be considered as having a 'direction'. If enterprise A invests in enterprise B, for example, a line may be directed from point A to point B: graph theory depicts the line as going 'out' from A and 'in' to B. It follows that in such a 'directed graph' the adjacency of a point can be divided into two distinct measures termed the 'in-degree' and the 'out-degree'. In a network of shareholdings the out-degree of an enterprise is simply the number of other enterprises in which it invests; its in-degree is the number oʳ enterprises which participate in its capital. If the directed network of connections encircling the 100 controlling constellations were to be considered, Table 5.3 would show participants ranked by their out-degree and Table 5.7 would show enterprises ranked by their in-degree. The Prudential, for example, was the most central participant, with an out-degree of 88. While points with high-adjacency scores are central to networks, those with low adjacencies are 'peripheral' and those with no connections at all are 'isolates'.

In order to develop the power of social network analysis to its full, it is necessary to employ concepts which go beyond the location of particular points within the network to consider the existence of groups of points. Any network can be broken down into the 'pieces' of which it is composed. Each isolated point comprises a distinct piece of the network, but the remaining points will form one or more connected 'components'. A component, at its simplest, is a subset of points which are linked to one another through a continuous chain of connections, and the number of components into which a network is divided is a measure of its fragmentation.[60]

The simple concept of the component has been developed in a number of ways by graph theorists to reflect varying forms of connection between points. One particularly important approach uses the 'multiplicity' score of each line as a criterion for identifying components. Multiplicity is a measure of the intensity of the line between two points, where intensity is based on the number of distinct connections between the points. If enterprises are regarded as related through the existence of common shareholders, for example, the presence of one common shareholder creates a line of multiplicity 1, while the presence of two common shareholders creates a line of multiplicity 2. It is possible, therefore, to group points into components according to the multiplicities of the lines which connect them. A network may comprise a number of separate components each of which is internally connected through lines of, say, multiplicity 4, but none of the lines running between components are of this intensity. At multiplicity 3, however, some components may merge because they are connected at this level of intensity, while other remain distinct. The use of varying levels of multiplicity to identify components, therefore, generates a hierarchy of 'nested' components; and if each component is thought of as a circle, the network can be visualised as a pattern of concentric circles—contour lines—which encircle contiguous points connected at a particular level of intensity.

An alternative approach to the identification of components involves the search for 'cyclic components'. A cycle is a chain of connections which starts and ends at the same point and which consists of a specified number of lines; thus, the chain of connections A-B-C-A includes three lines and so constitutes a cycle of length 3. A cyclic component is built from chains of intersecting cycles,[61] and a network may comprise one or more such cyclic components. By altering the length of the cycle used to identify components, a form of 'nesting' can be achieved, with shorter cycles being regarded as more intense connections than longer ones.[62]

Closely linked to the identification of components in graph theory is an approach which searches for 'blocks' in a network. Though not based on graph theory, this blocking procedure is, nevertheless, compatible with its basic assumptions. Blocking aims to partition a network into sets of 'structurally equivalent' points and to exhibit the relations between these sets.[63] Points are regarded as structurally equivalent if they have similar patterns of connections to other points in the network; the blocking is not concerned with any connections which may or may not exist among the structurally equivalent points. Members of a set occupy a structurally equivalent location within the network, but they do not necessarily have strong connections among themselves. If the sets are displayed in a matrix (termed an 'image matrix' of the original matrix) the chessboard-pattern of blocks will indicate the general pattern of relations between the various sets. Thus a blocking of the network is concerned not with individual agents and their connections, but with sets of structurally equivalent agents and their connections with other sets. As such, it is perhaps the most appropriate procedure for identifying hierarchical and hegemonic relations between sets of enterprises.

Although graph theory is the best-developed mathematical model for social networks and has a great deal of intuitive appeal, its assumptions about social reality are not necessarily the most useful. An alternative approach with considerable promise is Q-analysis, which can be regarded as an extension of graph theory into a more realistic multidimensional geometry.[64] The image of social structure contained in graph theory is built from points connected by lines, and when the analyst attempts to draw a large, complex structure on a sheet of paper the lines begin to criss-cross in such a way that it is impossible to produce a useful picture of the network: the thicket of intersecting lines produces a jumble rather than a clear image. This problem arises because more than the two dimensions of the flat sheet of paper are required to represent the structure, and Q-analysis is an attempt to produce a formal language for describing structures which is better able to handle the multidimensional nature of social reality. Attempts to apply Q-analysis to social data have so far concentrated on the identification of components, producing results which are equivalent to the analysis of nested components in graph theory. In these procedures the multiplicity of a line is taken as a measure of the intensity of connections. A recent development, however, has departed from such an absolute measure of intensity and has investigated the 'relative intensity' of connections. The significance of having, say, four shareholders in common is greater for enterprises which have many connections at multiplicity 1 than it is for enterprises with many multiplicity-6 connections. For this reason, the average number of connections for each agent in a network can be used as a measure of the relative intensity of each of the agent's connections. Thus components can be defined as groups of points which are connected by lines of above-average intensity.

The most fruitful line of advance in social network analysis is likely to involve a synthesis of the realistic assumptions of

Q-analysis and the conceptual elaborations of graph theory. Both approaches produce mathematical descriptions of networks which cannot, except in their very simplest forms, be drawn on paper, and any attempt at synthesis would have to involve procedures for producing useful maps of the social structure in which the arrangement of points is not arbitrary (as in the case of most hand-drawn networks) but reflects their real location in space. Various approaches to this problem have been suggested, most involving 'scaling' techniques which use cartographic methods for projecting multidimensional structures onto a two-dimensional page in much the same way as physical geographers project the three-dimensional globe onto the flat page of an atlas.[65]

The data to which the techniques of social network analysis were applied were the participations of the top 250 enterprises in the 100 constellations, which were discussed in the previous section, together with their holdings in those enterprises which were majority or minority controlled. The network analysed, therefore, comprised 69 controllers and participants plus the 140 enterprises which they controlled. As 43 of the 69 controllers were themselves among the 'controlled' enterprises —the remaining 26 being public corporations, mutuals, and enterprises with dominant controllers outside the top 250—a total of 166 enterprises made up the network.[66] This network could be analysed in two distinct ways. First, all 166 enterprises could be regarded as points in a single network, with the shareholding participations between them being regarded as directed lines. This approach was used in standard graph theoretical analyses and in two related algorithms: the CONCOR algorithm produced a 'blocking' of the network and the EBLOC algorithm searched for cyclic components. The second way to analyse the network is to treat the 69 'controllers' and the 140 'controlled' as two separate networks: in the network of controllers, enterprises are 'connected' if they have one or more investment targets in common; and in the network of the controlled, enterprises are connected if they have one or more participants in common. The CONCOR algorithm can produce a blocking of each of these networks, and the QCOMP algorithm identifies nested components in each network.[67]

Use of the EBLOC algorithm, searching for cyclic components, showed that the British intercorporate network was well connected and had little internal fragmentation. The structure produced was dominated by a large cyclic component of 137 members. The 137 enterprises were connected through intersecting cycles of length 3 to form a continuous skein of linkages. A further twenty two enterprises were 'hangers' to this component; that is to say, their only network links were with members of the large component, but they were not involved in any cyclic relations. The hangers were, therefore, relatively peripheral to the network and comprised sixteen 'hangers-off' which were controlled by members of the cyclic component, and six 'hangers-on' which participated in very few constellations.[68] In addition to this large component and its peripheral hangers, EBLOC identified three small non-cyclic components which had links to one another through majority shareholdings but had no links to other network members. The National Enterprise Board and its two subsidiaries (British Leyland and Rolls-Royce) formed one of these components, and the other two comprised Rank Organisation/Rank Xerox and S. Pearson/Lazard.[69]

The sixty-nine controlling interests were clearly the major actors in the intercorporate network, and further insight into its structure can be gained from an analysis of the network of controllers: did they form a unified group or were they divided into rival and solidaristic coalitions? If rival coalitions of controllers existed, following similar investment strategies and coordinating their participations to maximise the leverage which they could exercise over subordinate enterprises, both CONCOR and QCOMP should find evidence for their existence. CONCOR produced a partitioning of the controllers into four sets,[70] though these did not correspond to possible coalitions. The search for structural equivalence distinguished major investors from second-rank investors and divided the former into a set based on insurance companies and a set based on public sector pension funds. Merchant banks and other fund managers were divided between these sets. The only set to be at all sharply distinguished was one which included relatively marginal investors and enterprises involved in relations of majority and minority control. The hangers and members of non-cyclic components identified by EBLOC predominated in this latter set. It could not be said, however, that the bulk of the controllers showed any significant internal division. Where CONCOR searches for structurally equivalent locations, QCOMP searches for groups of closely linked points and so might be expected to produce stronger evidence for the existence of any coalitions. QCOMP regards controllers as falling into the same component if it is possible to trace a continuous chain of connections through common investment targets, where the strength of the connection is measured by the number of common investments. A network which showed the existence of a number of distinct components would indicate that there was some tendency for enterprises to coordinate their investments within groups of associates. In fact, QCOMP found no evidence for the existence of distinct components in the network of controllers: at all levels of intensity there was simply one large component.[71] This component 'grew' slowly and steadily from its two core members (Prudential and National Coal Board), with seventy-two investments in common, to sixty-five members linked through chains of connection involving at least one common investment. Four of the controllers fell outside this component as they had no participations in common with any of the other controllers, and three of these four were the controlling members in the small non-cyclic components identified by EBLOC.[72] The 'contour map' produced by QCOMP, therefore, showed that the network consisted of a single peak and four 'outliers'.

When using an absolute measure of intensity of connection to analyse nested components, QCOMP adopts the same cut-off threshold for all enterprises: components are identified at specified levels of connection. This application of QCOMP failed to produce any evidence for the existence of distinct coalitions of controllers, but it is possible that a more sensitive measure of relative intensity may highlight any internal divisions within the large component. In this approach, the cut-off threshold varies from one enterprise to another. It is assumed that those connections of above-average intensity for an enterprise are most salient to it, and so the 'mean connectivity' of a point can be used to produce an initial decomposition of the large component. To produce a nested contour map, the mean connectivities of points can be multiplied by successively higher common factors: the cut-off used for each enterprise becomes, then, twice its mean, three times its mean, and so on. With each increase in the factor, the components identified have a stronger level of internal connection, and their members have correspondingly weaker connections to outsiders. Applying this variant of QCOMP it was found that the large component of the standard analysis was initially divided into a subcomponent of forty-six and a small component of two.[73] The seventeen remaining members of the original component appeared as isolates in this analysis, indicating their peripherality within the large component.

As the factor was increased, leaving only the most intense connections, the large component diminished in size and spawned further small components, though these were generally very small and unstable. The small components which appeared at various levels of analysis were:

1. Guardian Royal Exchange Assurance, N.M. Rothschild
2. Morgan Grenfell, British Steel
3. British Airways, British Petroleum
4. Save & Prosper, M & G, Eagle Star Insurance, Touche Remnant, ICI
5. Robert Fleming, Mercury Securities

To use the contour map analogy once more, the original peak was found to comprise a dominant peak with lesser peaks on its middle slopes. The small components which formed these lesser peaks comprised enterprises which had a small number of rather intense mutual connections which were masked by the very large number of less intense links which they had with numerous other enterprises. Only one of the small components had more than two members, and this was rapidly reduced in size to include just the two unit-trust groups. Does the discovery of these components point to the existence of investment and controlling coalitions that have a significant leverage in particular enterprises? This would be the case only if corresponding components were to be found in the network of controlled enterprises, but no such evidence was discovered.

Neither the standard output from QCOMP nor its extension based on relative intensity disclosed any groups which correspond to those identified in the network of controllers. The components which were discovered did not support the idea that the British intercorporate network was structured into rival financial interest groups. The network of controlled enterprises was dominated by a large component of enterprises connected by chains of common participants. In the standard analysis, three small components appeared, one of which included the two wholly owned subsidiaries of the National Enterprise Board and had no connections with the large component. Finance for Industry and Agricultural Mortgage Corporation, two banking consortiums, formed the second component, and the third comprised three enterprises (Glaxo, Taylor Woodrow, Legal & General Assurance) which had twelve of their major participants in common. The QCOMP analysis of relative intensity was rather more informative, as this disclosed the existence of six small components which appeared at the first step and survived throughout the analysis. These components, all built around relations of majority and minority control, were:

1. British Leyland, Rolls-Royce: [*National Enterprise Board*]
2. British Aircraft Corporation, ICL: [*General Electric*].
3. BAT Industries, Bunzl Pulp & Paper: [*Imperial Group*].
4. Bank of Scotland, Tozer Kemsley and Millbourn: [*Barclays Bank*].
5. Clydesdale Bank, Standard Chartered Bank, Wood Hall Trust: [*Midland Bank*].[74]
6. National and Commerical Banking, Grindlays Holdings: [*Lloyds Bank*].

The first three of these small components were associated enterprises of non-financials (shown in brackets), while the other three were bank-controlled groups. Barclays, Midland, and Lloyds each held controlling stakes in Scottish banks; Midland and Lloyds controlled overseas banks; and Barclays and Midland controlled trading enterprises. At a later stage in the analysis a further bank-centred component appeared; having three consortium banks at its core it included a financial and a commercial enterprise as more marginal members.[75] The small components which appeared at later stages, as the large

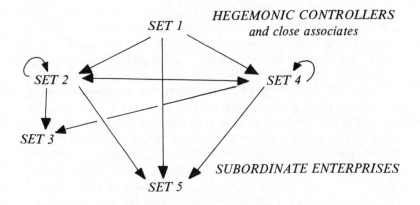

Figure 5.1: *The structure of financial hegemony in Britain*

component fragmented, were far less stable and seemed to have little relation to the main structural features of the network. They appeared as isolated chains of connection because of the disappearance of one or two links of lower intensity, and so their presence was very dependent on slight changes in the network: one more participation by an enterprise could have tied them back into the large component, while one fewer participation elsewhere could have produced relatively different components. Only those components which are stable have any structural significance.[76]

The network of intercorporate participations in Britain in 1976, therefore, showed only weak clustering among controllers and the enterprises which they controlled. The major divisions in the network were highlighted by CONCOR, which showed the patterns of structural equivalence among enterprises. The whole network of directed lines connecting the 166 enterprises showed a clear hierarchical structure, summarised in Figure 5.1. CONCOR initially partitioned the network into two overarching sets, which were subsequently partitioned into further sets, and the arrows in the diagram show the predominant direction of investment.[77] Sets 1, 2, and 4 were the constituent and hierarchically ordered elements in the group of hegemonic controllers and their close associates. Set 1, comprising twenty enterprises, included the large public corporations, the merchant banking fund managers, a small number of private sector pension funds, and the two Scottish mutual insurers. Members of this set were major participants in three of the other sets, and it owed its position at the top of the hierarchy to the fact that the majority of its members were not controlled through constellations of interests but by families and the state. Set 2, with eleven members, included two large clearing banks, five insurers, and four smaller fund managers. Its members tended to participate in one another's controlling constellations and were important participants in the control of sets 3, 4, and 5. The subordinate position of set 2 to set 1 reflected the fact that the majority of its members were controlled through constellations of interests in which members of set 1 participated. Set 6 is not shown in Figure 5.1, as it was a small set with very weak links to other parts of the network and little internal cohesion. This set brought together those enterprises involved in joint ventures, a number of enterprises with only one participation each, and those minority-controlled enterprises whose controllers had no other connections in the network.[78] Set 4, a small group of clearing banks, insurers, and ICI, was distinguished from set 2 by the fact that its members were relatively less involved in the minority–and consortium-controlled enterprises of set 3. The latter set, with twenty-two members, were subordinate to sets 2 and 4, many of the links being strong ties of minority control. Finally, set 5 comprised ninety-one enterprises whose controlling constellations were drawn from the three hegemonic sets. Twenty-one members of this set were themselves participants in controlling constellations, but none were major investors and there was little sign of any meaningful internal division of the set.

The hegemonic structure takes the form of a 'polyarchy' Rooted in the circulation of money capital, a diverse group of clearing and merchant banks, insurers, public corporations, and private sector manufacturers stood at the heart of the intercorporate network. Large 'non-financial' enterprises were able to play a leading part in this polyarchy because the massive investment funds of their pension schemes enabled them to operate as financial intermediaries as well as industrial undertakings. As units of 'finance capital' they took their place alongside the more narrowly defined 'financial' enterprises. Table 5.3 showed enterprises ranked by their 'out-degree' in the network formed amongst the controlling constellations and shows clearly the identity and significance of the leading members of the polyarchy; and Figure 5.1 shows how these controllers were connected into the wider structure. Thirty-nine of the sixty-nine enterprises which participated in the control of Britain's largest enterprises were members of sets 1, 2, or 4, and a further nine were members of set 6.[79] The network was not subdivided into rival financial empires or financial interest groups, the results from both QCOMP and EBLOC showing that controllers and investors were tied together into an extensive, diffuse, and cohesive structure. Prudential Assurance and the National Coal Board, having the largest number of controlling participations, lay at the core of the network and were surrounded by circles of other participants to whom they were linked through intense and cyclical chains of connection.

Capital relations are the major form of connection between enterprises, though other intercorporate bonds do exist. Most important among these are interlocking directorships, which many researchers have regarded as indicators of underlying capital relations. Interlocks do, however, have an intrinsic significance of their own, as they constitute institutionalised channels for the communication of information between enterprises.[80] The present research discovered that there was no one-to-one relation between the partial networks of capital relations and interlocks, though they had, of course, definite points of articulation. Both networks were extensive and diffuse, each being dominated by a large component of connected enterprises. The central enterprises in each network, however, were not identical: the ten enterprises with the largest number of interlocks,[81] as measured by their adjacency, included only two of the ten largest participants from Table 5.3. Key positions in the network of interlocking directorships were played by the big four clearing banks, while the leading positions in the network of participations were held by insurers and pension funds. The Prudential, which participated, in 88 of the controlling constellations was interlocked with only 5 of the top 250 enterprises—and 3 of these interlocks were with American subsidiaries.

It clearly cannot be assumed that interlocking directorships can be used as unproblematic traces of capital relations. The polyarchic financials which dominate the mobilisation of capital are differentially involved in the pattern of board representation which generates the network of interlocking directorships. Not all shareholding enterprises demand a voice in the affairs of the enterprises in which they participate, many preferring to stand on the sidelines with the ultimate sanction of 'exit' through the sale of their shares.[82] Financial intermediaries have, however, become locked in to the fate of the enterprises in which they invest because of the sheer scale of their holdings. An intermediary wishing to sell a large block of shares will be unable to find a customer, unless the share price drops radically, as other intermediaries also wish to sell rather than to buy. Participants in the controlling constellations, therefore, are under pressure to ensure that the interests of 'institutional' shareholders are safeguarded through the presence of suitable non-executive directors on corporate boards. Enterprises are constrained to recruit to their boards a sufficient number of 'outside' directors to represent the interests of the polyarchic financials.

Clearing bank and, to a lesser extent, merchant bank directors have traditionally been an important pool of such outside directors. The clearing banks are, of course, important participants in the controlling constellations—three of the big four clearers are listed in Table 5.3—and their dominance in the market for short-term credit, and their board connections with insurers and other intermediaries makes them crucial brokers in the mobilisation of capital. But as well as enhancing an enterprise's access to sources of short-term and long-term capital, bank directors are seen as useful sources of corporate intelligence, especially if they also have other directorships. At the same time, banks seek to recruit their own directors from among their major customers, clients and associates in order to facilitate and expand the development of their own business. In these ways banks acquire an importance in interlocking directorships which is out of all proportion to their centrality in the network of participations; and their presence on a corporate board is generally regarded by financial intermediaries as a satisfactory safeguard for the interests of the financial world.

Interlocks, therefore, become structured around the big banks in a way that does not happen with participations. Financial intermediaries are able to remain relatively passive because banks have been willing to look after and give voice to their interests. The mobilisation of capital and the exercise of control, therefore, takes place within the constraints of a pre-existing structure of interlocking directorships, and earlier research has shown that the British interlock network of 1976 was structured around the clearing banks. The big four were pivotal points in the network of primary interlocks—those carried by financial or non-financial executives—and they formed clusters of enterprises that have been described as bank-centred spheres of influence.[83] The core members of these spheres were the financial and commercial enterprises which were majority- and minority-controlled by the various banks, and around these gravitated some of the more important of the banks' deposit customers and the clients of their merchant banking departments and associates. The outer boundaries of such spheres were, of course, only loosely defined, and only the core members showed a sustained involvement in the sphere over the long term, but the spheres were real and important features of strategic decision-making in large enterprises. But banks were not the ultimate centres of power in the corporate network; and they were not themselves run by dominant interests. Each of the big four clearers was controlled through a constellation of interests, reinforcing the general structure of impersonal possession in which they played such an important part, and they were allied to one another through their joint participation in a number of consortium banks.[84] Through shareholding and board connections the bank-centred spheres of influence were embedded in a more inclusive and diffusely structured intercorporate network.

The structure of financial hegemony which has been described is the basis upon which large corporate shareholders are able to determine the conditions under which the largest British enterprises must operate. Enterprises which seek to expand or diversify, or even to continue their existing operations, are dependent on access to the capital which they require, and thus are dependent on the enterprises which are able to make this capital available. This gives these enterprises considerable power, but a power which they possess collectively rather than individually. The possibility which any one participant in a constellation has to influence that enterprise's strategy is extremely limited, and the major shareholders will tend to act as a constraint on the strategy rather than actively determining it. Share participations do, of course, give a potential to coordinate the behaviour of those enterprises in which they participate, but the exercise of this potential only becomes possible under certain conditions. The likelihood of such coordination being attempted depends on the shareholder obtaining the support of other participants, and is reinforced by any interlocking directorships which may exist among the enterprises. The power of a coalition of associates is enhanced by any imperfections in the knowledge available to enterprises and their shareholders. In cases where there is a dominant shareholder, the identity of the holder and the size of its holding will be known to all concerned in running the enterprise; but where there is no dominant interest, the identity of the largest holders and the size of their holdings will normally be unknown by other shareholders because of the widespread use of nominee share registrations. Similarly, the directors of a particular enterprise are unlikely to know the identity of the members of its controlling constellation and the distribution of votes among them: their knowledge is likely to extend only to especially large holdings and the holdings of enterprises with which they may be closely associated. Thus corporate controllers face uncertainty in their dealings with one another, and they may fail to intervene in an enterprise's affairs because they are unaware of the position that they hold. Failure to intervene because of uncertainty will enhance the power of any relatively stable alliances that might exist within the controlling constellation; as such allies are likely to have a more accurate knowledge of one another's holdings.

Merchant banks are often leading elements in the formation of such coalitions, because of the role they play in the mobilisation of capital. Through their own funds and those of their clients, and through their ability to 'place' share issues, merchant banks operate as brokers in the access to capital. Thus the link between a large shareholder and the enterprise in which it participates may often be mediated by a merchant bank, which may or may not itself be a large vote holder in the enterprise. In such circumstances the passivity of the shareholder strengthens the power of the merchant bank, and the bank's role is greater if it is itself a shareholder and has allies within the controlling constellation. An example of the exercise of power by a coalition of interests is the alliance between Hill Samuel and Eagle Star Insurance, which enabled them to influence Beecham Group and Eagle Star itself. Hill Samuel, jointly controlled by the Philip Hill investment group and the Samuel family, was the largest participant in Eagle Star's controlling constellation, though its holding amounted to only 3.98 per cent, and it was Eagle Star's merchant bank. The Philip Hill group held a further 0.94 per cent and two family groups, both represented on the board, held 1.34 per cent. Eagle Star itself was minority-controller of Philip Hill Investment Trust, and was interlocked with both the Trust and Hill Samuel. There was a long association between Eagle Star and the Midland Bank's 'Drayton' investment trusts, and the Midland was represented on the Eagle Star board and held 1.82 per cent of its capital. A loose group of associates, therefore, were represented on the Eagle Star board and held a combined block of 8.08 per cent of the votes, out of a total of 24.07 per cent held by the twenty largest shareholders. A similar situation held in Beecham, which had two interlocks with Hill Samuel, its merchant bankers, and with Philip Hill Investment Trust. These two shareholders together with Eagle Star held 4.07 per cent out of the 19.99 per cent block held by the controlling constellation. In both enterprises the leading interests could be outvoted by a coalition drawn from the remaining members of the constellation, but a lack of knowledge about the distribution of the votes in the two enterpises meant that opposition was unlikely to arise in the short term. The position of such an alliance is, however, extremely unstable: shortly after the completion of this research Eagle Star was the subject of a takeover which the coalition was unable to prevent.[85]

Under normal circumstances, therefore, decisions over voting potential and the success of rights issues are decisions under conditions of uncertainty. It can be argued that a major reason for the failure of many financial intermediaries to intervene in corporate affairs on the scale that might be expected from the size of their holdings is precisely this lack of knowledge of the amount of shares held by their fellow shareholders. Because of the size of their holdings, institutional shareholders in Britain have already been forced to become more active controllers of the affairs of the enterprises in which they participate. Their difficulty in withdrawing completely from a particular enterprise—because the only possible purchasers of their shares would be other, equally reluctant, financial intermediaries—means that they have become locked in to the fate of the enterprises in which they invest. Many of the largest intermediaries have, therefore, established regular and thorough monitoring of the operations of these enterprises in order to safeguard their interests. Any reduction in the uncertainty facing shareholders—for example, by a legal requirement to disclose publicly an enterprise's twenty largest voteholders—would be expected to reduce even further the institutional reluctance to intervene and would, perhaps, bring about a closer articulation between the network of capital participations and the network of interlocking directorships.

NOTES

1. For background to this discussion, *see*: G. Clayton and W.T. Osborn, *Insurance Company Investment*, London, George Allen & Unwin, 1965; G. Clayton, *British Insurance*, London, Elek Books, 1971; and B. Supple, *The Royal Exchange Assurance*, Cambridge University Press, 1970.
2. The relation was not perfect: the mutual Norwich Union had only 3.6 per cent of its assets invested in equities. *See* Clayton and Osborn, Table 25 and p. 126.
3. *Ibid.*, p. 177, Table 43; Clayton, pp. 236–7.
4. This discussion draws on: H. Burton and D.C. Corner, *Investment and*

Unit Trusts in Britain and America, London, Elek Books, 1968; and J. Revell, *The British Financial System*, London, Macmillan, 1973.

5. The financial distinction between a share and a certificate is largely spurious, but persists in present-day unit trusts. The main distinction between the two is that certificate holders do not necessarily have the voting rights of a shareholder and there is no framework of disclosure requiring, for example, publicly accessible certificate registers.

6. Revell, p. 447. The legal status of investment and unit trusts is discussed in Burton and Corner, Ch. 1. Investment trust companies may use the word 'trust' in their name, but they are not trusts in law. Their main surviving legal privilege is that they are not classed as investment-dealing institutions and so pay a lower rate of capital gains tax. To qualify for this exemption, a company must accept certain restrictions on its income retention and dividend distribution and must be officially recognised as an investment trust company.

7. Burton and Corner, pp. 28, 43, 47, and Tables 4.1, A.1, A.3, and A.4.

8. For a definition of these terms, *see* J. Scott and C. Griff, *Directors of Industry*, Cambridge, Polity Press, 1984, Figure 1.1, p. 21.

9. The groups can be described as follows. *Touche*: Based around the Industrial and General Trust and run by George Touche CA, a grandson of Alex Guild of Edinburgh. The group was closely associated with overseas electric supply and with the domestic electrical contracting business of George Balfour. *St Davids*: Based around the Government Stocks company, which, with its associates, was forged into a tight group by John Philipps (Lord St Davids) and the group operated like an investment bank with extensive industrial interests. *Crichton and Govett:* Based around the Foreign and Colonial company, originally promoted by merchant bankers Morton Rose and later controlled by Arthur Crichton and the Baring and Cecil families. This trust and its associates were allied with a number of trusts managed by stockbrokers John Govett. *Brown, Fleming & Murray:* The Scottish Western Investment company was originally promoted in Glasgow by William McKenzie of the Alliance Trust of Dundee, with Robert Fleming advising the managers. The Caledonian and Clydesdale trusts were formed by the same interests prior to the First World War, and 'second' and 'third' trusts were formed later.

10. See *Economist*, September 1936, p. 567-8.

11. Robert Benson moved from Liverpool to London and, with his partner Henry Vernet, became involved in investment trusts and in financing the Underground Electric Railways combine. The core of the Benson group was Merchant's Trust.

12. Robert Murray coordinated the Glasgow trusts of Brown Fleming & Murray, while Ivan Spens ran their London trusts. Murray and Spens secured the finance and directors, while Robert Fleming undertook investment management.

13. The original Scottish American trust was formed by Fleming prior to his move to London. *See:* J.C. Gilbert, *A History of the Investment Trusts in Dundee 1873-1938*, London, P.S. King, 1939; D. Hart-Davis, *Peter*

Fleming, London, Cape, 1974.
14. On the Scottish trusts, *see* J. Scott and M. Hughes, *The Anatomy of Scottish Capital,* London, Croom Helm, 1980, pp. 74–81.
15. This process has sometimes been reversed: Mitchell Cotts was originally an investment trust in the St Davids group (under the name City of London and Colonial Trust), but changed its name in 1932 and was floated as an industrial holding company. As shown in Chapter 4, this company was in 1976 minority-controlled by the Midland Bank through its Drayton Montagu investment trusts, the successors of the St Davids group.
16. Burton and Corner, Table A.5. The authors combine Hill Samuel and Philip Hill into one group. The Glasgow and Dundee trusts had become more independent of Fleming by this time, and Brown Fleming and Murray eventually became Murray Johnstone. The Crichton and Govett trusts had become separate groups, the former becoming known as the F & C Management group.
17. *See* A.A. Arnaud, *Investment Trusts Explained,* Cambridge, Woodhead-Faulkner, 1977, App. B.
18. For some time Alfred Booth and Co., had a major interest in the British contracting operations, and in the early 1930s George Booth bought a personal stake.
19. *Economist,* Unit Trust Survey, 13 May 1939.
20. Save & Prosper originated as Trust of Insurance Shares, Britannia Arrow (formerly Slater Walker) as the National group, and Allied Hambro as Allied Investors. Other important groups in 1976 were those run by Lloyds, National Westminster, Hill Samuel, West of England Trust (the Tyndall group), and Dawnay Day (the Target group).
21. R. Minns, *Pension Funds and British Capitalism,* London, Heinemann, 1980.
22. The Electricity supply industry pension fund was operated on behalf of both the Electricity Council and the Central Electricity Generating Board.
23. British Rail and the Post Office each managed a part of their funds internally, delegating the management of the balance: British Rail funds were managed by Hill Samuel and Mercury Securities, and Post Office funds by Mercury Securities, Morgan Grenfell, and Schroders.
24. The management of the Ford scheme, for example, was split among seven merchant banks.
25. Minns, pp. 30–1.
26. The controlling constellations of ICI and the Prudential Assurance are given in J. Scott, *Corporation, Classes, and Capitalism,* rev. edn, London, Hutchinson, 1985, Table 19. Full lists of all 100 constellations are printed in J. Scott, *The Controlling Constellations,* University of Leicester, 1984.
27. The figure includes the holding of the Cooperative group, which held mainly through its insurance subsidiary.
28. In a rights issue, each shareholder has the right to participate in the new issue of shares in proportion to their existing holding.
29. It can be seen that the twentieth holder in Imperial held 0.4 per cent of the

votes. Even if all the remaining shareholders held equal blocks of 0.3 per cent, it would require fifty-eight shareholders to outvote the top twenty. In fact, the size of holdings tapers very dramatically and no group outside the top twenty could hope to form a successful voting block.

30. Florence gave these lists to an economist in the 1970s, but they now seem to have been lost.

31. P.S. Florence, *Ownership, Control and Success of Large Companies*, London, Sweet & Maxwell, 1961, Appendix.

32. In EMI the largest holder in 1935, the year to which Florence's '1936' data actually relate, was Radio Corporation of America. RCA sold its holding in that year, but many of the shares seem to have been acquired by other American interests. The large holding in 1951 seems to have been a nominee holding shares on behalf of these interests, though this interpretation has not been confirmed. In the other company. Sears, the largest holding in 1951 was classified as an 'institution' by Florence. No further information is given, and the data relate to a period two years before Charles Clore's Investment Registry is reported to have built up its controlling holding.

33. These were Marks & Spencer and Tate & Lyle. The third enterprise, BOC, involved the survival of a large corporate holding, by Metal Industries, into the early 1950s.

34. A general qualification to these conclusion is that Florence examined registered shareholdings, and so the actual vote concentration in 1936 and 1951 is likely to have been somewhat higher than Florence's figures suggest. This is unlikely to seriously qualify the conclusions drawn here.

35. Scott and Griff, Table 2.10. The figures relate to grouped holdings, though special voting regulations existed in the earlier years.

36. The big four railway companies of the 1920s and 1930s are possible exceptions to this claim, but their shareholdings have hardly been investigated. For an exception, *see* H.R. Parkinson, 'Who Owns the Railways?', Parts 1–4, *Financial News*, 31 October 1944 and 1–3 November 1944.

37. Their total of votes was 20 × 500.

38. Seventy-nine per cent of Lloyds' ordinary capital was issued for consideration other than cash.

39. P & O, see above, had similar voting restrictions in 1938 and 1957, and these were altered shortly after it experienced a growth in institutional holdings.

40. This has sometimes been a deliberate adoption in order to avoid the risk of a takeover. Standard Life Assurance, for example, converted from a proprietary to a mutual form in 1925.

41. For this reason it is not possible for banks and other enterprises to accumulate votes when policies are assigned to them. Building societies, for example, have many life insurance policies assigned to them in return for granting endowment mortgages. The voting rights, however, will normally remain with the original policy-holder. In most mutual insurers, voting rights are limited to 'with profits' policy-holders.

42. *See* P. Barnes, *Building Societies*, London, Pluto Press, 1984.

128   *Capitalist Property and Financial Power*

43. 'Participation' in the following discussion is taken to mean a holding
    included among the 20 largest in one of the 100 enterprises. The total of
    participations would be 100 × 20, i.e., 2,000, but, as one share list
    contained only 18 holders after processing, the actual total was 1,998.
44. All except one were non-financials investing through their pension
    funds. The exception was the Abbey National Building Society, the only
    building society to participate in a constellation.
45. In addition to the four listed in Table 5.3, these were Royal London
    Mututal Assurance, Sun Alliance and London Assurance, Kuwait
    Investment Office, Britannia Arrow, Refuge Assurance, Merchant Navy
    Officers pension fund, and Sun Life Assurance Society.
46. Lloyds Bank was the only one of the big four clearing banks not to
    appear in Table 5.3. It was ranked 27, with participations in twenty
    enterprises.
47. Non-financials did sometimes participate in the course of their normal
    business, but the bulk of their holdings were through their pension
    departments. The remaining large public sector funds and the number of
    their participations were: BP (28), British Airways (26), British Steel (26),
    Post Office (16), British Gas (13), Bank of England (6). The Bank of
    England holdings may include some funds managed on behalf of the
    royal family and other banking clients. The 'public sector' also includes
    the County Council pension funds discussed later. British Rail did not
    appear as a major participant because much of the pension fund was
    managed by two merchant banks. The largest private sector funds, after
    Shell, were: ICI (36), Unilever (18), Imperial Group (17), and GEC (8).
48. The next ten largest fund managers comprised five merchant banks and
    five trust groups.
49. The Robeco investment group of the Netherlands participated in two
    enterprises, and other foreign holders were CIO of Switzerland, Aer
    Lingus of Ireland, Svenska Accumulator of Sweden, and General Cable
    and Exxon of the USA. Esso pension fund invested in three enteprises,
    and these holdings have been allocated to its American parent, Exxon.
50. Prudential held sixteen second-place participations and ten third place.
51. SICOVAM was reputed to hold many of the overseas investments of the
    French branch of the Rothschild family.
52. Most of these were, in fact, legally constituted as 'corporate' bodies, but
    they were not organised as joint-stock companies and were not subject to
    any of the Companies Acts. They were generally established as
    corporations by Royal Charter or Act of Parliament so as to give them a
    legal existence independent of that of their members and officials. The
    Kuwait Investment Office has been treated as a corporate business
    enterprise in this analysis as it seems to have operated as the London
    investment branch of an extensive corporate empire—though the precise
    legal forms under which it operated were cloaked in secrecy.
53. R. Minns and J. Thornley, *State Shareholding,* London, Macmillan,
    1978.
54. Together with Scottish Widows Fund, Coats Patons, and Burmah Oil,
    they were members of the top 250.

55. It has been found that this is especially strong in the smaller enterprises engaged in finance and oil, with the Scottish merchant banks being of great importance in mobilising this involvement. *See* J. Scott and M. Hughes, Chs. 4 and 5.

56. Norwich Union and Royal London Mutual were the participants concerned.

57. Scott and Griff, pp. 172–3.

58. The technical details of these models are set out in Appendix II of this book. A fuller account of this perspective is given in *ibid.*, pp. 8ff. *See also* S.D. Berkowitz, *An Introduction to Structural Analysis*, Toronto, Butterworth, 1982.

59. *See*: P. Doreian, *Mathematics and the Study of Social Relations*, London, Weidenfeld & Nicolson, 1970, Chs. 1–4; P. Hage and F. Haray, *Structural Models in Anthropology*, Cambridge University Press, 1983.

60. Isolated points are sometimes treated as components, though this is only trivially true. The present discussion follows the usage of Wellman, who employs 'piece' as the generic term for singletons and components. A component, therefore, has a minimum size of 2. *See* B. Wellman, 'Domestic Work, Paid Work, and Network', in S. Duck and D. Perlman (eds.), *Personal Relationships*, London, Sage, 1985.

61. This is based on the argument of Everett, and the complexities which he introduces are discussed later in the text and, more fully, in Appendix II. Everett talks about 'cyclic blocks', and while his usage of 'block' is in accord with its original meaning in graph theory, the term has led to much confusion. In the discussion which follows, Everitt's 'blocks' are treated as 'components' so as to distinguish them from the 'blocks' introduced later on.

62. The analysis of cyclic components can, of course, be combined with the analysis of multiplicities to produce more complex 'nestings'.

63. Block modellers confusingly use the word 'block' to refer to both the set of agents and, the relations between sets. Carrington, Heil, and Berkowitz call the first, 'blocs' and the second, 'blocks', but it is less confusing to refer to the former simply as 'sets'. *See* P.J. Carrington, G.H. Heil, and S.D. Berkowitz, 'A Goodness of Fit Index for Blockmodels' *Social Networks*, 2, 1979.

64. *See* R.H. Atkin, *Multidimensional Man,* Harmondsworth, Penguin, 1981.

65. *See* R.N. Shepard, A.K. Romney, and S.B. Nerlove (eds.), *Multidimensional Scaling*, vol. 1, New York, Seminar Press, 1972. An important application of these ideas is *Levine's Atlas of Corporate Interlocks*, Hanover, New Hampshire, Worldnet, 1984.

66. All the top twenty shareholders in those enterprises originally classified as subject to limited minority control were analysed. The sixty-nine controllers comprised the sixty participants in controlling constellations and nine other enterprises which appeared as minority or majority controllers or which participated in enterprises subject to limited minority control.

67. Further details on the algorithms are given in Appendix II. CONCOR

was implemented in FORTRAN by Clyde Mitchell and EBLOC by Martin Everett. QCOMP was implemented in PASCAL by Peter Cowley.

68. The six hangers-on and their participations were: Scottish Widows (4), Esso (3), Arthur Guinness (1), George Wimpey (1), Associated British Foods (1), and Abbey National Building Society (1).
69. This structure was extremely stable. With the cycle length increased to 4 just three of the hangers-off (British Aircraft, ICL, and Consolidated Petroleum) became members of the large component.
70. These were produced in the first three steps of the analysis. Further partitions did not produce useful or informative sets.
71. This analysis takes the rows in the matrix and computes the network of connections which occur by virtue of enterprises having investments in common. This row solution is an analysis of the relation KY(X). Where links between investment targets are analysed, the column solution, the relation is KX(Y).
72. These three were National Enterprise Board, Rank Organisation, and S. Pearson. The fourth, Tube Investments, was a member of the cyclic component because it was the only one of the four to be controlled through a constellation of interests.
73. These two were Reed International and George Wimpey, both of which had just one participation—in MEPC—and so had a more intense mutual connection than they had with any other enterprises.
74. Mitchell Cotts (*see* n. 15 above) was inadvertently excluded from this analysis. If included it would have appeared in small component number 5.
75. The five members were FFI, AMC, Yorkshire Bank, Union Discount, and Guinness Peat.
76. This conclusion was reinforced by the CONCOR column solution, which showed few significant divisions. The first partition distinguished those with few participants, but further partitioning of the remainder was uninformative.
77. The arrows connecting sets in Figure 5.1 represent those blocks of above-average density of the image matrix produced by CONCOR. The two initial sets were subsequently partitioned into, respectively, sets 1, 2, and 6, and sets 3, 4, and 5. Set 6, for reasons discussed in the text, is not shown in the diagram.
78. Set 6 included the non-cyclic components identified by EBLOC and many of the hangers to the large cyclic component.
79. Of the remainder, three (Guinness Peat, Bank of Scotland, National and Commercial) were in set 3, and eighteen, all private sector enterprises investing mainly through their pension funds, were in set 5.
80. *See* Scott and Griff *op. cit.: see also* F.N. Stokman, R. Ziegler, and J. Scott, (eds.), *Networks of Corporate Power,* Cambridge, Polity Press, 1985, Ch. 1.
81. Scott and Griff, Table 6.2, p. 155.
82. The terms 'exit' and 'voice' are drawn from A.O. Hirschman, *Exit, Voice, and Loyalty*, London, Harvard University Press, 1970.

83. Scott and Griff, Ch. 6.
84. The Bank of England played an important role for the network as a whole. It was at the centre of a sphere of connections as it recruited the chief executives of many enterprises to its board. It was not, however, involved in normal commercial or corporate banking on any scale and was marginal to the network of participations.
85. The coalition initially accommodated to the acquisition of a minority block by Allianz, but failed completely to prevent the acquisition of Eagle Star by BAT Industries.

6 Corporations and Constellations in the United States

The main legal form of big business in the United States is very similar to that found in Britain, though the framework of regulation is different.[1] The basis of the modern legal framework is provided by the Securities Act of 1933, which superceded some of the earlier enactments of the individual states. The first state to evolve any form of legal regulation over joint-stock enterprise was Massachusetts which, from 1852, created a complex set of statutes to regulate railways, investment companies, public utilities, and other types of corporation.[2] The main feature of this framework was separate statutory regulation of each specific type of enterprise, and only after the turn of the century did a number of states begin to pass general securities regulations. The primary aim of such legislation was the prevention of the fraudulent promotion of businesses, and the eventual outcome were the so-called 'Blue Sky laws'. Thus, for most of the nineteenth century and well into the twentieth century American business operated under fewer and much looser legal constraints than did their British Counterparts.

The earliest forms of federal regulation had been the creation of the Federal Trade Commission (FTC) and the passing of the Clayton Act, both of which had centred on the anti-competitive effects of formal and informal arrangements between enterprises: a particularly important target of this legislation were the 'trusts' and interlocking directorships which had been established by the New York investment bankers as they bought and built giant enterprises prior to the First World War. The Securities Act of 1933 was the first attempt to control company formation and regulate disclosure at a federal level, and was administered by the FTC until the

Securities and Exchange Commission (SEC) was created a year later. Initially, federal regulation was aimed at the issuing of shares by corporations, but the Securities Exchange Act of 1934, which established the SEC, extended the range of federal legislation to the trading in shares which had already been issued. The Acts of 1933 and 1934 were both concerned with general securities regulation for all joint-stock companies, but the SEC became the body responsible for later Acts concerned with public holding companies, trusts, and investment companies. Although there had, from the 1920s, been pressure from within the legal profession for the establishment of a uniform model Securities Act which was compatible with the evolving federal legislation and which it was hoped individual states would adopt, it was not until well into the post-war period that there was any marked move towards uniformity in corporate legislation.

The system of regulation which has been established in the United States is, in some respects, more centralised than that found in Britain. In Britain there is no equivalent of the SEC, though some of its powers are exercised on a 'voluntary' basis by the Council of the Stock Exchange, whose listing requirements are enforceable through the law of contract. In other respects, however, American regulation is looser and more decentralised: much legislation remains at the level of the individual states, its content varying from one part of the country to another, and the documents which are required for public disclosure are fewer than is the case in Britain. The initial registration documents of an American corporation contain the articles of incorporation, the names of directors, all large shareholders, and various other items of information. These documents must be filed with the SEC and are open to public inspection. Corporations must also make an annual return to the SEC which must, among other things, include a list of all shareholders owning 5 per cent or more of the shares, but there is no requirement to make a return of the full share register. The requirement to disclose substantial shareholders was aimed specifically at identifying holdings with a potential for control, and thus the legislation requires that the beneficial rather than the 'record' (i.e. registered) holder be listed.

The absence of any public disclosure of share registers, however, has seriously handicapped American researchers, who have had to rely upon piecemeal information such as the disclosures on substantial holdings and directors' stakes made to the SEC and on information drawn from the business press. Only Senate and congressional committees have had the power to require disclosure of systematic information to them, and this has been only for those years which such committees have investigated: the Temporary National Economic Committee, for example, studied 1937 and the Patman Committee investigated 1967.[3] Fortunately for the present research, a private body called the Corporate Data Exchange (CDE) has made use of the various SEC documents for 1980 in order to compile the closest possible approximation to a register of large voting shareholders. Their work has been published as a series of directories,[4] which it is intended to update periodically, though they are no substitute for access to the share registers themselves. The CDE researchers examined two main SEC sources: the disclosure of holdings by directors and substantial shareholders contained in the annual reports, and the disclosure which various types of investor are required to make.

Banks and trust companies, investment companies and advisers, insurance companies and pension funds all have to file with the SEC lists of the shares which they hold in other corporations, and the CDE researchers were able to make use of these to identify some holdings of less than 5 per cent in their target corporations. Holdings by executives in their own companies and holdings by individuals who sell unregistered shares must also be disclosed to the SEC, and this made it possible for the CDE to identify some of the more important personal holdings. The CDE aimed to identify, for each corporation which they investigated, all holders of 0.02 per cent or more of the voting capital, and, while they have incomplete knowledge of personal holdings, their lists are useful approximations to the registers of large vote-holders produced in the British research.[5] The lists printed in the CDE directories contained an average of about fifty shareholders, and to enable comparison with the results of the British research these were reduced to lists of the twenty largest vote-holders.

From these sources it was possible to obtain shareholding information for the top 252 American enterprises. These enterprises had been selected using similar criteria to those used in selecting the British top 250 of 1976, and comprised the 202 largest non-financials, ranked by turnover, and 50 large financials.[6] Not all of these enterprises were studied by the CDE and so lists of the twenty largest shareholder of those excluded could not be obtained. In order to minimise the loss of information a search was made in two other sources[7] for any usable information on ownership and control. In a number of cases it proved possible to identify the mode of control in this way, though it was not possible to obtain full lists of large shareholders for those not included in the CDE directories. After these searches there were just twenty-six enterprises for which no ownership information was available.

The types of shareholders which appeared in the American lists were, in general terms, similar to those on the British registers, though their relative importance differed. Alongside the big banks, insurers, and private sector pension funds were a small number of public sector pension funds, though none of these were as large or as important as those found in Britain. Examples of such small public sector funds were the New York State Common Retirement Fund and the New York City Comptrollers Office, and the only large shareholder which derived its funds from public sector employees (Teachers Insurance and Annuity Association) was a mutual company. Foreign interests participated in American enterprises pre-dominantly through their American subsidiaries and associ-ates—for example, the Rothschilds via Bank of California, and Barings via Endowment Management and Research—though some of the few cases of majority ownership involved direct stakes by European enterprises. The lists showed the frequent appearance of smaller corporations from outside the top 252 such as Fayez Sarofim, T. Rowe Price Associates, Thorndike-Doran-Paine & Lewis, Batterymarch Financial Management, David L. Babson, and State Street Research and Management. A number of these enterprises were investment bankers and stockbrokers, while others were managers and advisors to investment trusts and mutual funds (unit trusts). In most cases little further information was available, though many were known to be personal partnerships or family-controlled corporations.

A particularly important category of shareholding in the United States comprised the many holdings of bank trust departments. For a long time investment management and fiduciary trustee business was carried out by trust companies separate from the 'commercial' or clearing banks, though they gradually became affiliated to particular banks and have increasingly become incorporated into them as trust departments. This has occurred at the same time as bank holding companies have been formed to allow banking enterprises to avoid some of the legal restrictions imposed on them. No commercial bank may operate in more than one state, and so the device of the bank holding company enables one enterprise to undertake nationwide commercial banking to personal and corporate clients and to run a substantial trust business. Thus J.P. Morgan and Co., is the holding company for Morgan Guaranty Trust,[8] Citicorp is the holding company for first National City Bank, and Western Bancorp is the holding company for United California Bank. Herman has argued that the growth of mutual fund and pension fund business has led trust departments to become more centralised and bureaucratic, with their research departments producing lists of approved securities and a small number of investment managers coordinating accounts in terms of guidelines which specify the spread of holdings at which they should aim and the maximum size of their holdings in particular companies. This makes it possible, he argues, for trust departments to become subordinate elements in the corporate banking activities of their parents: they may be required to take up the new issues of banking customers, to support the corporate board in a proxy fight or takeover bid, and so on.[9]

THE STRUCTURE OF OWNERSHIP AND CONTROL

The information which has been collected makes it possible to classify the top 252 American enterprises by their mode of control. As in the case of the British enterprises studied in

Chapter 4, a provisional classification can be produced by examining the evidence for the existence of identifiable substantial shareholdings and by using a fixed cut-off threshold for minority control. Table 6.1 shows the results of this provisional classification, with the controllers broken down according to their type. In this table, minority control is defined as the situation where a dominant shareholder owns in excess of 10 per cent of the shares; limited minority control is defined as the situation where a holder of between 7 per cent and 10 per cent is represented on the board of directors.

The major differences between these data and the British data given in Table 4.1 are the extremely low level of majority control and the correspondingly higher number of enterprises with no dominant interest. Only seven of the American enterprises were subject to majority control, and there were no wholly owned subsidiaries or public corporations. The four foreign majority controllers were BP (controlling SOHIO), the Royal Dutch-Shell group (controlling Shell Oil), Renault

Table 6.1: *Corporate control in the United States: provisional classification (1980)*

	Type of controller					
		Corporate				
Mode of control	Personal	US	Foreign	Mixed	Other	Totals
Exclusive majority	2	1	4	0	0	7
Shared majority	0	0	0	1	0	1
Exclusive minority	26	21	0	0	0	47
Limited minority	3	0	0	0	0	3
Shared minority	1	0	0	2	0	3
Mutual	–	–	–	–	11	11
No dominant interest	–	–	–	154	–	154
Not known	–	–	–	–	26	26
Totals	32	22	4	157	37	252

(controlling American Motors), and Philips (controlling North American Philips). The American economy, therefore, showed an extremely low level of foreign ownership, though the German Flick family exercised minority control in W.R. Grace, and the Templeton family participated through a Canadian investment company. The number of minority-controlled enterprises was broadly similar in the United States and in Britain, though rather more of the British cases involved holdings of just under 10 per cent. Of the twenty-one enterprises which were minority-controlled by corporate interests, ten had their own pension fund or savings plan as their largest shareholder. It will be recalled that Lucas Industries was the only British enterprise to show this pattern of in-house control. American enterprises controlled in this way were Bendix, Borg-Warner, Celanese, Chrysler, General Motors, B.F. Goodrich, Procter & Gamble, Republic of Texas Corporation, Sears Roebuck, and US Steel. Six of the corporate controllers of the remaining enterprises were themselves members of the top 252, one of these being family minority-controlled,[10] one being controlled in-house,[11] and the remainder having no dominant ownership interest. It can be concluded that the scale of corporate enterprise in the United States prevented foreign enterprises from attaining any significant toehold in the economy, forced families to substantially dilute their controlling holdings, and resulted in a considerable dispersal in the distribution of shareholdings: as in Britain, the largest category of enterprises comprised those with no dominant shareholding interest.[12]

Using information on the twenty largest vote-holders in those enterprises for which such information was available, it was possible to reconsider the provisional classification. Only one of the enterprises originally classified as subject to shared minority control (McDonnell Douglas) required reallocation —it was regarded as having secure minority control because its joint controllers were the McDonnell family with 22 per cent and the corporation's pension fund with 24 per cent, the in-house holding buttressing family control. When the category of limited minority control was defined in terms of the likelihood of the largest shareholder being outvoted by the next nineteen shareholders, substantial reallocation was

Table 6.2: *Corporate control in the United States: final classification (1980)*

Mode of control	Personal	Corporate		Mixed	Other	Totals
		US	Foreign			
Exclusive majority	2	1	4	0	0	7
Shared majority	0	0	0	1	0	1
Secure minority	10	5	0	1	0	16
Limited minority	16	15	0	0	0	31
Shared minority	1	0	0	1	0	2
Unknown minority	3	1	0	0	0	4
Mutual	–	–	–	–	11	11
Constellation of interests	–	–	–	154	–	154
Not known	–	–	–	–	26	26
Totals	32	22	4	157	37	252

Note: Incomplete data meant that it was not meaningful to divide the 154 enterprises controlled by constellations according to the composition of their constellations. This question is, however, discussed in the text. The total of 154 includes 29 enterprises with dispersed ownership but for which lists of the 20 largest vote-holders were not available.

necessary. Table 6.2 shows that thirteen of the enterprises originally classified as subject to exclusive minority-control by personal interests and fifteen of those classified as minority-controlled by corporate interests were reclassified to the 'limited minority' category because their controlling interests could not be certain of victory in contested votes.[13] In a number of these cases these were associated and in-house holdings which buttressed the dominant interest, but their control was relatively more insecure than that of the controllers of the other sixteen minority-controlled enterprises. In the final allocation, therefore, limited forms of minority control were found to be more important in the United States than in Britain. The *de facto* threshold for secure minority control, however, was higher and more indeterminate than was the case in Britain. For personally controlled enterprises the threshold level lay somewhere between the insecure holding of 22.00 per cent which the Firestone family held in Firestone Tire & Rubber and the secure holding of 27.89 per cent which the Flick family held in W.R. Grace; it is impossible to be more precise as no minority blocks were found between these two levels. In the case of corporate control, however, there was a wide 'grey area' in which secure control shaded-over into limited minority control; while United States Steel was subject to secure minority control at 16.71 per cent, Celanese was subject to limited minority control at 20.87 per cent. All of the cases where corporate interests held 21 per cent or more, however, involved secure minority holdings. These findings confirm the conclusion drawn in Chapter 4 concerning the use of fixed threshold levels for determining control. A 10 per cent cut-off for minority control is adequate for delineating the broad contours of control in the British and American economies, though it is an uncertain guide to the control status of particular enterprises. When control is defined on the basis of the dynamics of corporate voting the 10–20 per cent band seems to be a crucial area of insecure, limited minority control, while minority blocks above 20 per cent are more likely to involve secure minority control.

There were 154 enterprises provisionally classified as having no dominant interest, and all of the 125 for which full lists of large shareholders were available were found to be controlled through constellations of interest. It seems reasonable to assume that all 154 were, in fact, controlled in this way. As in Britain, there were no enterprises where the controlling constellations held less than 10 per cent or more than 50 per cent. The enterprise with the most dispersed voting capital was Charter New York, whose controlling constellation held 10.21 per cent; and the most concentrated voting structure was found in Whirlpool, whose controlling constellation held 48.39 per cent. The 'typical' American constellation, however, held a larger block of shares than its British counterpart: in Britain more than three-quarters of the constellations held less than 30 per cent; in the United States this was true for only just over one-half. In each case of control through a constellation of interests, a minority block was held by a diverse group of

Table 6.3: *Share concentration in controlling constellations: United States (1980)*

% held by top 20	No. of enterprises		
	With family participation	Without family participation	Totals
More than 50	0	0	0
40–9	4	4	8
30–9	25	18	43
20–9	41	20	61
10–19	6	3	9
Less than 10	0	0	0
Incomplete information	3	1	4
Totals	79	46	125

Note: Four enterprises could not be classified because their shareholder lists were extremely short and so complete information was unavailable. These enterprises were Greyhound, Marine Midland Banks, Merrill Lynch, and Uniroyal.

corporate and personal interests, no one of which was large enough to dominate the others. The fact that twenty shareholders were necessary to accumulate these minority blocks is sufficient evidence to refute the claims for 'bank minority control'; but the managerialist position is no stronger. In none of the enterprises for which information was available did the degree of share dispersal seem sufficient to warrant the designation 'management controlled'. Herman's concept of constrained management control[14] certainly grasps some of the important features of control in these enterprises, but it fails to bring out forcibly enough the fact the 'constraint' is exercised by large and powerful financial intermediaries which frequently have board representation on the enterprises in which they participate and which have shown an increasing tendency to intervene actively in determining their corporate strategy. Those enterprises having no dominant shareholding interest may be regarded as controlled through constellations of interests.

Some insight into the development of these enterprises and their controlling constellations can be gained by comparing the results of the present study with those of the 1937 Temporary National Economic Committee. The TNEC compiled lists of the largest shareholders of record in many of the largest American non-financials,[15] and it is possible to examine the mode of control in 1937 of those enterprises controlled through constellations of interests in 1980. Many had in 1937 already attained a high level of share dispersal, though their largest shareholders were predominantly families and individuals rather than financial intermediaries. This can be illustrated by examining those non-financials with the greatest dispersal in 1980 (those which had less than 30 per cent of their capital held by controlling constellations) and for which 1937 information is available. The twenty-seven enterprises which met these criteria comprised, in 1937, nine clear-cut cases of minority control and eighteen enterprises with a high level of dispersal. Only one of the cases of minority control involved control by a corporate interest—Union Pacific's control of Illinois Central. All the remainder were cases of family control, with the Rockefellers alone controlling three enterprises.[16]

The enterprises with dispersed shareholdings in 1937 seemed to fall into three categories: five enterprises where a single family had a substantial holding below 10 per cent, six enterprises where various families participated in the controlling constellations, and seven enterprises where financial intermediaries were the dominant elements in the constellations. These three categories might, with certain reservations, be seen as stages through which an enterprise passes if it undergoes the transition from family minority-control to control through a constellation of interests. American Can, for example, where the Moore family held limited minority control on the basis of their holding of 7.36 per cent was clearly in the first stage, while IBM, where four separate families (Hewitt, Watson, Smithers, and Ford)[17] held a total of 10 per cent, had reached the second stage. Those which had reached the third stage were epitomised by IT & T, where a controlling constellation of financial intermediaries held 15.36 per cent.[18] The six enterprises similar to IT & T had between 9 per cent and 21 per cent of their shares held by their controlling constellations, suggesting a higher level of dispersal in 1937 than in 1980, and Table 6.4 does indeed show that in all seven enterprises there had been an increase in the proportion of shares held by the controlling constellations. It is worth noting in this context that the four enterprises with the highest level of dispersal in 1980 (those where the controlling constellations held 10–19 per cent) and for which 1937 information was available, had all been dominated by families and personal interests in the earlier period: three had been dominated by single families and one by a group of families.[19] That is to say, those enterprises had not moved from dispersal in 1937 to greater dispersal in 1980; they had moved from family dominance to control through a constellation of interests following the stages outlined above.

Table 6.2 shows that thirty-two enterprises in 1980 were controlled by personal interests, and that personal and corporate interests shared control in a further three enterprises. This total of thirty-five enterprises in which entrepreneurial capitalists had a dominant position included two cases of majority control,[20] three enterprises with a mixed controlling group,[21] sixteen cases of limited minority control, and eleven cases of secure minority control.[22] The only family

Table 6.4: *The development of controlling constellations: United States (1937 and 1980)*

Enterprise	% held by top 20	
	1937	1980
Continental Oil	21.29	27.55
General Electric	9.99	20.34
Int. Telephone & Telegraph	15.36	29.72
Radio Corp. of America	12.21	25.81
Union Carbide	15.17	23.20
Union Pacific	14.47	22.43
Westinghouse Electric	10.92	22.61

Table 6.5: *Major family controllers: United States (1980)*

Family	No. of enterprises in which dominant interest	No. of constellations in which participate	Totals
Ford	1	17	18
Rockefeller	0	7	7
Du Pont	1	3	4
Mellon	3	0	3
Templeton	0	3	3
Lykes	1	1	2
Phipps	0	2	2

to control more than one of these enterprises was the Mellon family, which had secure minority control of Mellon National Bank and limited minority control of Alcoa and Gulf Oil. But entrepreneurial capitalists were also important as participants in controlling constellations—79 of the 125 enterprises analysed had one or more family participants, and in 48 of these family representatives had seats on the board of directors. Thus a total of 114 of the enterprises for which information was available had some degree of family participation, a substantially higher proportion than was found in Britain. While the United States had a smaller proportion of family-controlled enterprises than did Britain, it had a much larger number of enterprises in which families had a considerable shareholding influence. The survival of such a large number of family participations in the United States indicates clearly that American families which had diversified their holdings of corporate stocks were nevertheless able to maintain large blocks in particular enterprises because of the generally higher level of personal shareholding found in the United States. Whereas personal ownership accounted for just 28 per cent of share ownership in Britain, the figure in the United States was 65 per cent.[23]

This is further reflected in the number of families which had control or influence in two or more enterprises. Table 6.5 shows that seven families had substantial holdings in more than one of the top 252 American enterprises, with the Ford family and the Ford Foundation participating in seventeen constellations in addition to exercising secure minority control over Ford Motor. There was little sign that these families were trying to buy into related enterprises in order to coordinate their policies, though the Mellon and Rockefeller holdings were concentrated in enterprises with which the families had long-standing relationships: the Rockefellers, for example, participated in three of the Standard Oil companies and in Chase Manhattan Bank,[24] though their other participations were in Beatrice Foods, Teledyne, and Merrill Lynch. While impressive, the figures in Table 6.5 underestimate the extent of family power and influence, as a number of families, such as the Du Ponts, used large minority-controlled enterprises as virtual family holding companies. In the present analysis these have been treated as corporate holdings. In addition to the four enterprises in which the Du Pont family had a direct involvement, E.I. Du Pont de Nemours (minority-controlled by the family) was a participant in 18 of the top 252 enterprises. Similarly, the Mellon-controlled Mellon National Bank participated in 23 of the top enterprises.[25]

As in the case of the enterprises controlled through constellations of interests, it is possible to use TNEC data to investigate the weakening of family control between 1937 and 1980. Information was available in both years for eight of the enterprises subject to family minority control in 1980, three of these involving secure and five limited minority control. All eight enterprises showed the same families to have been in control throughout the period, though in each case their percentage holding had fallen. In three cases (Ford Motor, Sun Co., Gulf Oil) there had been a transition from majority control to minority control, and in all other cases a minority block had been reduced in size. The smallest fall, of 7.68 per cent, was found in E.I. Du Pont de Nemours, but in each case where a minority holding had been reduced by more than 10 per cent the families were left with limited rather than secure minority control. It can be suggested that further reductions in their percentage holdings would eventually reduce their limited minority control to the point at which it is more realistic to see the enterprises as controlled through constellations of interests with dominant family participants.

THE STRUCTURE OF FINANCIAL HEGEMONY

The top 252 American enterprises included small blocks of foreign- and family-owned enterprises, but the majority were controlled by diverse constellations of corporate and personal interests. The growth in institutional shareholdings which has strengthened the position of the corporate participants in those constellations has been rather less marked in the United States than in Britain, resulting in a higher proportion of shares remaining in individual hands. Nevertheless, there is substantial evidence that a relatively small group of enterprises held a hegemonic position in the network of capital relations. Ninety-one of the top 252 enterprises were involved as participants or controllers of the top 252 themselves, though 38 of these were involved with only one enterprise. Of the remaining 53, 29 participated in the control of 10 or more enterprises (compared with 35 in Britain) and 4 participated in 50 or more (compared with 9 in Britain). Thus the power potential of the large financials was only slightly less marked than in Britain. Table 6.6 shows the 20 largest participants in American constellations of interests and brings out clearly the dominance of J.P. Morgan, which participated in 81 of the 125 constellations investigated. Though dominant within the American network of capital relations, Morgan did not occupy such an exalted position as Prudential Assurance in Britain.[26] The latter participated in 88 of the 100 British constellations.

Thirteen of the twenty largest American participants were banks, evidencing the lower level of concentration found in American banking and the fact that banking was regionally structured. This bank dominance also reflects the high degree of control which American banks exercised over pension fund capital through the operations of their trust departments. Indeed, only four self-managed pension funds appeared among the twenty largest participants: the teachers' mutual scheme TIAA and the private sector funds of General Electric, US Steel, and Du Pont. Seven of the top ten participants and a further four of the next ten had New York headquarters, and five of the remaining top participants were based in the north-east region.[27] Two of the top participants were based in the north-central region of Illinois and Michigan, and only two were based in the 'sunbelt'—Bank America in Los Angeles and Wells Fargo in San Franciso. This dominance of the capital market by north-eastern financials was evident also within particular constellations: J.P. Morgan was the leading participants in eight enterprises, and Manufacturers Hanover and Prudential Insurance were each the leading participants in six constellations. Turning from the controllers to the enterprises in which they invest, Table 6.7 shows the 'blue chips' of the American economy. The blue chips are those members of the top 252 with the largest number of other top 252 members in their controlling constellations. Six of the twenty enterprises listed in Table 6.7, all of them financials, were also listed in Table 6.6, but the main conclusion to be drawn about the blue chips is that they were predominantly non-financial enterprises operating in a very few industrial sectors. They included five oil producers, (including three of the Standard Oil companies), three enterprises from electronic and precision engineering, two farm equipment manufacturers, and three drug producers.

It is clear from the evidence presented so far that regionalism was a more important feature of banking in America than it was in British. Although New York and the north-east region dominated the financial system, there was some evidence for the existence of rival financial centres in the north-central region, and in California and Texas. In Britain, only Scotland appeared as a distinct base for banks, insurers, and investment companies, but it was discovered that the Scottish financials were so closely tied to London enterprises through their participations and through their own controllers that no distinctively Scottish component appeared in the network of participations. In view of the importance attributed to regionalism in American studies of interlocking director-ships,[28] it is important to investigate whether the north-central and sunbelt regions were foci for any fragmentation of the

American network of capital relations into regionally based components.

The 91 corporate controllers invested in 107 of the top 252 enterprises, either as minority controllers or as participants in controlling constellations, and the combined network of controllers and controlled included 151 of the top enterprises.[29] Use of the EBLOC algorithm, with cycle length 3, showed that the combined network was dominated by a large cyclic component with 129 members. Outside the large component were two non-cyclic components with just two members each,

Table 6.6: *The largest participants: United States (1980)*

Investor	No. of participations in controlling constellations
J.P. Morgan	81
Manufacturers Hanover	55
TIAA	54
Wells Fargo	50
Citicorp	49
Bankers Trust	48
General Electric	42
United States Steel	37
Prudential Insurance	36
Chase Manhattan	32
First National Boston	29
National Detroit	28
Continental Corporation	25
Chemical New York Bank	24
BankAmerica	23
Mellon National Bank	23
First Chicago	23
Bank of New York	22
Equitable Life	20
Du Pont	19

Note: BankAmerica and Mellon National were also involved in the minority control of other enterprises. This table lists only participations of members of the top 252.

Table 6.7: *The blue-chip investments: United States (1980)*

Enterprise	Top 252 members in controlling constellation
Exxon	14
Caterpillar Tractor	13
Eastman Kodak	13
IBM	13
J.P. Morgan	13
Merck	13
BankAmerica	12
John Deere	12
Mobil	12
Texaco	12
Wells Fargo	12
American Home Products	11
Bristol-Myers	11
Citicorp	11
Conoco	11
Continental Illinois	11
First Chicago	11
Manufacturers Hanover	11
Raytheon	11
Standard Oil of Indiana	11

one of which was a regional group from Texas.[30] There were, in addition, eighteen 'hangers' to the large component, of which four—all hangers-on—were mutual insurers. All the remaining hangers were non-financial enterprises. The five non-financial hangers-on were peripheral participants and minority-controllers, while the nine hangers-off were minority-controlled enterprises and unpopular investment targets. The large component itself showed little sign of internal fragmentation, as an analysis of reciprocal participations showed it to be organised around a five-member New York core surrounded by three hangers and two-non cyclic components. Five New York financial intermediaries—Bankers Trust, Citicorp, Continental Corporation, Manufacturers Hanover, and J.P.

Morgan—were closely allied through reciprocal share participations, and various of these five had close links with the hangers and small components. One of the small components was a pair of Californian enterprises,[31] one of which had a reciprocated link to J.P. Morgan. EBLOC, therefore, showed weak regionalism—the existence of Texan and Californian groupings—to be a feature of an extensive intercorporate network organised at a national level through a core of New York financials.

The CONCOR algorithm produced further evidence on the weak internal structuring of this network. The major feature of the network of controlled enterprises was the separation of the minority-controlled enterprises from those controlled through a constellation of interests, but the network of relations among the ninety-one controllers suggested an axis of regional differentiation. The latter network had as its main feature a split between the nationally orientated but New York based investors and a more diverse set containing enterprises with a strong regional character. Twelve of the twenty enterprises in this set had their headquarters outside New York, forming seven regional centres:

Boston   —Northwestern Mutual
Connecticut   —Connecticut General Insurance, Travellers Corporation
Pennsylvania —Bethlehem Steel, US Steel, First Pennsylvania
Minneapolis   —Northwest Bancorp
Seattle   —Seattle–First National
Texas   —Republic of Texas Corporation
California   —Security Pacific, American Brands, Western Bancorp

It should be emphasised that these did not appear as sharply defined groups but as members of a large regionally based set whose main common feature was a tendency to show differing patterns of investment from the major New York investors. An important finding is the relative separation of the Boston, Connecticut, and Pennsylvania enterprises from the New York members of the north-east region.

As the controlling enterprises did not seem to fall into discrete and tightly-organised regional groups, it is not surprising that the main feature of the combined network of controllers and controlled, when analysed by CONCOR, should be the separation of a set of hegemonic investors from a relatively undifferentiated set of subordinate enterprises. Nevertheless, the hegemonic set showed some regional differentiation.[32] Its core comprised a group of twenty-two enterprises drawn from all the financial centres of the United States: New York, San Francisco, Boston, Pittsburgh, Detroit, and elsewhere. All of these enterprises showed similar patterns of national orientation in their investments and in their own controlling constellations. Outside this core were six relatively more peripheral sets of hegemonic controllers, five of which contained enterprises based outside New York. Only one of the sets, however, was truly regional in character, a set of two enterprises based in Chicago.[33] The CONCOR analyses, therefore, suggest a division between a hegemonic and a subordinate set of enterprises, with the former having a 'national' core and a surrounding fringe of rather more regionally orientated enterprises. The EBLOC analyses show that the national core had a strong New York element at its heart and that the majority of all the enterprises were connected into a single large component.

Further insight into this structure can be gained from analyses using the QCOMP algorithm. The standard analysis, using an absolute measure of intensity of connection, disclosed no small components in the network of controllers; all shareholding enterprises in the top 252 were formed into a single component through continuous chains of connection. Its core members were J.P. Morgan, Manufacturers Hanover, Citicorp, TIAA, and Bankers Trust, all except the mutually controlled TIAA having appeared in the EBLOC core, and the component rapidly grew to include eighty-three of the controlling enterprises. The more sensitive procedure using a measure of relative intensity showed that this component did possess some internal divisions and that these were more important structural features than their British counterparts. In addition to the 'peak' of the large component, a number of smaller peaks appeared at high levels of intensity. The first of these contained Loew's Corporation and Gulf & Western from New York, but the other two contained enterprises from various parts of the north-east. Lesser peaks which occurred within the large component were short-lived and, while they contained enterprises based outside New York, none were exclusively regional groups.[34]

The QCOMP analysis of the controlled enterprises was altogether more complex, with small components appearing in the standard analysis. The core of the large component consisted of the blue-chip investments, but four small components appeared at various levels of intensity:

1. Exxon, Mobil Oil, Standard Oil of Indiana
2. BankAmerica, Reynolds Industries
3. Northwestern Bancorp, First Bank System
4. Aetna Life, Wells Fargo

Particularly striking is the appearance of a Standard Oil component, as the three enterprises were shown earlier in this chapter to have share participations by the Rockefeller family. The family holdings, however, were not coded into the data set analysed, and the three enterprises appear as a component because they were common investment targets for a number of big New York banks. Northwestern Bancorp and First Bank System constitute a regional group and were particularly tightly linked, having appeared as a separate component in the network of controllers. Both enterprises were based in Minneapolis, there were strong cross-holdings, and each enterprise was its own largest shareholder. Common participants in their controlling constellations included National Detroit, First Chicago, and, outside the top 252, the Minnesota State Board of Investment. Clearly, the enterprises were well embedded in a nexus of connections to the north-central region.[35] The QCOMP analysis of relative intensity in the network of controlled enterprises disclosed a number of short-lived small components. The most striking feature, however, is that the small components and the core of the large component were dominated by enterprises based outside New York. The large component core comprised Seattle – First National Bank, National Detroit, Borden, First Pennsylvania, and IC Industries—of these, only Borden was based in New York. Northwest Bancorp and First Bank System appeared in a small component with General Mills, another Minneapolis enterprise in which the two banks were participants. The Minneapolis component became the core of a component which equalled the original large component in size, and the structure crystallised around these two nucleii. New York enterprises appeared mainly in small components which merged with one or other of the nucleii, and at lower levels of intensity the two components merged into a single large component.

The American intercorporate network, therefore, showed far more internal division than was the case in Britain, though these divisions did not take the form of tightly integrated interest groups. The big New York banks were the core of a hegemonic polyarchy of national investors whose activities generated some degree of regional differentiation amongst both controllers and controlled. No regional centre, however, appeared as a rival to the big New York banks. The prime contender for regional distinctiveness seemed to be the small Minneapolis group, these enterprises being forged into a group by their own investment activities and by the operations of the Chicago and Detroit banks. The north-central region did, indeed, seem the prime candidate for regional autonomy, but all analyses showed it to be well-integrated into the national network.

This discovery of regional differentiation, though not regional interest groups, within the American economy echoes the results from studies of interlocking directorships.[36] Such studies have shown that the structure of primary interlocks—interlocks created by executives—exhibits a decidedly regional character: enterprises are strongly linked to others in the same part of the country rather than to enterprises from other regions. At the same time, the regional groupings so formed are tied through the looser interlocks created by non-executive directors into an extensive national network centred on New York. The evidence from intercorporate shareholdings shows that the regional operations of banks and certain other financial intermediaries lead to a degree of regional differentiation in investment practices and that executive directors, especially those who sit on bank boards, reinforce and tighten this differentiation to form a number of bank-centred regional groupings. A recent investigation of interlocks among the top

252 enterprises analysed in this chapter documented the existence of New York, Boston, Pittsburgh, Chicago, Detroit, Minneapolis, and West Coast groups. In addition, the interlock network showed that the major banks of New York and Chicago were foci for the formation of wider, nationally orientated groups into which the regional groups were tied.[37] The network of interlocking directorships, therefore, articulated the incipient regional differentiation in shareholding so as to form a two-tier structure of regional and national groupings.

NOTES

1. The following discussion draws heavily on L. Loss, *Securities Regulation*, Little Brown, 1961.
2. It will be recalled the American law refers to 'corporations' rather than to 'companies'. The joint-stock corporation, therefore, is fundamentally different from the British 'public corporation'.
3. R.W. Goldsmith and R.C. Parmelee, *The Distribution of Ownership in the 200 Largest Non-Financial Corporations*, Monographs of the TNEC, no. 29, Washington, Government Printing Office, 1940; *Commercial Banks and their Trust Activities* (The Patman Report), Staff Report for the Subcommittee on Domestic Finance, Committee on Banking and Currency, House of Representatives, 90th Congress, 2nd Session, Washington, Government Printing Office, 1968.
4. *Banking and Finance*, CDE Stock Ownership Directory no. 3, New York, Corporate Data Exchange, 1980; *Fortune 500*, CDE Stock Ownership Directory no. 5, New York, Corporate Data Exchange, 1981. Though referred to as '1980' throughout this chapter, the data on banking and finance relate to 1979. Full details on methods of selection are contained in the directories.
5. In the CDE lists holdings were grouped by the researchers in a similar way to the grouping performed on the British data. The main exception was that they grouped with a parent company not only the holdings of its subsidiaries but also holdings by 40 per cent associates. Certain alterations were made to the CDE lists. Bank custodian holdings for corporate pension funds which were listed in the CDE directories were regarded as being under the voting control of the corporations themselves unless the directory indicated that the voting rights had been passed through to the bank concerned. Family holdings which were predominantly through minority-controlled corporations (insofar as

this was apparent from the entry in the directory or from other sources) were listed under the name of the corporation rather than the family, though holdings through majority-owned corporations were left in the name of the family. Thus some of the holdings which the CDE allocated to such families as the Du Ponts, the Kempers, and the Kirbys were treated here as corporate holdings of E.I. Du Pont de Nemours, Kemper Insurance, and Alleghany Corporation. Foundations, such as those of Ford and Rockefeller, were left as family holdings, though it is unclear whether, for example, it is realistic to treat Rockefeller University as part of the Rockefeller family interests. In the absence of alternative information the data were left as listed by the CDE.

6. These enterprises were those studied by Bearden and Mintz for the international research project of which the British study was a part, and their paper gives details on data selection. See J. Bearden and B. Mintz, 'Regionality and Integration in the United States Interlock Network', in F.N. Stokman, R. Ziegler, and J. Scott (eds.), *Networks of Corporate Power*, Cambridge, Polity Press, 1985. The list relates to 1976, though the CDE shareholding information relates to 1980.

7. E.S. Herman, *Corporate Control, Corporate Power*, Cambridge University Press, 1981; M. Moskowitz, M. Katz, and R. Levering, *Everybody's Business*, San Francisco, Harper & Row, 1980.

8. Morgan accepts trust business only on condition that it is granted full voting rights on all shares held in trust.

9. E.S. Herman, 'Commercial Bank Trust Departments', in M.J. Rossant (ed.), *Abuse On Wall Street*, Conn., Quorum Books, 1980; Herman, *Corporate Control*, pp. 137–8.

10. Mellon National Bank.

11. Republic of Texas Corporation.

12. Whether this indicates management control or control through a constellation of interests will be discussed shortly. Among the enterprises for which no adequate information was available were a number, such as AT & T, Pan Am, and TWA, which were suspected of having no dominant interest, but for which the overall distribution of shareholdings was unknown. If these had been classified they would undoubtedly have been unlikely to boost the levels of majority and minority control to any considerable extent; *see* the similar results in Herman, pp. 56–61. Herman *Corporate Control*, reports that one of the enterprises for which no information was available, Marcor had been taken over by Mobil in 1974–75. As a wholly owned subsidiary of a top 252 enterprise Marcor would not have qualified for inclusion in the top 252 of 1980.

13. The three enterprises classified in Table 6.1 as subject to limited minority control were Archer-Danials-Midland, Dow Chemical, and Weyerhauser, all being family controlled. Four enterprises could not be unambiguously reclassified in Table 6.2 because of inadequate information.

14. Herman, *Corporate Control, Corporate Power*.

15. *See* note 3 above. The focus on registered shareholdings and the fact that

only limited grouping of holdings was carried out means that the TNEC research understates the degree of concentration.

16. The Rockefellers controlled Standard Oil of New Jersey (Exxon), Standard Oil of Indiana, and SOCONY Vacuum Oil (Mobil). The other family-controlled enterprises were American Cyanamid (Bell family), Colegate–Palmolive (Colgate family), International Paper & Power (Phipps family), Reynolds Tobacco (Reynolds family) and Singer (Clark family).

17. No relation to the Ford family of Ford Motor.

18. These 'stages' are not to be seen as steps in some inexorable evolutionary unfolding. They are analytical categories which grasp some of the key features of corporate development.

19. The four were Standard Oil of New Jersey (Exxon), American Brands. America Can, and IBM.

20. Getty Oil, controlled by the Getty family, and Campbell Soup, controlled by the Dorrance family.

21. United Brands, where the directors shared control with American Finance Corporation; General Tire & Rubber, where the O'Neil family shared control with Gulf and Western and the controlling alliance was supported by an internal pension fund holding; and McDonnell Douglas (see text).

22. The three enterprises which were not allocated because of incomplete information were: Coastal States Gas, where the chief executive held 10.5 per cent; Lykes, where the family held 12.3 per cent; and Rapid American, where the Rickless family held 14.5 per cent. It is probable that all these enterprises were cases of limited minority control.

23. J. Scott, *Corporations, Classes and Capitalism*, rev. edn, London, Hutchinson, 1985, pp. 68, 78. It should be noted that family influence also existed through the numerous small family-controlled investment companies which participated in the controlling constellations.

24. The three oil producers were Exxon, Mobil, and Standard Oil of Indiana (see n. 16, above). The Rockefeller holdings are discussed in J.C. Knowles, *The Rockefeller Financial Group*, MSS Modular Publications, Module 343, 1973.

25. The Kirby family used Allegheny Corporation in the same way, but Allegheny was not itself a member of the top 252. Indirect family participation happened on a lesser scale with other enterprises, especially financials, which were family controlled: the Harris family Harris Bancorp participated in eighteen enterprises and the Tisch family Loew's Corporation participated in four.

26. It should be emphasised that Prudential Insurance of America has no board or ownership links with Prudential Assurance of Britain. The American corporation was named after the successful British company, but both have always been distinct businesses.

27. Two from Pittsburgh, one from Boston, one from New Jersey, and one from Wilmington.

28. *See* the reference cited in note 36, below.

29. Owing to the absence of full information on all controlling constella-

* tions, the total of 151 is an underestimate of the actual size of the combined network.
30. This group comprised Republic of Texas Corporation and Texas Instruments. The other small component included Metropolitan Life Insurance and Nabisco.
31. BankAmerica and Western Bancorp. The other small component comprised Chase Manhatten Bank and General Electric.
32. Unlike the British case, the blocking of the American network did not produce a first step differentiation of these two sets. The rearranged matrix had a somewhat 'stripey' appearance and a number of partitionings were required to produce dense blocks. The matrix was manually rearranged to bring these 'stripes' together to clarify the overall structure. A similar procedure was followed in the even-more-stripey Japanese case, and the procedure is more fully discussed in the following chapter.
33. Continental Illinois and First Chicago.
34. One component contained National Detroit and Mellon National, one contained BankAmerica, Bank of New York, Equitable Life, and Continental Corporation, and one contained Crocker National, Bethlehem Steel, First Bank System, and Northwestern Bancorp.
35. The two enterprises and the three other north-central shareholders mentioned in the text jointly held 21.15 per cent of First Bank System and 17.26 per cent of Northwestern Bancorp.
36. *See*: J. Bearden, W. Atwood, P. Freitag, C. Hendricks, B. Mintz, and M. Schwartz, 'The Nature and Extent of Bank Centrality in Corporate Networks', Paper to the American Sociological Association, 1975; Bearden and Mintz *op. cit.*; B. Mintz and M. Schwartz, *The Power Structure of American Business*, University of Chicago Press, 1985; J. Levine, *Levine's Atlas of Corporate Interlocks*, Hanover, New Hampshire, Worldnet, 1985.
37. J. Bearden and B. Mintz, 'The Structure of Class Cohesion: The Corporate Network and Its Dual', in M. Mizruchi and M. Schwartz, (eds.), *The Structural Analysis of Business*, New York, Cambridge University Press, 1986.

7 Combines and Aligned Participations in Japan

The Japanese 'economic miracle' of the post-war years has been the outcome of a systematic reconstruction of the economy, a reconstruction necessitated by the massive damage incurred during the war and the immediate post-war policies of the American Occupation authorities. This reconstruction, however, involved the conscious and deliberate adaptation of practices and forms of organisation which had evolved during the fifty years prior to the war. These structures and practices had themselves resulted from an attempt to adapt traditional Japanese ideas to the requirements of rapid industrialisation and, as a result, the Japanese economy appears to show a remarkable continuity in many of its key features. In particular, the industrial 'groups' which are such an obvious feature of the post-war economy have their roots in the pre-war financial empires and the pre-industrial merchant houses. For this reason it is even more than normally the case that an understanding of the modern economy depends upon an understanding of its historical origins. The features of the Japanese economy which have generated the post-war 'miracle' must be understood as consequences of Japan's unique historical experience.

ENTERPRISE GROUPINGS IN JAPAN

Until the middle of the nineteenth century Japanese feudal society remained isolated from all contact with the West, and all commercial and financial activities were under the control of dynastic merchant families.[1] The 'restoration' of power to the Emperor Meiji in 1868 led, in fact, to the dominance of a political oligarchy which sponsored economic development under the control of the old merchant houses and of new entrepreneurs drawn from the samurai. In a desire to bring about rapid industrialisation, the state took an active role in the economy, setting up not only the post, telegraphs, and railways, but also a shipping line and manufacturing enterprises involved in armaments, brewing, cement, cotton, iron and steel, and shipbuilding. From 1880, however, the role of sponsor to private enterprise predominated, and most of the state enterprises were sold to the capitalist interests which supported the state policy of industrialisation. This policy of privatisation enabled these interests to build large financial and industrial groups. These groups—the so-called *zaibatsu*—operated in a variety of industries, and were organised hierarchically through a central holding company, which undertook marketing for the group enterprises, and a bank, which provided financial support.

The largest and most powerful of the *zaibatsu* was Mitsui, which was based around an old trading house and was run on a day-to-day basis by managers under the supervision of a family council recruited from the extensive Mitsui kin.[2] The holding company, Mitsui Bussan, owned or controlled enterprises in mining, steel, and other sectors of heavy industry, its associated enterprises including Toshiba and, in conjunction with the British firm of Vickers, Nippon Steel. In the period up to the 1930s the Mitsui *zaibatsu* was the major force behind the Seiyukai Party,[3] its representatives including Marquis Inoue and Prime Minister Ito, and the policy of the Party involved support for government subsidies and state expenditure as mechanism for developing domestic industry. The other main political party, Kenseikai (later Minseito), supported the expansion of foreign trade and the maintenance of solid government finance, and this party received the support of the rival Mitsubishi *zaibatsu*.[4] Mitsubishi was formed by Iwasaki, a samurai, in 1870, and continued to be run by the Iwasaki family. Its major political representatives included Prime Minister Kato and Baron Shidehara, both of whom were related to the Iwasaki family. The industrial undertakings of the group were especially important in engineering and

shipbuilding, though, like Mitsui, it was represented throughout the economy. Alongside Mitsui and Mitsubishi were two
other *zaibatsu*, making the 'big four' groups of the Japanese
economy of the 1920s. The Sumitomo *zaibatsu* was based
around an old family merchant house, the family being related
to Prince Saionji, one of Japan's elder statesmen, while the
Yasuda *zaibatsu* was a post-restoration family group with its
main strength in banking, shipping, and colonial trade. The big
zaibatsu grew considerably during the first two decades of the
twentieth century, and each of the big four had its own
banking, insurance, and trading enterprises as well as its heavy
industrials by the 1920s. The absence of an effective stock
market meant that businesses seeking capital for expansion
had either to enter into association with the *zaibatsu* or to join
with similarly placed enterprises to form smaller *zaibatsu* of
their own. Thus the big four co-existed with a number of other
zaibatsu, each having a bias towards particular industrial
sectors. Asano was important in cement and steel, Kuhara and
Okura were strong in mining and engineering, Furukawa
played a key role in copper and electric power, and Kawasaki
had its base in heavy industry. Another of the smaller *zaibatsu*,
Shibusawa, joined with Furukawa and Kawasaki in the control
of the Dai-Ichi Bank, making it the only group outside the big
four to have its own bank.

Though competing in many industries, the *zaibatsu*
cooperated wherever this was in their interest, and such
cooperative ventures often had the support of the state. In 1900
the government and the *zaibatsu* formed the Nippon Kogyo
Ginko (Industrial Bank of Japan, or IBJ) as a mobilier
investment bank, and subsequently the *zaibatsu* cooperated in
the formation of large electricity supply companies in all the
major urban areas. The Imperial family itself participated in
many such ventures, the emperor owning almost a half of the
shares of the Bank of Japan and sharing control of the shipping
company Nippon Yusen with the Mitsubishi group. Thus the
big *zaibatsu* were allied through personal and business links
with the leading statesmen and politicians, and the major
parties were closely tied to the two biggest groups. The *zaibatsu*
and their political parties, in turn, vied with the military
leadership, the big landowners, and state officials for

dominance within the political oligarchy whose symbolic focus was the emperor.[5]

Until the 1920s this structure of economic and political power had been held together by the dominant role played by the Genro, an informal council of imperial advisers recruited as 'elder statesmen' from the retired leadership of the main political factions. The Genro, however, had become less influential as the conflicting factional interests became stronger. Popular opposition to 'big business' and distrust of parliamentary politics created a fertile soil for fascist ideas, and the increasing strength of the military led to a weakening of the political power of the *zaibatsu* in the early 1930s. The military leadership used their dominant position within the state to encourage new business groups (the so-called *shinko zaibatsu*) which they hoped would support their policy of a strong state-controlled economy. Prominent among these new groups was Nippon Sangyo Kaisha (Nissan), controlled by the Aikawa family, which became a major military contractor. Nevertheless, the *zaibatsu* remained closely allied with the state, as it was only through them that Japan's massive military requirements could be met. Despite the liquidation of political parties in 1940, the *zaibatsu* and their political representatives remained an important element in the state, and government policy itself sponsored further monopolisation. This was particularly marked in banking, where the Yasuda Bank acquired the Showa and other banks, and the Mitsui and Dai-Ichi Banks merged to form the Teikoku Bank in 1944. At the height of the war Japanese banking was dominated by seven banks: Teikoku, Mitsubishi, Sumitomo, Yasuda, Nomura, Sanwa (a merger of three banks in 1933 and controlled by the Yamaguchi and Konoike families), and Tokai.

The military defeat of Japan was followed by its occupation by American civil and military forces. A central plank of American policy was the break-up of the *zaibutsu*, which had supported the Japanese war effort, and proposals for *zaibatsu* 'dissolution' were announced and, in part, implemented. Members of the leading capitalist families, fifty-six 'designated persons' in all, were required to sell their shareholdings in *zaibatsu* holding companies, receiving non-negotiable government bonds in compensation. The holding companies

162   *Capitalist Property and Financial Power*

themselves were declared illegal and their shareholdings were sold. At the same time, many of the largest operating subsidiaries were broken-up into smaller units: Mitsubishi Chemical was split into Mitsubishi Rayon, Asahi Glass, and a new Mitsubishi Chemical; Daiken Industries was split into C. Itoh, Marubeni Corporation, and two smaller traders; Mitsui Bussan had part of its assets formed into Toshoku, and the remainder of the enterprise was dissolved; and this pattern of splitting and dissolution was repeated in many sectors. The occupation authorities directed their attack primarily at the ten family-controlled groups which they believed to have been the largest pre-war *zaibatsu*: the big four together with Asano, Fuji Industries, Furukawa, Nissan, Nomura, and Okura.[6]

Although the big trading companies of the Mitsui and Mitsubishi *zaibatsu* were broken up, Japan's largest financials remained intact and were allowed to retain many of their industrial participations.[7] This proved to be of central importance to Japanese recovery after the Occupation came to an official end in 1952. The banks became foci for the re-establishment of many of the pre-war group affiliations during the 1950s, and the former Mitsui trading interests were reconstituted as Mitsui and Co. in 1959. Japanese business commentators were once again writing about the Mitsubishi, Mitsui, and Sumitomo groups, though the absence of the controlling families meant that they were no longer described as *zaibatsu*. Instead, the term *kigyoshudan*[8] came to be applied to the groups of enterprises which were linked through reciprocal shareholdings, trading links, and orientation to the same bank. Where the pre-war *zaibatsu* were structured vertically as pyramids through the family-controlled holding companies, the post-war *kigyoshudan* had a flatter, horizontal structure. Ownership and banking ties in the three biggest groups were weaker than before, the groups being less cohesive and occupying a less prominent position in the economy. The Yasuda group was not reconstructed, though the Fuji Bank, successor to the Yasuda Bank, did bring together some of the group enterprises and some from the Asano and Okura groups into a loose alliance.[9] The Dai-Ichi Bank, now separated from Mitsui, retained links with the surviving Furukawa and Kawasaki enterprises and in 1971 merged with another bank to become the Dai-Ichi Kangyo Bank (DKB). The Sanwa Bank, not tied to any of the pre-war groups, built up a set of industrial clients and affiliates during the 1960s. The IBJ had been reconstructed after the war and established links with a number of dependent clients, but its role as a specialist in rescue operations meant that it did not establish a true *kigyoshudan*. By the middle of the 1960s, therefore, six large *kigyoshudan* with varying levels and forms of integration were normally identified: Mitsubishi, Mitsui, Sumitomo, Fuyo (Fuji Bank), DKB, and Sanwa. In addition to the big bank-centred enterprise groups, other enterprises forged groups of subsidiaries and affiliates together. In some cases this involved smaller bank-centred groups, such a Tokai, but in others the structure came to approximate to that of the Anglo-American parent/ subsidiary form of enterprise. The latter was true of Matsushita, fully independent of Sumitomo since 1960, and Hitachi (formerly part of the Nissan group). Yet other enterprises formed hybrid groups between these two forms: in both Nissan and Toyota (the latter separated from Mitsui at the dissolution) a horizontal structure of affiliates was combined with the vertical parent/subsidiary structure.

Varying interpretations have been given to the predominance of enterprise groupings in the Japanese economy. Nishiyana has advanced the claim that enterprise grouping reflects an attempt to counter the uncertainty of a rapidly changing environment by maximising the flow of information between associated enterprises.[10] They are an alternative to the extensive interlocking directorships found in the United States. Pointing to the fact that mutual insurance companies are important shareholders in each of the groups, Nishiyana argues that 'Capitalism in Japan ended when the life insurance companies advanced to become the leading stockholders of the banks and large firms and came to monopolise their stocks.'[11] An alternative to this managerialist view has been proposed by Okumura, who describes Japan as 'corporate capitalism'. Enterprise groupings are not the result of managerial calculation but are the adaptation of older forms of business organisation to post-war conditions. They represent an attempt to counter excessive competition by building cooperation within groups and alliances with independent enterprises.[12] What-

ever the causes may be, it is clear that enterprise groupings
in the modern Japanese economy are a deliberate adaptation
of pre-war patterns, conscious creations of the leaders of
Japanese business in the two decades following the war. It is
for this reason that any study of ownership and control in
Japan must take account of the historical heritage and concern
itself with the implications of group formation for the overall
structure of intercorporate relations.

PATTERNS OF CORPORATE CONTROL

The legal framework regulating business activity in Japan was
explicitly constructed along European lines, though the post-
war occupation introduced a number of American features.[13]
The original Meiji commercial code on joint-stock companies
(*kabushiki kaisha*) dates from 1899 and established corporate
forms similar to those found in Britain and the United States. It
was this framework which permitted the *zaibatsu* to build large
groups of intersecting companies. The 'dissolution' and antitrust measures of the American occupying powers were aimed
at the break-up of the *zaibatsu* and, not surprisingly, new
corporation laws were introduced. In 1948 a Securities and
Exchange Law was introduced which followed closely the
American legislation of the 1930s. The Ministry of Finance was
required to set up a Bureau of Securities (the *Shokenkyroku*)
which was to supervise company registration and public
disclosure. Registration documents are predominantly financial and there is no requirement to file a share register or to
include shareholding details in the annual return. The
unimportance of the stock exchange in company finance
means that preference and deferred shares are rare, and the fact
that a very small group of investors is involved in shareholding
means that bearer shares are almost unknown. Despite this
simple structure of shareownership—exclusively registered
ordinary shares—there is no requirement for public disclosure.
Fortunately for the researcher, a private directory has for long
been published which gives information, obtained directly
from the companies, on shareownership. *Kigyo Keiretsu Soran*,
published by the Oriental Economist, contains a classified list
of quoted companies showing, for each company, the amount

of credit received from each bank, the names of directors and executives, and its twenty largest shareholders. For each of these shareholders is given the name, the number of shares held, and the proportion of the ordinary capital which this represents. This unique source, however, is published only in Japanese and is extremely difficult to obtain outside Japan. The English-speaking researcher, therefore, must rely on a recently published English-language version of this directory. The *Japan Company Handbook*[14] is published half yearly and gives an abstract of operating statistics for each quoted company together with the five to ten largest shareholders.

The research reported in this chapter relates to the 200 largest non-financial enterprises, ranked by turnover, and 50 large financials of 1980, selected from the list published in *Industrial Groupings in Japan*.[15] This irregular source also gives information on the bankers and ten largest shareholders for constituent enterprises of the major *kigyoshudan* and certain other groups, its information seeming to be obtained directly from *Kigyo Keiretsu Soran*. For those enterprises whose shareholders were not listed in this source, the shorter lists in the *Japan Company Handbook* were used. In this way, it was possible to obtain shareholding information comparable to that in the British and American data sets. Shareholders were grouped on the same basis as in previous chapters—individuals were grouped if they had the same family name, and subsidiary companies were grouped with their parents. No attempt was made, however, to group holdings by *kigyoshudan* members. Thus all holdings by Mitsubishi-affiliated enterprises[16] in Mitsubishi Bank, for example, were treated as separate holdings for the purpose of determining its mode of control under the conventional criteria. This decision maximised comparability with the British and American research and enabled the degree of influence exercised by *kigyoshudan* members to be treated as an empirical question. Because of the high level of intercorporate shareholding in Japan, documented below, the network analyses were based upon the full lists of the ten largest shareholders, even where enterprises were majority- or minority-controlled by their largest shareholder. Even a cursory glance at lists of shareholders in Japan highlights some important features of shareholding which must be discussed before examining the results of the research.

It is necessary to look at the types of shareholder and the forms of shareholding.

Banks are major owners of company shares, and there are four main types of bank in Japan.[17] City banks are analogous to clearing and commercial banks and operate branch banking for personal and industrial clients on a national scale. The city banks of each of the six largest *kigyoshudan* were based in Tokyo, as were the Tokai, Kyowa, and Bank of Tokyo, but the data set also included city banks from Osaka and Kobe. Local banks operated only in specific regions and only the Saitama Bank, based in Tokyo, was large enough to appear in the data set. In 1977 there were thirteen city banks and sixty-three local banks operating in Japan.[18] Very few of these banks engage in trustee business, and there are a small number of separate trust banks. Of the big six *kigyoshudan*, only DKB had not formed a trust bank as it was the only city bank to have an internal trust department. The trust banks run investment companies and manage funds on behalf of clients, though, unlike the British and American fund managers, they did not manage corporate pension funds. Pensions in Japan are arranged by individuals rather than through group schemes. The largest of the trust banks—Mitsubishi, Mitsui, Sumitomo, and Yasuda—were formed in the 1920s, but their role increased markedly in the wake of the *zaibatsu* dissolution as they acquired many of the shares formerly owned by holding companies. The final type of bank is the long-term industrial finance bank, the IBJ being the forerunner of enterprises such as the Long Term Credit Bank and Nippon Credit which were formed following permissive legislation in 1952.

A type of shareholder unique to Japan is the general trading company (*sogo shosha*), engaged in buying and selling in much the same way as the forerunners of the British merchant banks. The trading companies, however, operate on a much larger scale and were the lynchpins of the old *zaibatsu*. In modern Japan the trading companies are large shareholders which use their shareholdings in order to expand their trading activities.[19] Also specific to Japan are the securities companies which engage in security dealing and underwriting as well as fund management. They thus combine some of the features of both a stockbroker and an investment banker—with the important proviso that investment banking is of far less significance in Japan than it is in the United States. Banks are not legally permitted to engage in security dealing and so the large banks have all established relations with securities companies. This cooperation reaches into the area of fund management as unit trusts—the only form of investment company found in Japan—are often jointly run by trust banks and securities companies, the former acting as custodian and administrator and the latter acting as managing trustee. Almost a half of all security business is handled by four large companies: Nikko, Nomura, Yamaiichi, and Daiwa.

Other categories of investor are similar to those found in Britain and the United States, though their role and significance differ. Mutual life insurers and proprietary fire and marine insurers are major holders of company shares, with many of the largest companies being affiliated to *kigyoshudan*. Industrial and other non-financial enterprises hold a much higher proportion of company shares in Japan, and they participate through trade investments and controlling holdings rather than through pension funds. The level of personal shareholding is very low, though some of the trust bank holdings will have been managed on behalf of individuals and families. The *zaibatsu* dissolution had little effect on the level of personal shareholdings, as the reliance of enterprises on bank loans and group support has meant that popular stock-exchange investment has never been necessary for *kigyoshudan* members.

This brief review of the chief features of investment in Japan has continually referred to the involvement of the various types of investor in the *kigyoshudan*. As this form of organisation will figure prominently in this chapter it is important to clarify some of its main characteristics. A *kigyoshudan* is a combine, a group of enterprises tied together through reciprocal share-holdings, credit relations, trading relations, and interlocking directorships. The members of such a combine will not necessarily be subsidiaries or minority-controlled associates of particular parents. Many are enterprises with no single, dominant shareholding interest. But in these enterprises other members of the *kigyoshudan* will be amongst their largest shareholders and will collectively hold substantial blocks of shares. This distinguishes such enterprises sharply from those which have been described as controlled through constellations of interests. In a controlling constellation the participants comprise a diverse collection of interests among which any coalitions are unstable and short-lived. By contrast, the controlling participants in many *kigyoshudan* members form a stable and durable coalition of other *kigyoshudan* members. Such enterprises can be described as controlled through coalitions of aligned participations which are dominant within their twenty largest shareholders. The system of aligned participations which runs through the core of the *kigyoshudan* is reinforced by the provision of loan capital by the group bank and the handling of sales by group trading companies, and this allows mutual insurance companies and enterprises controlled by families and other corporate interests to become affiliated to the *kigyoshudan*. All members of the combine are united through these economic bonds and by their common orientation to the idea of the group. This group orientation is expressed in the power accorded to the presidents' club (*shacho kai*) of the combine. This 'club' is, in fact, a committee, made up of the presidents of the major member enterprises, which meets regularly, generally monthly, to evolve a group policy. Each president has the power to exercise the voting rights of the shares owned by this [20] enterprise, and so the club has effective voting control over all shares held by group enterprises. Okumura has argued that this structure impels executives to become dependent upon one another: where A can influence B and B can influence A through shareholdings, the directors and executives of both A and B have an interest in cooperation rather than conflict and competition. This leads to strong bonds of trust and confidence and, in consequence, a reluctance to allow directors to retire. Colleagues prefer to continue working with those with whom they have built a trust relationship and so the retiring age is continually extended, with many senior directors being in their eighties.[21]

Kigyoshudan organisation can best be illustrated through a particular case, that of Mitsubishi.[22] The core members of this group are Mitsubishi Bank, Mitsubishi Trust and Banking, Mitsubishi Corporation, Tokio Marine and Fire Insurance, and Meiji Mutual Life Insurance. In each of the four joint-stock companies the Mitsubishi group held 18 per cent or more of the shares.[23] The group controlled Nikko Securities and six non-financial enterprises from the top 250 which bear the group name: chemical, oil, petrochemical, mining, electric, and heavy industries. Sales for these enterprises were handled by Mitsubishi Corporation and two other group trading companies, and the group's interests extended to enterprises without the Mitsubishi name in chemical engineering, vehicles, construction, food and drink, retail distribution, and shipping. In total, 24 of the top 250 enterprises regarded themselves as members of the Mitsubishi *kigyoshudan*; and these enterprises provided the bulk of the membership of the 'Friday Club', the Mitsubishi presidents' club. Increasingly, combine presidents' clubs have co-opted the chief executives of large independent enterprises from outside the group, a relationship which expands group influence and gives the independent enterprises access to the capital and intelligence embodied in the combine.[24] The Tokyu retailing and construction enterprises, for example, had membership of the Friday Club without being members of the Mitsubishi combine, and the group had close links with Nippon Steel and three of the big electricity supply companies. This form of organisation was found also in Mitsui and Sumitomo and, to only a slightly less developed extent, in the DKB, Sanwa, and Fuyo combines. Each had its coordinating presidents' club, and some of the larger independent enterprises were members of two or more such clubs; Toshiba, for example, was a member of the Mitsui and DKB clubs, while Hitachi was a member of the DKB, Sanwa, and Fuyo clubs. Thus the internally integrated *kigyoshudan* had varying levels and forms of connection with one another and with independent enterprises, creating an extensive web of group affiliations which stretched throughout the Japanese economy.

This feature of Japanese business leads to many difficulties in applying the usual categories for modes of control to Japan's largest enterprises. Any classification which fails to explore the implications of group organisation can only give a partial picture of corporate control in Japan. In Chapters 4 and 6 the British and American enterprises were provisionally analysed into modes of control using the conventional 10 per cent cut-off threshold for minority control, and for purposes of comparison a similar procedure will be used for Japan. This should not, however, be seen as a 'provisional' classification from which a refined 'final' classification is to be derived. Although a second classification based on voting dynamics and group structure will indeed be presented, this is constructed on a radically different basis from that used in earlier chapters. The two classifications are alternative ways of grasping the complexities of Japanese corporate structure and so are designated as 'Method A' and 'Method B'. In Method A the conventional categories will be applied in the same way as in Tables 4.1 and 6.1; but in Method B an attempt is made to estimate the number of enterprises which are controlled through aligned participations, and Method B is supplemented by other tabulations of the voting structure of these coalitions.

Table 7.1 shows the classification using Method A, and it is clear that there is a great similarity between the results for Japan and those given for the United States in Table 6.1. In both countries the number of majority-controlled enterprises was extremely low, and the number with no dominant interest was correspondingly high. Japan had rather fewer family-controlled enterprises than the United States, and all such enterprises were minority controlled. Table 7.1 shows that thirteen enterprises were subject to some form of shared control, of which five involved some degree of foreign control. Foreign control, therefore, was present as an important factor in 10 of the 250 largest Japanese enterprises, with this foreign ownership being concentrated in the oil industry. The American enterprises Getty Oil, Caltex, and Exxon each had a Japanese subsidiary or associate, and Exxon and Mobil shared control of another.[25] The Saudi Arabian and Kuwait governments shared control of Arabian Oil, and the Royal Dutch-Shell group controlled two enterprises.[26] It is particularly significant that most of the foreign-controlled oil companies were formed in association with the big *kigyoshudan,* four of the enterprises being affiliated to one or other of these groups. This was also true of Fuji Electric, where Siemens shared control with a member of the DKB group. The remaining cases of foreign control—both being minority controlled—were straightforward cases of American

Table 7.1: *Corporate control in Japan: Method A (1980)*

Mode of Control		Type of controller						
	Personal	Corporate					Other	Totals
		Japanese	Foreign	Mixed	State	Mixed		
Exclusive majority	0	0	2	0	0	0	0	2
Shared majority	0	1	2	0	0	0	0	3
Exclusive minority	11	44	3	0	1	0	0	59
Shared minority	0	6	1	2	0	1	0	10
Mutual	–	–	–	–	–	–	10	10
No dominant interest	–	–	–	–	–	159	–	159
Not known	–	–	–	–	–	–	7	7
Totals	11	51	8	2	1	160	17	250

Note: No attempt was made to use the category of limited minority control.

enterprises with foreign associates: General Electric controlled Toshiba-IHI and General Motors controlled Isuzu Motors. It can be concluded that foreign control was rare in Japan, was limited to certain industrial sectors (oil, electronics, and vehicles), involved only the very largest American enterprises, and generally involved some kind of tie-up with Japanese interests.

The role of the state in corporate control was extremely limited. Despite actively promoting Japanese interests through MITI (Ministry of International Trade and Industry) and other organisations such as the Zaikai, the state seeks only to facilitate private enterprise. The sole case of state control in the top 250 enterprises was Japan Air Lines, where the government owned 37.7 per cent of the shares. This low level of state enterprise sharply distinguished Japan and the United States from Britain.

Evidence on family control and influence is shown in Table 7.2, together with summary figures for Britain and the United States. Figures for family control and for family participation in enterprises with no dominant interest were about a third of the levels recorded in the United States, though in both economies family ownership more often took the form of participation rather than outright control. Families in Japan held exclusive minority control in eleven enterprises and

Table 7.2: *Family control and influence: Britain, United States, and Japan (1976–1980)*

| | Number of enterprises | | | |
| | Britain (1976) | USA (1980) | Japan (1980) | | |
			Big 6	Others	Total
Family control	49	35	3	9	12
Family participation	36	79	10	16	26
Totals	85	114	13	25	38

shared control with a *kigyoshudan* member in one more.[27]
Three of the wholly family-controlled enterprises were
affiliated to the big six groups, as were ten enterprises with no
dominant interest which had substantial family participants.
Family control, like foreign control, often seemed to involve a

Table 7.3: *The largest family shareholdings: Japan (1980)*

	Family	Enterprise	Industry
Minority controllers	Hattori	K. Hattori	Trading in clocks and watches
	Ishibashi	Bridgestone Tire	Tyre manufacture
	Ito	Ito Ham	Meat processing
	Ito	Ito-Yokado	Retail distribution
	Iwatani	Iwatani (Sa)	Trading in gases
	Nakauchi	Daiei	Retail distribution
	Nagase	Nagase	Trading in chemicals
	Ohbayashi	Ohbayashi-Gumi (Sa)	Construction and contractors
	Okada	Jusco	Retail distribution
	Toda	Toda Construction (M)	Construction
	Tsusho	Taiyo Fishery	Fish and food processing
	Yamagata	Koa Fire & Marine	Insurance
Large participants:	Fujita	Fujita	Construction and contractors
	Kajima	Kajima (Su)	Construction and contractors
	Morita	Sony	Electronics
	Saneyoshi	JGC	Engineering
	Sato	Sato Kogyo (D)	Construction and contractors
	Takeda	Takeda Chemical (Su)	Pharmaceutical manufacture

Note: (M)=Mitsubish, (Sa)=Sanwa, (Su)=Sumitomo, (D)=DKB.

Table 7.4: *Size of family participations: Japan (1980)*

	Size of family shareholding block (%)							
	<1	1.0–1.9	2.0–2.9	3.0–3.9	4.0–4.9	5.0–5.9	6.0–6.9	>7	Totals
Big six	1	0	3	2	0	1	1	3	11
Others	0	2	6	4	1	2	0	3	18
Totals	1	2	9	6	1	3	1	6	29

partnership with the big enterprise groups: only Mitsui had no such links with family-influenced enterprises in the top 250. Table 7.3 shows the minority controllers and those families which held 7 per cent or more of the shares in enterprises with no dominant interest,[28] and the predominance of construction, trading, and food is obvious. Among all thirty-eight enterprises with some degree of family influence there were thirteen involved in wholesale and retail distribution, nine in construction, and five in food processing, and there was a slight tendency for construction enterprises to be more heavily concentrated in the big combines and for food producers to be independent of the groups. Although none of the independent construction firms were family-controlled, all three showed very large family participations (see Table 7.3). Three of the enterprises with no dominant interest had more than one family among their ten largest shareholders, and two family names, Ito and Ishibashi, appeared in more than one enterprise.[29] Neither of the latter, however, comprised kinship groups and it can be concluded that there were 40 families involved in controlling the top 250 Japanese enterprises. Table 7.4 shows that there were 29 family shareholdings in the 26 enterprises with family participants,[30] the average size of the family blocks being greater than in Britain (see Table 4.6). *Kigyoshudan* members and independent enterprises showed a similar pattern of distribution in family participations, though the three largest family holdings in the independent enterprises were all above 9 per cent.

In view of the importance of the *kigyoshudan* in Japan,

Table 7.5: *Control within the big combines in Japan: Method A (1980)*

Mode of Control	Numbers of enterprises						
	Mitsubishi	Mitsui	Sumitomo	Sanwa	DKB	Fuyo	Totals
Exclusive majority	1	0	0	0	0	0	1
Shared majority	0	0	0	0	0	1	1
Exclusive minority	4	3	4	7	1	0	19
Shared minority	2	1	0	0	3	1	7
Mutual	1	1	1	2	1	1	7
No dominant interest	16	15	13	11	13	15	83
Totals	24	20	18	20	18	18	118

Note: This is a subject of the data contained in Table 7.1.

Table 7.6: *Share concentration in large enterprises: Japan (1980)*

% held by top 10	Mitsubishi	Mitsui	Sumitomo	Sanwa	DKB	Fuyo	Independents	Totals
More than 50	0	0	0	0	0	1	0	1
40–9	6	1	2	3	2	4	7	25
30–9	5	9	7	6	8	2	31	68
20–9	5	5	4	2	3	8	32	59
10–9	0	0	0	0	0	0	6	6
Less than 10	0	0	0	0	0	0	0	0
Totals	16	15	13	11	13	15	76	159

Note: Figures relate to the 159 enterprises with no dominant interest in Table 7.1. In some cases fewer than ten shareholders were given in the source listings.

evident from the data already presented, it is important to look more closely at the control patterns of *kigyoshudan* members. According to *Industrial Groupings in Japan*,[31] 118 of the top 250 enterprises were affiliated to the big 6 combines, and their distribution across the modes of control is shown in Table 7.5. The typical *kigyoshudan* member had no dominant shareholding interest, though a not insignificant number were subject to forms of minority control. Some of the latter were

Table 7.7: *Top shareholders of Toyota Motor (1982)*

Rank	Shareholder	% of shares
1.	Sanwa Bank	5.00
2.	Mitsui Bank	5.00
3.	Tokai Bank	4.79
4.	Toyoda Automatic Loom	4.48
5.	Nippon Life Ins.	3.86
6.	Long Term Credit Bank	3.50
7.	Taisho Marine & Fire Ins.	2.60
8.	Daiwa Bank	2.59
9.	Dai-Ichi Mutual Life Ins.	2.41
10.	Mitsui Mutual Life Ins.	2.21
	Top 10	36.44
11.	Kyowa Bank	2.04
12.	Mitsui Trust & Bank	2.03
13.	Fuji Bank	2.03
14.	Mitsubishi Bank	1.96
15.	Tokio Marine and Fire	1.78
16.	Dai-Ichi Kangyo Bank	1.61
17.	Sumitomo Bank	1.53
18.	Asahi Mutual Life Ins.	1.51
19.	Meiji Mutual Life Ins.	1.49
20.	Toyo Trust and Bank	1.13
	Top 20	53.36

Source: Data supplied by Y. Ueda from *Kigyo Keiretsu Soran* (Tokyo Keizai Shinposha, 1982).

the family- and foreign-controlled enterprises which have already been discussed, but the bulk of them—twenty of the twenty-six minority-controlled enterprises—were controlled by Japanese corporate interests. In most cases this involved the exclusive or shared control of a group enterprise by other members of its combine, though some involved control by 'independent' enterprises.[32] The proportion of minority-controlled enterprises was rather higher in the Sanwa group than in any other. These were also rather more likely to be exclusively controlled, and four of the five corporate controllers were group members.[33] Differences in the level of minority control between groups should not, however, be seen as indicating higher or lower levels of integration within the group, as this is more directly reflected in the level of cross-holdings within the group. This will be more fully discussed in the following section, but a provisional picture of the level of share concentration is given in Table 7.6.

Looking only at enterprises with no dominant interest, the highest level of share concentration was found in the Mitsubishi group, and the most polarised distribution was in the Fuyo group. The level of concentration was generally higher among the big six than among the independents. The overall distribution shown in Table 7.6 demonstrates that the largest shareholders in Japanese companies held a much larger percentage of shares than their counterparts in Britain and the United States (see Tables 5.2 and 6.3). This finding is particularly striking in view of the fact that the Japanese data relate to the holdings of the ten largest shareholders, while the British and American data relate to the twenty largest. The overall concentration would appear far higher in Japan if the data were strictly comparable, as is apparent from the illustrative data in Table 7.7, which relate to one independent enterprise for which full information was available. The ten largest shareholders of Toyota Motor held 36.44 per cent, placing it firmly in the modal category of Table 7.6,[34] but the next ten largest holders owned a further 17.12 per cent. Thus an analysis of the top twenty shareholders would show them to have held more than a half of the Toyota shares in issue.

Clearly, the largest shareholders occupied a far strong position in Japan than in either of the other two countries investigated. But who are the shareholders who occupy such a key position? Table 7.8 shows those members of the top 250 with the largest number of shareholding participations, including controlling interests and holdings in majority- and minority-controlled enterprises as well as in companies with no dominant interest.[35] Fifteen of the twenty largest participants were affiliated to the big six *kigyoshudan*. Each group was represented in the list by its city bank, and each of the big three combines was represented also by its trust bank and one of its insurers. The enterprises unaffiliated to *kigyoshudan* were two long-term credit banks, two city banks, and a large mutual insurance company. It can be seen from Table 7.8 that nine enterprises each had fifty or more participations; and a total of thirty-nine enterprises had ten or more participations. This level of participation was similar to that found in Britain and higher than that in the United States, though the use of data on the ten largest shareholders in Japan undoubtedly underestimates the extent of large-scale intercorporate participation. The hegemonic financials, it would appear, had an especially strong position in Japan.

The analysis so far has been concerned with control measured by Method A—equivalent to the 'provisional' analyses in earlier chapters—but the influence of group organisation is already apparent and it is necessary to examine the impact of this on patterns of ownership and control. What has been termed 'Method B' involves an attempt to classify enterprises having no dominant shareholding interest and to undertake any other reclassifications required when the pattern of aligned participations is investigated. The 159 enterprises with no dominant interest fall into 2 distinct categories: 83 *kigyoshudan* members controlled through aligned participations and 76 'independent' enterprises. Two enterprises subject to shared control[36] as well as those which were minority-controlled by *kigyoshudan* members could also be regarded as affiliated to the big combines. Seven of the mutual insurers, despite having no share capital themselves were affiliated to the groups and participated in their aligned controlling shareholdings. On this basis, 122 of the top 250 Japanese enterprises were elements in the systems of aligned participations from which the big six combines were formed.

Table 7.8: *The largest participants: Japan (1980)*

Investor	No. of participations in top 250
Nippon Life Insurance (Sa)	149
Dai-Ichi Mutual Life Ins.	98
Dai-Ichi Kangyo Bank (D)	72
Industrial Bank of Japan	62
Fuji Bank (F)	58
Mitsui Trust and Banking (Mi)	57
Sumitomo Bank (Su)	52
Sanwa Bank (Sa)	50
Asahi Mutual Life Ins. (D)	50
Meiji Mutual Life Ins. (M)	48
Tokio Marine and Fire Ins. (M)	47
Sumitomo Mutual Life (Su)	47
Mitsui Bank (Mi)	45
Mitsubishi Trust and Banking (M)	41
Daiwa Bank	41
Long Term Credit Bank	38
Mitsubishi Bank (M)	36
Tokai Bank	33
Mitsui Mutual Life Ins. (Mi)	29
Sumitomo Trust and Banking (Sa)	27

Note: (D)=DKB, (F)=Fuyo, (M)=Mitsubishi, (Mi)=Mitsui, (Sa)=Sanwa, (Su)=Sumitomo.

Of the remaining majority- and minority-controlled enterprises, fourteen were controlled by families, the state, or foreign interests, six were controlled by independent banks, investment companies, or non-financials,[37] and twenty-three were linked to what have often been described as smaller corporate groupings.

It is important to investigate, therefore, whether the latter could indeed be regarded as small-scale variants of the *kigyoshudan*. There were, in fact, nine contenders for this status. Taking account of the affiliations of these enterprises and their links to enterprises outside of the top 250, as shown in

Industrial Groupings in Japan, it seemed that three of them (the Matsushita, Yamaha, and Nippon Mining groups) could be regarded as conventional parent-centred groups of the British and American type, while six (the Nippon Steel, Tokai, Nissan, Toyota, Tokyu, and Seibu groups) were closer to the distinctively Japanese combine form of organisation. The latter were, however, hybrids between the *kigyoshudan* and parent-centred groups: the parent enterprises often shared their controlling holdings with other group members, but the focal enterprise itself was generally controlled by a diverse constellation of interests. If these 'hybrid' groups are regarded as systems of aligned participations, it is necessary to reallocate certain other enterprises to the 'little six' groups: the four 'parent' enterprises,[38] seven enterprises with no dominant interest but classified by *Industrial Groupings in Japan* as affiliated to the six groups, and one of the mutual insurers.[39]

The reclassification by Method B, therefore, showed the existence of twelve groups (the big six *kigyoshudan* and the little-six hybrid combines), together accounting for 153 enterprises, one state enterprise, eight family concerns, five foreign-controlled enterprises, two independent mutual insurers,[40] sixty-five enterprises controlled through constellations of interests, and ten associates of various Japanese corporate interests. These figures, shown in Table 7.9, can also be used to give some indication of the importance of the two forms of minority control. Though the numbers involved are small, secure and limited forms of minority control, in those enterprises for which the distinction could be made, was of equal importance. The important factor in deciding whether control was secure or limited was not the size of the holding *per se* but the number and size of any rival blocks of allied interests. Indeed, the presence of rival coalitions in many of the minority-controlled enterprises suggests that the distinction is of far less value in Japan than in Britain or the United States. General Electric, for example, with a 10.2 per cent holding in Toshiba, could exercise only limited minority control: it could be outvoted by the remaining large holders, and these included three Mitsui enterprises with 6.8 per cent. On the other hand, the 'secure' position held by the Nagase family in Nagase, with a holding of 11.5 per cent, was nevertheless faced with a

Sumitomo block of 8.9 per cent. It is likely, therefore, that a number of the enterprises apparently subject to minority control were involved in loose *de facto* coalitions with one or other of the big groups. The conventional categories of control, even when modified to reflect the voting balance between shareholding interests, must be used with caution in analysing Japanese data. The pattern of aligned participations permeates the whole economy.

This conclusion is reinforced by a consideration of those enterprises classified as controlled through constellations of interest. While this designation is, indeed, appropriate, certain crucial differences between Japanese and Anglo-American constellations must be borne in mind. In Japan the pool of participants is very much smaller and so there is great

Table 7.9: *Corporate control in Japan: method B (1980)*

Mode of control		Type of controller					
			Corporate				
	Personal	Japanese	Foreign	State	Mixed	Other	Totals
Exclusive majority	0	0	2	0	0	0	2
Secure minority	4	3	1	1	0	0	9
Limited minority	4	3	2	0	0	0	9
Unknown minority	0	4	0	0	0	0	4
Aligned groupings	–	153	–	–	–	–	153
Constellation of interests	–	51	–	14	–	65
Mutual	–	–	–	–	2	2
Not known	–	–	–	–	6	6
Totals	8	217	1	14	10	250

Note: 'Unknown minority' refers to companies classified in *Industrial Groupings in Japan* as minority-controlled, but for which no shareholder lists were available. The fourteen 'mixed' constellations were those with family participants: two of the sixteen shown in Table 7.2 (Matsuzakaya and Daiwa House) were members of small groups and were classified under 'aligned participations'.

concentration of shares in the hands of a small number of investors who reappear in the controlling constellations of a great many enterprises. There is also more likely to be one or more stable coalitions present in any particular constellation, reflecting the penetration of the aligned participations, and this makes many of the enterprises appear as virtual consortiums or joint ventures of the big groups.[41] The data for Toyota (Table 7.7), a parent for one of the groups in the little six, shows one such 'closed' constellation: the big six *kigyoshudan* jointly held 33.7 per cent of the shares, in blocks ranging from Sumitomo's 1.53 per cent to Mitsui's 11.84 per cent. In the sixty-five enterprises classified as controlled through constellations of interests in Table 7.9[42] the situation was generally very similar. In Tokyo Electric Power, for example, the Mitsui, Sumitomo, DKB, and Sanwa groups collectively held 13.1 per cent; in Nippon Oil the Mitsui, DKB, and Fuyo groups held 17.8 per cent; and in Hitachi the big six held 18.8 per cent. A similar pattern was found in the banking sector: Mitsubishi, Sanwa, and DKB held 13.2 per cent of the IBJ; Sanwa, DKB, and Fuyo held 12.5 per cent of the Long Term Credit Bank; and Mitsubishi, Sanwa, and Fuyo held 17.7 per cent of the Bank of Tokyo.

INTERCORPORATE RELATIONS AND FINANCIAL HEGEMONY

The inadequacy of many of the conventional approaches to corporate control in Japan, highlighted by the interweaving participations of the big six and the little six combines, has been recognised by Japanese writers. Futatsugi, for example, has proposed that the inadequacies be avoided by examining networks of intercorporate relations rather than merely dyadic connections.[43] Although he does not employ the formal techniques of network analysis, he suggests that the ramifications of reciprocal holdings can be studied through a matrix of capital connections, based on both shareownership and bank lending. In a study of 112 non-financials, he found a continuous chain of linkages connecting 78 of them. The big three *kigyoshudan*, with high levels of reciprocal connections, appeared as distinct poles in the network, while the Yasuda

(Fuyo), Sanwa, and DKB groups were less prominent and were united through their linkages to the group bank rather than through reciprocal connections. In a study of interlocking directorships, Sheard[44] shows that the leading Mitsubishi and Sumitomo enterprises had the highest level of internal recruitment to directorships—13 per cent of directorships in members of their presidents' clubs were held, in 1980, by current or former group executives. For the DKB group, just ahead of the rest of the big six, this was true of 9 per cent of directorships.[45] these and other studies[46] confirm the dominance of the big six in the network of intercorporate relations and are important pointers to differences in the level and mode of integration achieved in the groups. In the present research these issues have been studied in two ways: the organisation of aligned participations within the big six groups was investigated, and then the network of connections among all 250 enterprises was explored.

Table 7.10 shows the extent of share concentration by group members within each of the *kigyoshudan*. By far the most common situation was for group members to hold between 10 and 19 per cent of one another's shares, though a substantial number of cases involved group holdings of less than 10 per cent. These categories together—accounting for two-thirds of all *kigyoshudan* members—comprise those enterprises where

Table 7.10: *Intra-group shareholdings*

% by group members	Mitsubishi	Mitsui	Sumitomo	Sanwa	DKB	Fuyo	Totals
50–9	1	2	1	1	1	0	6
40–9	2	1	0	0	0	0	3
30–9	3	0	4	1	2	0	10
20–29	6	2	2	2	0	1	13
10–9	9	11	6	10	8	13	57
Less than 10	2	3	4	4	6	3	22
Mutual	1	1	1	2	1	1	7
Totals	24	20	18	20	18	18	118

Note: Figures relate to holdings by group members among the top ten shareholders in each enterprise.

group members form a dominant coalition of aligned interests within a more diverse set of large shareholders. This is brought out clearly by comparing Table 7.10 with Table 7.6, the latter showing that there was no *kigyoshudan* member in which the ten largest shareholders held less than 20 per cent. This comparison also highlights the absence of any case in which intra-group holdings amounted to more than 60 per cent: the cases of extremely high concentration in Table 7.6 were those foreign- and family-controlled enterprises which had allied themselves to a *kigyoshudan*. Table 7.10 shows that the lowest level of intra-group shareholding was found in Fuyo, where only one enterprise, Penta Ocean Construction, had more than 20 per cent of its shares held by other group members. DKB and Sanwa showed somewhat higher levels of integration, just behind Mitsui, and the tightest structure of intercorporate relations was found in Sumitomo and Mitsubishi. This characteristic of the latter two groups reinforces the findings of Sheard, while the high integration of each of the big three confirms the results of Fututsagi's research. It is clear, however, that none of the combines could rely exclusively on their intercorporate holdings to achieve group coordination. In Mitsui and Co., and in Mitsui Trust group, control was secure, as it was in Fuji Bank, Mitsubishi Bank, and the Mitsubishi and Sumitomo trust banks. But in Mitsui Bank the group holding of 10.3 per cent was countered by the 16.7 per cent held by six other large shareholders—and a similar situation held in the Sumitomo, DKB, and Sanwa banks. Although a number of cases where the group held less than 10 per cent were enterprises in which the aligned participations formed a small but stable coalition, others were enterprises with family controllers and participants or corporate controllers from outside the group. In Sekisui Chemical, for example, the Sanwa group held just 9 per cent, while Asahi Chemical, an independent enterprise, held 17.4 per cent.[47]

The solution to this paradox should be clear from the earlier discussion of the weakness of the stock exchange in Japan. While shareholdings are important supports for a controlling group, share capital is not the major source of corporate finance. Capital for expansion comes overwhelmingly from the banking system, and it is possible for groups to coordinate their members through the granting or withholding of bank loans. Among the 118 enterprises affiliated to *kigyoshudan* there were only 6 in which the group bank was not the primary source of borrowing.[48] All the Mitsubishi and Mitsui enterprises, for example, received the bulk of their loan capital from the Mitsubishi and Mitsui banks, respectively. Where enterprises borrowed additional capital from other sources, they were reluctant to resort to banks affiliated to rival groups. In most cases the position of second or third lender was taken not by a *kigyoshudan* city bank but by the IBJ or the Long Term Credit Bank. In this way, the combines could permit their affiliated enterprises to borrow from outside the group without running the risk of losing any control to their rivals. The only *kigyoshudan* banks to play an important role as supporting lenders to enterprises outside their groups were Mitsubishi Bank and Dai-Ichi Bank: indeed, Mitsubishi played such a strong supporting role for all of the combines except Mitsui. It was noticeable, however, that both of these banks were more likely to act as third lender than second lender, emphasising the extent to which the *kigyoshudan* attempted to maintain a high level of internal funding.

It is clear, therefore, that the generally tight organisational structure of the big combines did not preclude the establishment of banking and shareholding links between groups. In an attempt to discover the structure inherent in these capital relations, the techniques of network analysis employed in earlier chapters were applied to the matrix of shareholdings among the top 250 Japanese enterprises. By contrast with the results found for Britain and the United States, a similar structure of blocks and components was discovered with each of the three alogrithms used. This suggests that the mixture of fragmentation and cohesion present in the analyses reflected important and stable features of the Japanese economy.

The CONCOR blocking procedure for the whole network of controllers and controlled enterprises produced an extremely complex picture, as the clustering of enterprises into combines was strong enough to prevent the appearance of a single set of structurally equivalent hegemonic controllers. The rearranged matrix showed that shareholding relations formed a number of horizontal 'stripes'—broad bands in which shareholding connections were concentrated—separated by sets of enterprises among which shareholdings were sparse. The underlying structure of hegemony in this network was discovered through a further rearrangement of the matrix to bring the 'stripes' into alignment with one another.[49] It appeared that the seven sets of enterprises which made up the 'stripes' in the network formed an internally clustered hegemonic set, as shareholding relations were predominantly directed from this set of fifty-three enterprises to the remainder of the network. Three of the seven sets corresponded closely to the core membership of the big three *kigyoshudan*: one containing six Sumitomo enterprises, one containing three Mitsui enterprises, and one containing seven Mitsubishi enterprises.[50] The remaining sets drew their members from the smaller combines and from the independent enterprises, the big three *kigyoshudan* being merely marginal members in most of them.

Two of the sets seemed to be of particular importance, as they included only financial controllers and were more diverse in their composition than the others. The largest of these sets contained the mutual insurers from five of the big combines—only Mitsui was not represented—as well as other insurers, the Mitsubishi and Sumitomo trust banks, and two independent banks.[51] The second financial set contained the Sanwa, DKB, and Fuyo banks, together with an insurer and four city banks. The strongest hierarchical links[52] in the network were between the first of these financial sets and the Mitsubishi core, and slightly less-strong links joined the two financial sets and connected the larger with the Sumitomo core. The remaining sets were connected only loosely to the strongly bonded sets, and the small Mitsui set maintained very weak links with the rest of the network. It can be concluded, therefore, that the Japanese intercorporate network was divided into hegemonic and subordinate sets, with the Mitsubishi, Sumitomo, and Mitsui enterprises forming distinguishable subsets among the hegemonic controllers. Members of the Sanwa, DKB, and Fuyo combines were fused into a large financial core which included the IBJ, the Long Term Credit Bank, and numerous insurers and city banks, and with which the Mitsubishi and Sumitomo combines were allied.

This conclusion is confirmed by the results of the EBLOC

and QCOMP analyses, both of which showed the existence of distinguishable components within a larger intercorporate network. EBLOC disclosed the existence of a large cyclic component containing 230 of the top 250 enterprises,[53] while the standard QCOMP analysis of the 123 controlling enterprises showed that all except one[54] were joined into a single component. This superficial similarity to the British and American networks is belied by the very strong evidence of internal fragmentation in the standard QCOMP analysis of the controlled enterprises. In the latter network Mitsubishi and Toyota affiliates appeared as strongly tied components, forming two 'peaks' which became elements in a larger component built from Fuyo, DKB, and Sanwa industrials as well as such enterprises as Nippon Steel, Hitachi, and Sharp. Outside this large component were a number of secondary peaks—two containing Sumitomo enterprises,[55] two containing Fuyo enterprises, and others organised around Mitsubishi, Tokai, and Sanwa affiliates[56]—and at lower levels of intensity these small components were fused with the large component to form a single component with 229 members.[57]

An analysis of the network of controllers using the more sensitive QCOMP procedure, based on relative intensity, showed that the clustering of subsidiaries and associates reflected coordinated patterns of investment by their controllers. Mitsubishi and Sumitomo financials appeared as intensely linked components, though the latter also had many investments in common with the Sanwa, Dai-Ichi Kangyo, and Fuji Banks as well as with independent city banks. The Sumitomo financials, therefore, were more closely linked to the financial core than were those from the Mitsubishi group. Mitsubishi and Sumitomo industrials each formed separate components, as did the Mitsui financials, though the Sumitomo component contained Nissan and Nippon Steel and the Mitsui component contained the Long-Term Credit Bank. The big three combines, therefore, each showed an internal coordination of their shareholdings in other enterprises, with Mitsui showing the greatest distinctiveness and the Sumitomo financials showing the least. This analysis also produced evidence that the Fuyo financials possessed a higher level of coordination than those from the DKB and Sanwa groups: the

Component	Core Members	Fringe members
1. MITSUBISHI	Mitsubish Mitsubishi Bank Mitsubishi Trust Tokyo Marine & Fire Mitsubishi Heavy Industry Asahi Glass	Mitsubishi Electric Nippon Yusen Bank of Tokyo*
2. MITSUI	Mitsui Mitsui Bank Mitsui Trust Taisho Marine & Fire	Mitsui Engineering Fuji Photo Film Toray Industries Mitsui OSK Toshiba*
3. SUMITOMO	Sumitomo Sumitomo Trust Sumitomo Marine & Fire Sumitomo Chemical Sumitomo Heavy Industry Sumitomo Metal Industry Nippon Electric	—
4. DKB	Dai-Ichi Kangyo Bank Kawasaki Steel ︶ ︵ Long Term Credit Bank*	C. Itoh Nippon Credit Bank*
5. FUYO	Marubeni Fuji Bank Yasuda Trust Yasuda Fire and Marine Nissan Motor*	Nippon Kokkan Nissho-Iwai (Sa)* Kobe Steel (Sa)*
6. TOYOTA	Toyota Motor Toyota Motor Sales Tokai Bank*	Toyota Automatic Loom

7.

FINANCIAL CORE

Sumitomo Bank (Su)	Saitama Bank	Daiwa Bank (Di)
Sanyo Electric (Su)	IBJ	Nomura Securities (Di)
Tokyo Sanyo (Su)	Kyowa Bank	Fuji Fire & Marine (Di)
Sanwa Bank (Sa)	Nippon Steel	Hitachi
Teijin (Sa)	Kubota (F)	Daihatsu Motor (T)
Hitachi		
Shipbuilding (Sa)	Nichido Fire & Marine (F)	Osaka Gas
Toyo Trust (Sa)	Matsushita Electrical	Nippon Fire & Marine
	Industries	Asahi Chemical

Figure 7.1: *Network components in Japan*

Note: Asterisk indicates that enterprise is not a member of the group whose name is given to the component.

Groups in financial core: (Di)=Daiwa; (F)=Fuyo; (Sa)=Sanwa; (Su)=Sumitomo; (T)=Toyota

Yasuda trust bank and insurers together with Marubeni Corporation formed a small component of coordinated investors. A particularly long-lasting small component was that which contained Nomura Securities, Hitachi, Teijin, and Hitachi Shipbuilding, the latter two from the Sanwa group, all of which shared participations in Sanwa Bank and the Sanwa-affiliated Toyo Trust & Banking; although the Sanwa combine did not show a particularly high level of coordination in its investments, it was itself subject to a loosely coordinated coalition of shareholders.[58]

Perhaps the clearest picture of the structure of the network comes from an EBLOC analysis in which only reciprocal shareholdings are considered; that is to say, where two enterprises are regarded as connected only if each participates in the other. In view of the significance attached by Japanese writers to such reciprocal links in the horizontally structured combines, it is to be expected that this analysis would distinguish the strongest intercorporate bonds in Japan. In this analysis EBLOC searchers for cyclic components in the network of reciprocal shareholdings and the non-cyclic components to which they are connected. Figure 7.1 shows the results of this procedure.

The initial application of EBLOC identified six cyclic components at cycle length 3, those cores numbered one to six in Figure 7.1.[59] In addition to the hangers to these components there were three non-cyclic components, one connected to Mitsui, one (comprising Sanwa members) to Fuyo, and a larger one connected to Fuyo, DKB, Sumitomo, and Toyota. Of the big six, therefore, Sanwa appeared to have the lowest level of reciprocal holdings. Mitsubishi was the only big combine not to have any reciprocated participations in other groups, though Mitsui's only reciprocal links were with Toyota Motor and Toshiba rather than with other *kigyoshudan*. The main foci of the links between DKB, Fuyo, and Sumitomo involved members of the large non-cyclic component. The fringes of the various components in Figure 7.1 were constructed from the members of the non-cyclic components by allocating enterprises to the fringe of a cyclic component to which they had a reciprocated link; their attachments to their components were weaker than those of the core members. It can be seen that the first six components were built around particular enterprise groups, but that all except Sumitomo included enterprises from outside the group. The Fuyo component, for example, was centred around an alliance between the Fuyo financials and Nissan, while members of the Sanwa group appeared in its fringes. Similarly, Toyota was allied with Tokai Bank and both Mitsui and Mitsubishi had non-group members in their fringes. The weakest of the six components was DKB: not only did it include few group members, but one (C. Itoh) was a joint venture with Sumitomo and the component included two independent long-term credit banks. This points to the closeness of the DKB component to the large non-cyclic component,[60] numbered 7 in Figure 7.1, which contained banks, insurers, and industrials from a number of smaller groups and to which independent enterprises and some *kigyoshudan* members were connected. Of the big six *kigyoshudan*, therefore, only Mitsubishi and Mitsui stood sharply apart from the rest of the network, though even they maintained looser links with other enterprises. Sumitomo was rather less separated from the core of the network, while Fuyo and DKB were closely linked to one another and to independent enterprises. Members of the Sanwa group showed little identity within the network, their capital relations with other enterprises often being stronger than those with one another.

The discussion of corporate control in Japan has concentrated very much on the impact of group affiliations on members of the big combines and their smaller counterparts. The analyses of the network of intercorporate relations, however, have shown that these groups did not exist in splendid isolation from one another. There were extensive, and often reciprocated, links between groups, though the various groups were differentially involved in such relations. The big three *kigyoshudan*, most closely rooted in old *zaibatsu* and heavily involved in 'traditional' sectors of industry such as mining, chemicals, engineering, and steel, showed the lowest levels of connection with other groups and, conversely, tighter levels of internal coordination.[61] Those linkages which Mitsubishi, Mitsui, and Sumitomo did maintain with other groups were predominantly through their trust banks and mutual insurers. The newer *kigyoshudan* (Sanwa, DKB, and Fuyo) were not so tightly organised internally and their affiliations and connections overlapped considerably. These groups, more extensively involved in the 'modern' sectors of the economy, joined with independent enterprises and smaller groups to form a network of relations which was closer in form to that found in the British and American economies. The hegemonic enterprises of the big six and little six groups, therefore, were embedded in a network of intercorporate relations in which a split between 'traditional' and 'modern' capital was an important feature.

The Japanese economic miracle was founded on the power and influence of the big groups and on their ability to coordinate the activities of their constituent enterprises.[62] The analyses presented in this chapter have shown that the degree of coordination that can be achieved through shareholding is at its greatest in the declining traditional sectors, and that, conversely, the expansion of the modern sector may have weakened group organisation. It is not suprising, then, that the newer groups have been centred around banks in a way that is not true of the big three[63] and that a key role in underpinning the activities of all the groups, traditional and modern, has been played by the long-term credit banks. The banks have been, and remain, of key importance in explaining Japanese business behaviour. It remains to be seen whether the mobilisation of capital through the banking system will continue to buttress the group structure of the *kigyoshudan*. The further development of the modern sectors of the economy and the independent enterprises may lead to the dismantling of the structures and practices of group organisation which the post-war Japanese business leaders sought so hard to adapt to the problems of industrial reconstruction.

NOTES

1. General historical surveys can be found in: R. Storry, *A History of Modern Japan*, Harmondsworth, Penguin, 1960; G.C. Allen, *A Short*

Economic History of Modern Japan, 3rd edn, London, George Allen & Unwin, 1972; W.W. Lockwood, *The Economic Development of Japan*, New Jersey, Princeton University Press, 1968; and J. Livington, J. Moore, and F. Oldfather, (eds.), *The Japan Reader*, 2 vols., Harmondsworth, Penguin, 1976 (1973). Japanese business is discussed in more detail in: J. Hirschmeier, *The Origins of Entrepreneurship in Meiji Japan*, Cambridge, Mass., Harvard University Press, 1964; J. Hirschmeier and T. Yui, *The Development of Japanese Business, 1600–1980*, London, George Allen & Unwin, 1981. An overview of business organisation, and further sources, can be found in J. Scott, *Corporation Classes, and Capitalism*, 2nd edn, London, Hutchinson, 1985, pp. 142ff.

2. There were eleven branches of the family, and their respective roles were regulated by a will of 1900. The main branch held 23 per cent of the shares of Mitsui Bussan, the holding company, five other branches each held 11.5 per cent, and five associated families each held 3.9 per cent. These and other family members held shares in subholding and operating companies. *See* E.M. Hadley, *Antitrust in Japan*, New Jersey, Princeton University Press, 1970, pp. 59–60.

3. This was based around Jiyuto, an earlier 'Liberal' party. The Party was a vehicle for Mitsui influence and was built around an alliance with the landed class.

4. The social base of Kenseikai support came from urban and industrial areas. Following the Second World War, Minseito, Kenseikai's successor, split into the 'Progressive' and 'Democratic' parties, but both merged with Seiyukai in 1955 to form the Liberal Democratic Party, which has dominated Japanese politics since that date.

5. The term *zaibatsu* could be used collectively to refer to the 'money clique' as a whole, and similar terms were used to describe the other political factions: *gumbatsu* (the military), *kambatsu* (officialdom), and *mombatsu* (landlords).

6. Nissan was controlled by the Aikawa family, Fuji Industries by the Nakajima family, and Furukawa by the Furakawa and Nakagawa families. The remaining groups were controlled by families bearing the same name. Thus the attack on ten groups was directed at eleven families.

7. The main impact of the 'dissolution' policy in the financial sector was the separation of the Mitsui and Dai-Ichi banks which had merged into the Teikoku Bank.

8. Hadley, *op. cit.,* incorrectly uses the term *keiretsu* to describe the enterprise groups. Strictly, *keiretsu* refers to a business subsidiary or associate. I am grateful to Hiroshi Okumura for pointing this out to me. A useful overview of the groups conventionally identified can be found in *Industrial Groupings in Japan, 1980–81*, Tokyo, Dodwell & Co., 1980.

9. Hadley, p. 262.

10. T. Nishiyana, 'The Structure of Managerial Control: Who Owns and Controls Japanese Business' (1980), in K. Sato and Y. Hoshino (eds.), *The Anatomy of Japanese Business,* London, Croom Helm, 1984.

11. *Ibid.,* p. 131.

12. H. Okumura, 'Enterprise Groups in Japan', *Shoken Keizai*, 147, 1984, pp. 176–7. *See also* H. Okumura, *Nihon no Rokudai Kigyoshudan* (Japan's Big Six Business Groups), Tokyo Daiyamondo-sha, 1983.

13. M. Yazawa, 'The Legal Structure for Corporate Enterprise: Shareholder-Management Relations Under Japanese Law', in A. Von Mehren (ed.), *Law in Japan*, Cambridge, Mass., Harvard University Press, 1963; B.A.K. Rider and H.L. Ffrench, *The Regulation of Insider Trading*, London, Macmillan, 1979, Ch. 13.

14. *Japan Company Handbook*, Tokyo, Oriental Economist, half yearly.

15. See *Industrial Groupings in Japan*.

16. Enterprises were classified into *kigyoshudan* according to the classification given in *Industrial Groupings in Japan*. C. Itoh & Co. was subject to joint control by the DKB and Sumitomo groups, but the source classified it as part of the DKB group. C. Itoh's associated companies were classified according to which of the two groups they were orientated. The classification given in the source was followed in the present research and this led to Toa Oil, of which C. Itoh owned 38.9 per cent, being allocated to the Sumitomo group.

17. The following discussion of types of investor draws on Nomura Research Institute, *Investing in Japan*, Cambridge, Woodhead-Faulkner, 1978, and K. Ohtani, *Securities Market in Japan*, Tokyo, Japan Securities Research Institute, 1983.

18. Nomura Research Institute, pp. 118–120.

19. H. Okumura, 'Stockholdings and Monopoly Problems in Japan', *Shoken Keizai*, 129, 1979; K. Kojima and T. Ozawa, *Japan's General Trading Companies*, Paris, OECD, 1984.

20. In Japan it is always 'him'. Female presidents of large enterprises are unknown.

21. Okumura, pp. 171–2; *idem*, 'Enterprise Groupings in Japan', p. 180. *See also* Y. Miyazaki, 'The Japanese-Type Structure of Big Business', in K. Sato (ed.), *Industry and Business in Japan*, London, Croom Helm, 1980.

22. H. Okumura, 'Interfirm Relations in an Enterprise Group: The Case of Mitsubishi', in Sato and Hoshino (eds.).

24. On the general principle *see* J. Scott and C. Griff. *Directors of Industry*, Cambridge, Polity Press, 1984, pp. 18ff.

25. The enterprises were Mitsubishi Oil (Getty), Koa Oil (Caltex), General Sekiyu (Exxon), and Toa Nenryo (Exxon/Mobil).

26. Shell group subsidiaries shared majority control of Showa Oil, and the latter shared minority control of Mitsubishi Petrochemical with other members of the Shell group.

27. The Yamagata family shared control of Koa Fire and Marine with Nippon Express, a member of the DKB group. Koa was not itself a member of the group and so, for the purposes of Method A, was regarded as outside the big six.

28. The latter would be the prime candidates for limited minority control if analysed on the same basis as for the United States. Incomplete information on board membership precluded the use of this category.

29. The Ito name appeared in Ito Ham, Ito-Yokado, and Matsuzakaya. The Ishibashi name appeared in Bridgestone Tire and Daiwa House Industry. The Ishibashi family of Bridgestone are an important family connected with ex-Prime Ministers Hatoyama and Ikeda among other political and industrial leaders.
30. The Atsumi family held 2.0 per cent in Fujita, alongside the Fujta family's 8.7 per cent; the Yoshimura family held 2.8 per cent in JGC, alongside the Saneyoshi family's 9.6 per cent; and Uny had participations from both the Nishikawa family (5.4 per cent) and the Furukawa family (2.5 per cent).
31. *See* note 8 above.
32. There were two cases of cross-group control: Chiyoda Chemical Engineering, in the Mitsubishi group, was controlled by a member of the DKB combine, as was Toa Oil in the Sumitomo group. The latter was due to the classification of C. Itoh referred to in note 16.
33. The exception was Sekisui Chemical, controlled by Asahi Chemical, the two formerly comprising the Nitchitsu group. Sekisui Chemical controlled Sekisui Prefabricated Homes, giving Asahi Chemical an indirect influence over another member of the Sanwa group.
34. The full data in Table 7.7 relate to 1982 and are translated from *Kigyo Keiretsu Soran*. The 1980 source listing showed the top ten as holding 36.1 per cent.
35. The British and American data in Tables 5.3 and 6.6 related only to participations in controlling constellations. Because of the peculiarities of intercorporate holdings in Japan, the data in Table 7.8 also includes controlling holdings and participations in enterprises controlled by other interests. Thus the data set comprises the top ten shareholders in *all* the top Japanese enterprises for which such information was available.
36. Koa Fire and Marine; Japan Pulp and Paper.
37. Hankyu Department Stores, Kanto Electric Construction, Snow Brand Milk Products, Izumiya, Chugoku Electric Power, Daito Gyorui.
38. Tokai Bank, Toyota Motor, Nissan Motor, Nippon Steel. Unlike the major members of the big six, these four enterprises were controlled through constellations of interests. Because of the structure of their groups, however, it seems realistic to see them as participants in the system of aligned participations.
39. Chiyoda Mutual Life, which was affiliated to the Tokai group. One of the enterprises classified as 'not known' in Table 7.1, Kyushu Oil, was also included here as *Industrial Groupings in Japan* indicated that it was affiliated to Nippon Steel.
40. *Industrial Groupings in Japan* suggests that Taiyo Mutual Life was in fact affiliated to the Taiyo Kobe Bank.
41. It should also be pointed out that non-financial enterprises in Japan tend to invest on their own account, as trade investments, rather than through a pension fund.
42. It should be recalled that eleven enterprises (including Toyota) controlled through constellations of interests formed constituents of the little six groups and so were classified in Table 7.9 under 'aligned participations'.

43. Y. Futatsugi, 'The Measurement of Interfirm Relationships' (1969), *Japanese Economic Studies*, 2, 1973; *idem*, 'An Economic Analysis of Stockholdings', *Annals of the School of Business Administration*, Kobe University, 22, 1978.
44. P. Sheard, 'Financial Corporate Grouping, Cross-Subsidisation in the Private Sector and the Industrial Adjustment Process in Japan', *Discussion Paper*, no. 44, Osaka University, 1984, Table 3.
45. *See also* Y. Ueda, 'A Quantitative Analysis of Interlocking Directorships in Enterprise Groups' (in Japanese), *Shoken Keizai*, 146, 1983.
46. *See* notes 10 and 12 above.
47. This arrangement seems to date from the time when the two chemical producers made up the Nitchitsu group.
48. One of these six was C. Itoh, the joint venture of DKB and Sumitomo. While allocated to the DKB group, its primary bank was Sumitomo Bank.
49. This second rearrangement was possible because the ordering of the sets generated by CONCOR is arbitrary. When, as in the present case, the number of blocks is large, it is only through such a manual rearrangement that the structure can be discovered.
50. The latter also contained Life and Bank of Tokyo from outside the Mitsubishi group.
51. These banks were IBJ and Daiwa Bank.
52. The strength of these links was measured by block densities. Using a variable threshold density it is possible to construct a 'nested' hierarchy of sets.
53. There were eleven hangers to this component, all except one being hangers-off and most being majority- or minority-controlled enterprises.
54. The exception was Ube Industries, a member of the Sanwa group, which was the only known participant in Seibu Oil.
55. One contained the trading company and trust bank, the other contained industrials.
56. One small component contained Daihatsu (Toyota) and Orient Leasing (Sanwa).
57. The Nippon Gakki (Yamaha) enterprises emerged as a short-lived small component at a low level of intensity. The only isolate was Seibu Oil; *see* note 54.
58. Hitachi Shipbuilding had formerly been a member of the Hitachi *zaibatsu*, and the Hitachi electrical enterprise maintained a small participation in it. Nomura Securities was associated with Daiwa Bank, in which both Nomura and Teijin participated.
59. At cycle length 4 the Fuyo and Sumitomo components were fused, but the Mitsui, Mitsubishi, DKB, and Toyota components remained separate. It should be noted that mutual insurers, because they have no share capital, can never be involved in reciprocal shareholdings. They do not, therefore, appear in this analysis.
60. This consisted of enterprises linked through reciprocal shareholdings but with no such links to members of the six cyclic components.
61. Okumura, 'Enterprise Groups in Japan'.

62. This is recognized even by managerialist writers such as Nakatani. See I. Nakatani, 'The Economic Role of Financial Corporate Groups', in M. Aoki (ed), *The Economic Analysis of the Japanese Firm*, Amsterdam, North Holland, 1984.
63. Futatsugi, 'The Measurement of Interfirm Relationships'.

8 Financial Power in Three Economies

The aim of this book has been to map the structure of financial hegemony, the contours of financial power, in three capitalist economies. All of the advanced capitalist economies, it has been argued, have a system of property relations which can best be described as impersonal possession. Networks of capital, commercial, and personal relations tie the majority of the large enterprises together into a structure in which it is no longer possible to say that 'this' enterprise is controlled by 'that' person. Personally controlled enterprises survive, but they must increasingly accommodate themselves to the structure of impersonal possession and have become more and more subordinate elements in the structure of financial hegemony.

Foreign-controlled enterprises and state enterprises also have a relative autonomy from the system of personal possession which prevails in any particular society, but even they are closely entwined with the intercorporate networks. Foreign subsidiaries and associates may represent areas of autonomous decision within a national economy, able to ignore some of the constraints which act upon their domestic counterparts, but they are themselves mere subordinate elements of parent enterprises which are integral members of their own national economies. Public enterprises have their ultimate locus of control within the apparatus of the state itself and so have the potential to act in ways other than the enterprises which are controlled through the system of impersonal possession; but this potential is rarely pushed to its full, and enterprises in which the state is merely majority or minority controller tend to act similarly to their privately controlled counterparts.

Levels of personal, foreign, and state control differ

considerably among the three economies. Using the conventional indicators of control to make a comparison of general patterns—the 'provisional' or 'Method A' classifications used in Chapters 4, 6, and 7—it was found that family control was lowest in Japan and highest in Britain; family influence within the system of impersonal possession was similarly at its lowest in Japan, but was highest in the United States. Even in Britain, family control had declined from considerably higher levels in the past, the foundations for the decline of family control having been laid between 1936 and 1951. While Britain retained a large and important group of family-controlled enterprises (about one-third of the top 250), in both Japan and the United States entrepreneurial capital was far more closely entwined within the system of impersonal possession. In the United States in particular there were numerous enterprises controlled through constellations of interests which had family participants in their controlling constellations. Families have gradually reduced the size of their holdings while striving to maintain control,[1] making the judgement that a greater overall dispersal of shareholdings permits control to be exercised with a progressively smaller holding. As a result, many formerly controlling families have become simply the largest, or one of the largest, participants in controlling constellations. Such families eventually disappear as significant forces as impersonal possession comes to prevail. In all three economies enterpreneurial capital was concentrated in distribution, construction, and food processing, but in Britain, where eight of the ten large merchant banks were family-controlled, it was also a major element in the financial sector.

The British economy also showed the highest levels of state and foreign control, just under one in ten and one in five, respectively, with figures for both being extremely low in the other economies. In Japan there was just one, minority-controlled, state enterprise, and there were none in the top 252 American enterprises. Only four large foreign-controlled enterprises operated in the United States and ten in Japan, a half of the foreign subsidiaries and associates in Japan being affiliated with Japanese business interests. Thus Britain showed the greatest representation of autonomous blocks of capital—enterpreneurial, state, and foreign—outside its domestic system of impersonal possession. This was reflected in the aggregate levels of majority control: the top 250 British enterprises included 91 enterprises with majority or equivalent forms of control, compared with 8 in the United States and just 5 in Japan. Levels of minority control were relatively similar in the three economies—51 enterprises in Britain, 53 in the United States, and 69 in Japan—though the composition of the category varied. In Britain and the United States, for example, family minority control was important, while in Japan minority blocks were overwhelmingly held by corporate interests. Adopting the voting criterion of control used in the 'final' and 'Method B' classifications, it was found that secure minority control prevailed in Britain but limited minority control was more important in the United States.

In all three economies the largest single category of control comprised those enterprises in which there was no dominant interest, the enterprises which were tied through interweaving share participations into a system of impersonal possession. Shareholdings were more dispersed in Britain than in the United States, as measured by the proportion of shares held by the twenty largest shareholders in each enterprise, and the highest level of concentration was found in Japan. In each economy there was one enterprise whose participations were far greater than its fellows—the Prudential, J.P. Morgan, and Nippon Life—but many enterprises had a large number of participations. Despite the high level of concentration, it was rarely the case that the largest holders owned more than 50 per cent of the shares; this was true of only one enterprise in Japan and none in Britain and the United States.[2] Conversely, the large holders never held less than 10 per cent in any of the three economies. These figures show that the system of impersonal possession consisted predominantly of enterprises in which the largest shareholders collectively held minority blocks in one another, with these minority blocks being internally fragmented into smaller intersecting participations. Despite the fact that each economy showed a group of large, hegemonic investors participating in many other enterprises, the hegemonic enterprises were themselves beset by conflicting interests: there was no monolithic locus of control within the intercorporate network.

In Britain and the United States the hegemonic investors of the system of impersonal possession formed diverse constellations of shareholding interests which controlled those enterprises which had no majority or minority controllers. Central elements in these constellations were the investment management groups, especially banks, which were extensively involved in the management of pension fund capital. Few large private sector pension funds in Britain were internally managed, in contrast with the situation found in the United States, where many of the largest enterprises had self-administered pension and saving schemes. In many of the American cases these 'internal' funds were the largest shareholders in their own companies, buttressing the power of the current board of directors who ultimately controlled the use and disposition of the funds. In many such cases the internal funds had external financial advisors, often represented on the board, and so represented financial influence at one remove. Many of the large pension funds, however, in both Britain and the United States, were under the direct management of banks and their trust departments. While banks generally had full voting control over the shares which they managed, there was no evidence in support of the idea of 'bank control'. Instead, a polyarchy of financial enterprises holding hegemonic positions in the system of capital mobilisation were able to determine the conditions under which other enterprises had to act. The hegemonic system was structured into bank-centred spheres of influence through the establishment of interlocking directorships. In the United States the system of capital mobilisation was fragmented along regional lines, under the dominance of the New York 'national' banks, and the establishment of associated regional interlocks generated a regional structure of spheres of influence.

Impersonal possession in Japan, while involving the interweaving of fragmented shareholdings, did not show such a marked development of control through a constellation of interests and the associated bank-centred spheres of influence. Instead, the interweaving shareholdings involved a number of relatively stable coalitions which allowed the establishment of a structure of aligned participations. The hegemonic enterprises were grouped into a small number of combines whose members pursued coordinated investment policies and whose aligned participations tied other enterprises to them in a subordinate role. Thus financial hegemony in Japan involved not so much a polyarchy of independent financials as an oligarchy of combines. This represents a deliberate adaptation of traditional ideas and pre-war business forms to post-war economic recovery and growth. The group structuring of the Japanese economy consisted of the 'big six' and 'little six' combines (accounting for 153 of the top 250 enterprises) and a number of independent enterprises, of which the majority were controlled through constellations of interests. The big six were the hegemonic units in the Japanese economy, with family- and foreign-owned enterprises often having to enter into alliance with one of the combines rather than operating independently. Such alliances were often the only way for enterprises to gain access to bank credit and to the marketing opportunities which expansion required.

The Japanese intercorporate network was discovered to have a marked split between 'traditional' and 'modern' sectors of capital. The traditional sector comprised the groups of Mitsubishi, Mitsui, and Sumitomo, which were closest to their *zaibatsu* predecessors. Each group had a tight internal structure and appeared as recognisable and autonomous 'poles' within the network, though each had intercorporate relations with many independent enterprises which tied them loosely to the wider network. Of the three groups, Mitsui was perhaps the most autonomous and Sumitomo had the strongest links to other enterprises. The modern sector of capital was centred on the Sanwa, DKB, and Fuyo groups and the independent city banks. The three big groups in the modern sector of capital showed less continuity with *zaibatsu* predecessors, and tended to have a bank-centred structure. The banks were the focus for their groups, and member enterprises were linked more closely to the group bank than they were to one another through reciprocal shareholdings. Intercorporate relations maintained by these groups involved numerous inter-group holdings, so the groups did not appear as such marked poles in the network as their 'traditional' counterparts. They had closer links with the smaller independent banks and

together comprised an extensive, but still internally fragmented, network. This 'modern' sector of the Japanese
intercorporate network may come to resemble the Anglo-
American networks more closely in the future; and the three
'traditional' groups may find a greater need to accommodate
themselves to this evolving intercorporate network by reducing
their levels of isolation. If this were to happen, impersonal
possession in Japan would begin to take the form of financial
hegemony structured through bank-centred groupings. But the
continuing strength of aligned participations and the key role
of banks in corporate finance is likely to ensure that these
groups continue to function as interest groups rather than mere
spheres of influence.

   This book has used the still relatively novel techniques of
social network analysis to investigate the connections between
forms of capitalist property and structures of financial power.
Network analysis makes it possible to trace the links between
enterprises and so to show the ways in which such links
interweave to create complex structures of interdependent
enterprises. These same techniques also disclose the shape and
texture of these structures and highlight the differing roles
played by, for example, the central and peripheral enterprises.
Banks and financial intermediaries have been found to be of
key importance in all three economies: they occupy the central
positions in their networks and are the pivots around which the
shareholding relations both fragment and unite other enterprises. They stand at the head of structures of financial
hegemony which vary with the legal forms of property
relations and with such factors as the time and pace of
industrialisation, the cultural inheritance, and the size of the
national economy. While it is correct to identify a common
pattern of impersonal possession in all modern capitalist
economies, it is wrong to assume that this invariably takes the
same form. The system of impersonal possession which now
prevails shows significant variations in form between the
polyarchic financial hegemony, bank-centred spheres of
influence, and control through a constellation of interests
found in Britain and the United States, and the oligarchic
hegemony, combine organisation, and aligned participations
found in Japan. Such variations in structural form may or may

not disappear in the future—no simple process of 'convergence' can be assumed—but only the techniques of network analysis will allow researchers to chart any changes which occur and to assess their significance.

NOTES

1. C.N. Pitelis and R. Sugden, 'The Alleged Separation of Ownership and Control in the Theory of the Firm' *Warwick Economic Research Papers*, 238, 1983.
2. There would undoubtedly have been more Japanese enterprises in which the largest shareholders controlled 50 per cent or more of the votes if the analysis had been based on the twenty largest holders.

Appendix I Data Selection and Classification

Lists of companies for analysis were selected, as far as possible, using comparable criteria. The 200 largest non-financials, ranked by turnover, were selected from the major business sources published in each country: The *Times 1000* for Britain, *Fortune* for the United States, and *Industrial Groupings in Japan* for Japan. The total in the United States was increased to 202 by the inclusion of two unconsolidated subsidiaries of companies already selected. In addition to the non-financials, fifty large financials were selected for each country, taking the largest companies in banking, insurance, etc. The British and American data comprise companies selected for analysis in an international study of interlocking directorships, and I am grateful to Jim Bearden and Beth Mintz for allowing me to use their list of American companies.[1]

A full classification of the British enterprises by mode of control, using the provisional classification, has already been published.[2] The remainder of this appendix sets out the final classification by control type, as used in Table 4.2 (p. 64).

CLASSIFICATION BY CONTROL TYPE (1976)

1. Public Corporations

British Airways	National Bus
British Broadcasting	National Coal Board
British Gas	National Enterprise Board
British Rail	National Freight
British Steel	Post Office
Electricity Council	South of Scotland Electricity
London Transport Executive	

2. Wholly Owned

(i) Personal
Baring Brothers
Heron
John Lewis Partnership
Littlewood Organisation

N.M. Rothschild
Union International
Wellcome Foundation

(ii) Corporate British
Clydesdale Bank

(iii) Corporate: Foreign
Alcan Aluminium
Anglo-Chemical & Ore
Ciba-Geigy (UK)
Conoco
Louis Dreyfus
Esso Petroleum
Ford Motor
Gallaher
Gulf Oil
Hoechst UK
IBM
Inco Europe
Kodak
Lonconex

Mars
Massey-Fergusson Holdings
Michelin
Mobil
Monsanto
Nafta
Petrofina
Philips Electronic
Standard Telephones & Cables
Tampimex
Texaco
Total
Tradax, England
Vauxhall Motors

(iv) State
Bank of England

3. Exclusive Majority

(i) Personal
Associated British Foods
British & Commonwealth
  Shipping
Czarnikow Group
Robert Fleming
Great Universal Stores
Gestetner Holdings
Hambros
John Laing

J. Lyons
Newarthill
Rank Organisation
J. Sainsbury
Stenhouse Holdings
Trust Houses Forte
George Wimpey

(ii) Corporate: British
Carrington Viyella   Lazard

(iii) Corporate: Foreign
Amalgamated Metal   Hoover
Bunge   Rothmans International
Cavenham   Thomson Organisation
Chrysler (UK)   F.W. Woolworth
H.J. Heinz

(iv) State
British Leyland   British Petroleum

4. Shared Majority

(i) Corporate: British and Foreign
Agricultural Mortgage   Morgan Grenfell Holdings
British Aircraft   Rank Xerox
British Aluminium   Save & Prosper Group
Consolidated Petroleum   Touche Remnant Holdings
Danish Bacon   Yorkshire Bank
Finance For Industry

(ii) Mixed
M & G Group

5. Secure Minority

(i) Personal
Blackwood Hodge   Marchwiel
Thomas Borthwick   S. Pearson
Richard Costain   Rowntree Mackintosh
Arthur Guinness   Schroders
Kleinwort, Benson, Lonsdale   W.H. Smith
Leslie and Godwin   Whitbread
Lonrho

(ii) Corporate: British
Bank of Scotland   Linfood Holdings
English Property   National & Commercial Banking
FMC   Standard Chartered Bank
Globe Investment Trust   Tozer, Kemsley & Millbourn
Grindlays Holdings

(iii) Corporate: Foreign
Albright and Wilson   Johnson Matthey
House of Frazer

(iv) State
British Sugar

(v) Mixed
Hill Samuel   Wood Hall Trust
Land Securities Investment Trust

6. Shared Minority

(i) Corporate: British
ICL   United Dominions Trust

(ii) Mixed
Bunzl Pulp & Paper   Gill & Duffus Group

7. Limited Minority

(i) Personal
Guthrie   Pilkington Brothers
Inchcape   Tesco Stores
Ladbroke Group   Thorn Electrical
Lex Service Group   Unilever
Marley   United Biscuits
Mercury Securities

(ii) Corporate: British
Wheatsheaf Distribution &
  Trading

(iii) Corporate: Foreign
Clarke Chapman   Lead Industries

(iv) Mixed
Trafalgar House

8. Mutual

Abbey National Building   Nationwide Building Society
  Society   Scottish Widows Fund & Life
Alliance Building Society   Assurance

Halifax Building Society
Leeds Permanent Building
Society

Standard Life Assurance
Woolwich Equitable Building

9. Constellation of Interests

All the remaining enterprises were controlled through constellations of interests; they are listed with their shareholders in J. Scott, *The Controlling Constellations,* Working Paper for the Company Analysis Project, University of Leicester, 1984. This booklet is available at major libraries.

NOTES

1. Further details on the British data selection can be found in J. Scott and C. Griff, *Directors of Industry,* Cambridge, Polity Press, 1984. The whole of the international project is reported in F.N. Stokman, R. Ziegler, and J. Scott (eds.), *Networks of Corporate Power*, Cambridge, Polity Press, 1985.
2. J. Scott, *Corporate Control in Britain,* Working Paper for the Company Analysis Project, Leicester University, 1985. This booklet is available at the national copyright libraries, from the British Library Lending Division, and at various other large libraries.

Appendix II Techniques of Network Analysis

The discussion of social network concepts in the main chapters of this book has been kept deliberately brief and non-technical. This appendix sets out fuller technical details of the mathematical models and the three algorithms used to analyse shareholding data—EBLOC, QCOMP, and CONCOR—and shows the relationships between their major concepts.

Network analysis is rooted in set theory, a formal way of expressing and analysing sets of elements and sets of relations. The usual starting point for network analysis is the construction of an incidence matrix from which can be derived two adjacency matrices. An incidence matrix is a rectangular matrix in which rows and columns refer to separate groups of elements (such as agents, events, or attributes), and the entries in the cells of the matrix denote the presence or absence (the 'incidence') of relations among the elements. Figure AII.1 presents a small incidence matrix showing the relation between enterprises and shareholders, the '1' and '0' entries indicating that shareholder A, for example, invests in enterprises 1 and 2 but not in enterprises 3, 4, and 5. The two adjacency matrices are derived, respectively, from the rows and columns of the incidence matrix and show the number of connections between elements. Enterprises 1 and 2, for example, have three shareholders in common (A, B, and C), and so the adjacency matrix shows a '3' in the corresponding cell.

In graph theory the structure is modelled by analogy with physical networks of, say, electrical connections, and in the 'graph' of a network the elements are regarded as points and the relations as lines connecting the points. In the terminology of graph theory, enterprises 1 and 2 are 'adjacent' points connected by a line of 'multiplicity' 3. The adjacency matrix, therefore, shows the multiplicities of the lines connecting points, and the row total of each element (the number of non-zero entries) is its adjacency or 'degree'. A more general form of the adjacency matrix would consist simply of '0' and '1' entries, disregarding the multiplicity of lines. The cell entries may be used as measures of the intensity of the line, with multiplicity being only one such measure.[1] As both adjacency

(i) Incidence matrix

		Shareholders				
		A	*B*	*C*	*D*	*Total*
	1	1	1	1	1	4
	2	1	1	1	0	3
Enterprises	*3*	0	1	1	0	2
	4	0	0	1	0	1
	5	0	0	0	0	0
	Total	2	3	4	1	

(ii) Adjacency matrices

		Enterprises					
		1	*2*	*3*	*4*	*5*	*No.*
	1	–	3	2	1	0	3
	2	3	–	2	1	0	3
Enterprises	*3*	2	2	–	1	0	3
	4	1	1	1	–	0	3
	5	0	0	0	0	–	0

		Shareholders				
		A	*B*	*C*	*D*	*No.*
	A	–	2	2	1	3
Shareholders	*B*	2	–	3	1	3
	C	2	3	–	1	3
	D	1	1	1	–	3

Figure AII.1: *Matrices for graph analysis*

matrices are derived from the same incidence matrix and so contain the same data, each may be regarded as the 'dual' of the other: they represent the same structure from different points of view.

Unlike an incidence matrix, an adjacency matrix is normally symmetric and each connection appears twice: the connections below the diagonal are a mirror image of those above, because the line joining, say, 1 and 2 is identical to the line joining 2 and 1. This is not the case in adjacency matrices in which the line may be regarded as 'directed' from one point to another. In such matrices and their associated graphs the line running from 1 to 2 is not the same as that from 2 to 1: if 1 likes 2, it does not follow that 2 likes 1. In a directed graph, therefore, the adjacency of a point may be split into its 'in-degree' and its 'out-degree'.

The EBLOC algorithm[2] employs graph theoretical concepts to identify those parts of the network which can be regarded as 'cyclic components'. A cycle is a path, made up of distinct points and lines, which starts and ends at the same point, and the length of the cycle is measured by the number of lines it consists of. A line which connects two or more cycles is termed a 'bridge', and Everett defines a cyclic component as a set of points connected through cycles and in which the cycles are connected by bridges which are themselves parts of the cycles. Put more simply, a cyclic component is a chain of intersecting cycles, where the intersections are lines common to the overlapping cycles.[3]

To identify the cyclic components in a network, EBLOC deletes all bridges which do not lie on a cycle of the specified length. If cycles of length k are to be considered, EBLOC deletes k-bridges. After the deletion of these bridges, the remaining parts of the network will be cyclic components, weaker non-cyclic components, or isolated points. When the cycle length is great there is a tendency for networks with even a moderate level of connection to comprise a single large cyclic component, and Everett recommends that cycle lengths of 3 or 4 be specified. With a cycle length of 3 EBLOC investigates whether there are distinct components built from 'triangles'; with a cycle length of 4 EBLOC searches for 'rectangles'. Such short cycles are, in any case, of greater significance to agents and so there is a sociological rationale for restricting analyses to such cycles. EBLOC operates on an adjacency matrix, but can handle the rather hybrid directed matrix; as in the adjacency matrices of Figure AII.1, the rows and columns refer to the same set of elements, but they are considered from different points of view (e.g. as 'senders' and 'receivers' of help) and so the matrix is assymetric. To ignore the directionality of the lines, to treat them as 'semi-paths', is to lose important information and EBLOC therefore uses directionality in defining cycles. EBLOC recognises both directed cycles $(A \rightarrow B \rightarrow C \rightarrow A)$ and those 'acceptable semi-cycles' which contain two points connected by two distinct directed paths $(A \rightarrow B \rightarrow C \leftarrow A)$.[4] The output from EBLOC shows a listing of the members of all cyclic components and also indicates which points (termed 'adjacent vertices') are the end-points of the deleted k-bridges. In addition to isolated points and non-cyclic components, the output lists all 'waverers' and 'hangers'. Waverers are points, or non-cyclic components, linked to two or more cyclic components, while hangers are points linked to one component only. It was suggested in Chapter 5 that it is possible to distinguish 'hangers-on' and 'hangers-off' in a directed graph.

The branch of mathematics called Q-analysis is based on algebraic topology[5] and is an extension of set theory which defines elements as 'simplices' and relations as 'shared faces' of simplices. Structures are understood as 'complexes' of simplices (simplicial complexes) and graph theory can virtually be regarded as a special case of Q-analysis. Graph theory applies most obviously to those structures which can be treated as if they were two-dimensional and hence can be interpreted on the basis of the conventional network metaphor. Social networks, however, cannot always be treated this way, and the multi-dimensional approach of Q-analysis is generally preferable. QCOMP is an implementation of Q-analysis which searches for components in networks. The dimensionality of a simplex (elements) is termed its p-value or top Q and describes the nature of the space in which it is located; a point, for example, has dimensionality zero, while a pair of points connected by a line must be represented in one dimension. The dimensionality of an element can be derived from the incidence matrix by calculating its row or column total and subtracting one from this. The simplex representing enterprise 1 in Figure AII.1, for example, has dimensionality 3, while that representing enterprise 4 has dimensionality 0. The network created by the connected simplices, the simplicial complex, can be analysed through the concepts of 'Q-nearness' and 'Q-connectedness'. By constructing the adjacency matrices from the original incidence matrix it is possible to analyse how 'near' elements are to one another in the structure. The Q-nearness of two simplices is measured by what graph theorists term the multiplicity of the line which connects them. Enterprises 1 and 2 are connected by a line of multiplicity 3 and are said to be '2-near', while enterprises 1 and 4, connected by a line of multiplicity 1, are 0-near. Q-analysis involves the construction of matrix of Q-nearness, a matrix showing the dimensionality of the shared faces of simplices, which is similar in form to the weighted adjacency matrices of Figure AII.1. It can be seen from Figure AII.2 that the two 'dual' or 'cognate' matrices have the top Q value for each element along the diagonal and that all other entries are one less than the totals shown in the weighted adjacency matrices. The adjacency of an element, as defined in graph theory, is equal to the number of positive, non-zero entries for its row or column in the matrix of Q-nearness.

Simplices are partitioned by QCOMP in the standard Q-analysis on the basis of their Q-nearness. Elements are regarded as members of the same component at a particular level of Q-nearness if they are connected by an unbroken chain of links with dimensionality Q. The members of such a component are Q-connected, though not all members are Q-near to all others: Q-nearness is a direct link, while Q-connection may be indirect.[6] Figure AII.3 shows the result of a standard Q-analysis for the matrices in Figure AII.2. In the network of enterprises, for example, there is a single-member 'component' at Q=3, but the first real component emerges only at Q=2. At Q=1 the component has grown to include enterprises 1, 2 and 3, and at Q=0 it includes all enterprises except the completely isolated enterprise 5. Thus it can be concluded that enterprises 1 and 2 are much more strongly connected to one another than either is to enterprise 3, but that

Enterprises

	1	*2*	*3*	*4*	*5*

		1	*2*	*3*	*4*	*5*
Enterprises	*1*	3	2	1	0	−1
	2	2	2	1	0	−1
	3	1	1	2	0	−1
	4	0	0	0	2	−1
	5	−1	−1	−1	−1	0

Figure AII.2: *Matrices of Q-analysis*

Shareholders

	A	*B*	*C*	*D*

		A	*B*	*C*	*D*
Shareholders	*A*	1	1	1	0
	B	1	2	2	0
	C	1	2	3	0
	D	0	0	0	0

Value of Q	Components Enterprises	Shareholders
3	{1}	{C}
2	{1, 2}	{B, C}
1	{1, 2, 3}	{A, B, C}
0	{1, 2, 3, 4} {5}	{A, B, C, D}

Note: Enterprise 5, with Q-nearness of −1 to all other enterprises is an isolate.

Figure AII.3: *Q-analysis of enterprises and shareholders*

enterprise 4 has the weakest links to other enterprises. Nevertheless, there is a 0-connected component of four enterprises at Q=0.[7] The Q-analysis, therefore, gives a 'contour map' in which areas of decreasingly intense connection are identified: the first contour line encircles only enterprise 1, the second encircles both 1 and 2, and so on. In graph theory this is termed an analysis of 'nested' components[8] defined through lines of decreasing multiplicity.

The extension of Q-analysis through the introduction of factor weightings was made by Cowley, and the procedure involves calculating the mean level of connectivity of each simplex and using this as the basis for a measure of relative intensity. All connections between pairs of points which are below each point's mean connectivity are deleted, and components are identified in the remaining pattern of connections. Multiplying the mean connectivities by successively higher factors leads to the gradual deletion of more and more connections, leaving only those which are most intense for each point. It is, therefore, possible to produce the same 'nested' or 'contour' analysis generated by the standard Q-analysis. The relative intensity measure, however, is more sensitive to the existence of groups of elements which are relatively marginal to a larger component and have relatively close connections among themselves.

CONCOR does not itself derive from either graph theory or Q-analysis. It is essentially a method of matrix permutation suitable for a variety of types of data and comparable in some respects to factor analysis and principal components analysis.[9] It is, however, readily translatable into graph theoretical terms as a set of operations on incidence and adjacency matrices. CONCOR aims to partition, or 'block', a matrix into structurally equivalent sets of elements. Members of a set of structurally equivalent elements have similar patterns of connection to the rest of the network and so play a similar 'role' in the network. CONCOR regards each column of a matrix as a vector showing the values of a particular element on each of a number of variables (the rows). In the case of sociometric data, the variables are the same or other elements. From the incidence matrix CONCOR calculates two correlation matrices—one for the rows and one for the columns. The cell entries are not 1s and 0s, as in the conventional adjacency matrix, but the product moment correlation between elements. Thus CONCOR's starting point is weighted adjacency matrices, with correlation as the measure of intensity. The CONCOR algorithm then produces a partitioning of each matrix, using a method of iteration.

The iteration works by calculating for each correlation matrix another correlation matrix, showing the correlation of correlations in each cell. The repeated application of this operation rapidly produces a matrix in which all entries are either '+1' or '–1' and thus the elements can be partitioned into two sets—those which are positively and those which are negatively correlated with one another. Separate matrices are constructed for each of the two sets, the original correlation coefficients are read back in, and the operation is repeated separately for each set. The continued application of CONCOR in this way produces a hierarchical partitioning of the columns and rows of the original matrix, and the elements can be rearranged according to this partitioning to show the final 'blocking' of the matrix. CONCOR can be used on an incidence matrix to produce a separate partitioning of rows and columns or on an adjacency matrix to produce a combined row and column partitioning. In the latter case the rows and columns are identical and the top half of the matrix is the mirror image of the bottom half. In the case of a directed adjacency matrix it is necessary to analyse rows and columns separately for the reasons already outlined.

The rearranged matrix produced by CONCOR is analysed by marking out the partitions to reveal the pattern of blocks, which can then be analysed as an image matrix. In this matrix the rows and columns relate not to the individual elements but to the sets of structurally equivalent elements identified by CONCOR. The cell entries in the image matrix show the relations between sets, strong relations represented by a '1' and weak relations by a '0'. The strength of the relation between sets is measured by the density of the connections carried by their members, though any particular cut-off level of density is, of course, arbitrary. A widely accepted procedure is to use the overall density of the original matrix as the cut-off level, so identifying blocks of above-average density as indicators of strong ties between sets. In some cases it is possible to construct a number of image matrices using a variable density threshold, beginning with a stringent density value for the strength of a relation and progressively relaxing this until the mean density level is reached. Such an analysis produces what can be regarded as a hierarchy of 'nested' relations, and this was possible with the Japanese data of Chapter 7. Whatever procedure is followed, an image matrix discloses both the sets of structurally equivalent elements and the relations between them, and, so long as the number of sets is not too large, the matrix can be readily interpreted. This is especially the case with matrices with directed relations, though undirected data has been successfully analysed with CONCOR.

It is now possible to illustrate more concretely the application of these ideas to intercorporate relations. In the analysis of interlocking directorships the starting point is an incidence matrix in which the rows represent enterprises and the columns represent directors (or *vice versa*). In this matrix an entry of one in a cell indicates the presence of a specific director on a particular board. The total number of ones appearing in the matrix is therefore equal to the total number of directorships. The dimensionality of the simplex representing a director, therefore, is equal to one less than her or his column total (i.e., one less than the number of directorships held). A director with four directorships, for example, can be represented by a 3-simplex, a tetrahedron with four points connected by six edges: the number of points corresponds to the number of directorships and the number of edges equals the number of interlocks between enterprises which that director creates. An interlock, therefore, can be interpreted as a relation of Q-nearness, and 'adjacent' enterprises are Q-near to one another. For this reason, the multiplicity of the line which represents the interlock can be translated into a Q-value: the Q-value of two Q-near enterprises is equal to one less than the multiplicity of the line which connects them.

Q-analysis operates on the two cognate adjacency matrices derived from the incidence matrix, and so the analysis of a matrix of shareholdings involves the conversion of the directed incidence matrix into two undirected adjacency matrices. These two matrices describe the connections among shareholding enterprises which exist (1) by virtue of their common shareholdings in the enterprises they control and (2) by virtue of the presence of common controlling shareholders in their own capital. Thus the top Q of a shareholder is equal to its out-degree minus one, and the top Q of a controlled enterprise is equal to one less than its in-degree. EBLOC, of course, operates on the directed links themselves, seeing shareholding participations as the lines of the graph. This is true of CONCOR, which can produce a combined analysis of rows and columns. In such a CONCOR analysis, enterprises are partitioned into sets according both to their shareholdings in other enterprises and to the participations of others in their capital. It is possible, however, for CONCOR to proceed in a similar way to QCOMP and to treat rows and columns separately.

The three algorithms, therefore, allow for the production of a number of different representations of the same structure: QCOMP standard and extended analyses of the two cognate matrices of Q-nearness, EBLOC analyses with varying cycle lengths, and CONCOR analyses of rows, columns, and both rows and columns. The number of possible representations can, of course, be expanded considerably by the inclusion of multiplicities and other measures of intensity, which permit more complex nestings to be produced. No one representation can be regarded as definitive. It remains the task of the researcher to choose those analyses which seem most appropriate and interpretable.

NOTES

1. In the present example the diagonal entries of the adjacency matrices are not considered, as it is assumed that an element is not adjacent to itself. In practice the diagonal may be very important where, for example, it is possible for an enterprise to hold its own shares. Algorithms for network analysis differ considerably in the way that they treat the diagonal, and users should be aware of the assumptions which are made.
2. A general reveiw of graph theoretical operations can be found in S. Berkowitz, *An Introduction to Structural Analysis*, Toronto, Butterworth, 1982. Everett's description of the EBLOC algorithm can be found in: M.G. Everett, 'A Graph Theoretic Blocking Procedure for Social Networks', *Social Networks*, 4, 1982; *idem.*, 'EBLOC: A Graph Theoretic Blocking Algorithm for Social Networks', *Social Networks*, 5, 1983; *idem.*, 'An Extension of EBLOC to Valued Graphs', *Social Networks*, 5, 1983; *idem.*, 'An analysis of Cyclically Dense Data Using EBLOC', *Social Networks*, 6, 1984.
3. Cyclic components may have weaker linkages when the cycles are connected through a common point, a cut-point, rather than through a common line. In this case, intersecting cycles have one member in common rather than two.
4. EBLOC can also handle two or more matrices, though this may not be

possible in practical computer terms if the network is large. The cell entries in each matrix are added to produce a combined valued graph. A 'compressing' number is then used as a threshold for converting the data to binary form. Varying the compressing number produces successive 'slices' of the network which can be combined to give a contour map of the whole network.

5. *See* R.H. Atkin, *Mathematical Structure in Human Affairs*, London, Heinemann, 1974; idem., *Combinatorial Connectivities in Social Systems*, Basel, Birkhauser, 1977; idem., *Multidimensional Man*, Harmondsworth, Penguin, 1981. Further discussions can be found in: J.H. Johnson, 'Some Structures and Notation of Q-Analysis', *Environment and Planning B*, 8, 1981; idem., 'q-Transmission in Simplicial Complexes', *International Journal of Man-Machine Studies*, 16, 1982; A.C. Gatrell, 'On the Structure of Urban Social Areas', *Transactions of the Institute of British Geographers*, 6, 1981; J. Beaumont and A.C. Gatrell, *An Introduction to Q-Analysis*, Norwich, Geo Publications, 1982; P. Doreian, 'On the Evolution of Group and Network Structure', *Social Networks*, 2, 1980; idem., 'Polyhedral Dynamics and Conflict Mobilisation in Social Networks', *Social Networks*, 3, 1981; idem., 'Levelling Coalitions as Network Phenomena', *Social Networks*, 4, 1982. The relationship between graph theory and Q-analysis is discussed in C.F. Earl and J.H. Johnson, 'Graph Theory and Q-Analysis', *Environment and Planning B*, 8, 1981.
6. Note that in the case of indirect relations of Q-connection the graph theoretic distance between points is not taken into account.
7. This component would be recognised by EBLOC as cyclic at length 3.
8. Two further concepts introduced by Atkin are 'bottom Q' and 'eccentricity'. The bottom Q of a simplex is the highest level of connection at which it is Q-near to any other point; it is the level at which it becomes a member of a component. The eccentricity of a simplex is the extent to which it stands out from its local environment and is measured by (Top Q— Bottom Q)/(Bottom Q + 1). The most eccentric enterprise in figure A2.2 is 5, because it is completely isolated.
9. CONCOR is described in: P. Lorrain and H.C. White, 'Structural Equivalence of Individuals in Social Networks', *Journal of Mathematical Sociology*, 1 (1971) 1; H. White, S.A. Boorman, and R.L. Breiger, 'Social Structure from Multiple Networks, I: Blockmodels of Roles and Positions', *American Journal of Sociology*, 81, 1976; S.A. Boorman and H.C. White, 'Social Structure from Multiple Networks, II: Role Structure', *American Journal of Sociology*, 81, 1976; R.L. Breiger, S.A. Boorman and P. Arabie, 'An Algorithm for Blocking Relational Data, with Applications to Social Network Analysis, *Journal of Mathematical Psychology*, 12, 1975. P. Arabie, S.A. Boorman, and P.R. Levitt, 'Constructing Blockmodels: How and Why', *Journal of Mathematical Psychology*, 17, 1978. *See also* J.M. Light and N.C. Mullins, 'A Primer on Blockmodelling Procedures', in P.W. Holland and S. Lienhardt (eds.), *Perspectives on Social Network Research*, New York, Academic Press, 1979, and R.L. Breiger, 'Toward an Operational Theory of Community Elite Structures', *Quality and Quantity*, 13, 1979.

Index

COMPANIES AND NAME

Companies listed in Appendix I have been indexed only if they appear in the main text.

221

SUBJECT AND AUTHOR

company Ch 2 passim; Companies
Acts 11–12, 20; company law in
Japan 164; company law in
United States 132–3; *see also*
chartered company, registered
company, statutory company
Companies Registration Office 18,
30n, 33, 34, 40
component 109–10, 212, 214
CONCOR algorithm 112, 186–7,
196, 216–18, 219
control 6, 49–52; control through a
constellation of interests 51, 52,
60–1, 78, 87–8, 94ff, 112ff, 140–1,
168, 182–3, 199, 201; *see also*
management control, majority
control, minority control
Corporate Data Exchange 134–5, 154–5n
corporation, in American law 29n;
in British law, 16, 51
Cowley, P. 216
Cubbin, J. 60
custodian trustee 21–2, 27
cycles in networks 110, 212–13
cyclic components: *see* components,
cycles, EBLOC

debentures 14–15, 19
directionality in networks 109, 212;
see also indegree, outdegree
directors 13, 15, 50, 75, 76–7, 80, 88,
201; *see also* interlocking
directorships
disclosure 5–6, 11–12, 15–16, 17ff,
133–4, 164

EBLOC alogrithm 112, 212–3, 218–9
enterprise groups in Japan 163,
193n; *see also* combines,
kigyoshudan, zaibatsu
entrepreneurial capital and family
holdings 2, 41–2, 59–60, 65, 71ff, 79–80,
64n, 142ff, 161–2, 172–4, 199; *see
also* family firm
Everett, M. 212

family firm 1ff, 9, 75–7, 97; *see also*
entrepreneurial capital
family participants in controlling
constellations 75, 76, 142–3, 172–4
finance capital 3, 4, 119
financial intermediaries 2, 3–4, 23ff,
58, 77, 88ff, 120, 203
Florence, P.S. 33–4, 36–9, 51, 55, 57, 96–7

foreign ownership 2, 12, 23, 54, 67–9,
78, 138, 170–2, 198–200
Futatsugi, Y. 183, 185

graph theory 108–10, 210ff

hangers 113, 213
hegemony, financial 4, 107ff, 111,
117–18, 146ff, 183ff, 200ff
Herman, E.S. 50–1, 141
Hilferding, R. 4; *see also* finance
capital
holding company 159, 161

immediate control 68–9
impersonal possession 1, 2, 4, 5,
198, 200, 203
in-degree 100, 109, 212
in-house holdings 61, 138–9
institutional ownership; *see*
financial intermediaries
insurance companies 3, 16, 24–5, 89–90
intensity 114–15
interest groups: *see* combines
interlocking directorships 3, 78–80, 91,
119–21, 147, 153–4, 167, 184, 218
investment banking 3, 135; *see also*
bank trust departments
investment trusts 3, 24, 44, 70, 71,
90–2, 102

Japan, shareholding in 4–5, 6, Ch 7
passim, 199–200, 201ff

kigyoshudan 162ff, 167–9, 175ff, 183ff
kinecon group 61
Kotz D. 50–1, 52

Leach, D. 60
legal device 71

majority control 49, 52; shared 62
management control 50–1, 99, 141
management shares 14
managerial enterprise 1, 52
matrix representation of network
110, 130n, 211ff
Means, G.C. 37, 49–50, 58
merchant banking 27, 70, 72, 91, 93,
102, 113, 118, 122–3
Ministry of International Trade and
Industry [MITI] 172
Minns, R. 67
minority control 37–9, 48, 52, 55ff,